John Esten Cooke

Fairfax: The Master of Greenway Court

A Chronicle of the Valley of the Shenandoah

John Esten Cooke

Fairfax: The Master of Greenway Court
A Chronicle of the Valley of the Shenandoah

ISBN/EAN: 9783744742597

Printed in Europe, USA, Canada, Australia, Japan

Cover: Foto ©Thomas Meinert / pixelio.de

More available books at **www.hansebooks.com**

OR,

THE MASTER OF GREENWAY COURT.

A Chronicle of the Valley of the Shenandoah.

BY

JOHN ESTEN COOKE,

AUTHOR OF "THE VIRGINIA COMEDIANS," "SURRY OF EAGLE'S NEST," ETC.

NEW YORK:
G. W. CARLETON & CO., PUBLISHERS.
LONDON: S. LOW, SON & CO.
MDCCCLXVIII.

Entered according to the Act of Congress, in the year 1868, by
G. W. CARLETON & CO.,
in the Clerk's Office of the District Court of the United States, for the Southern District of New York

LOVEJOY, SON & CO.,
ELECTROTYPERS & STEREOTYPERS,
15 Vandewater Street, N. Y.

To

ONE WITH WHOM

I RODE TO GREENWAY COURT,

IN MAY, 1866.

CONTENTS.

CHAPTER	PAGE
I.—THREE CAVALIERS	9
II.—GREENWAY COURT	16
III.—HOW CAPTAIN WAGNER BECAME UNEASY IN HIS SLEEP	23
IV.—HOW CAPTAIN LONGKNIFE SAW WITHOUT SEEING, AND WHAT FOLLOWED	28
V.—THE ESCAPE	36
VI.—CAPTAIN LONGKNIFE'S PRIVATE MATTERS	41
VII.—THE CAPTAIN RENEWS THE ATTACK	48
VIII.—HOW GEORGE WAS LED BY PROVIDENCE	52
IX.—HOW GEORGE MADE THE ACQUAINTANCE OF CANNIE	56
X.—A SINGULAR PERSONAGE	60
XI.—THE WILD HUNTSMAN	63
XII.—THE DRAMA COMMENCES	66
XIII.—HOW FALCONBRIDGE HAD A STRANGE DREAM	72
XIV.—THE NEXT MORNING	74
XV.—HOW LORD FAIRFAX INFORMED THE CAPTAIN OF A FAMILY PROPHECY	76
XVI.—HOW CAPTAIN WAGNER DECLARED WAR ON HIS PRIVATE ACCOUNT AGAINST LORD FAIRFAX	81
XVII.—MONSIEUR JAMBOT'S DEATH'S HEAD	87
XVIII.—HOW CAPTAIN WAGNER PREDICTED HIS FUTURE FAME	91
XIX.—OLD MEMORIES	99
XX.—FIRST LOVE	101
XXI.—CAPTAIN WAGNER GOES TO CALL UPON HIS FRIENDS	105
XXII.—THE CAPTAIN REVELS IN THE CREATIONS OF HIS FANCY	108
XXIII.—CAPTAIN WAGNER DISCOURSES ON THE NATURE OF PANTHERS	114
XXIV.—REFLECTIONS OF CAPTAIN LONGKNIFE	120
XXV.—HOW THE TOWN OF STEPHENSBURG, OTHERWISE NEWTOWN, WAS SOLD FOR A FLAGON OF PUNCH	122
XXVI.—THE DAGGER IN THE HEART	130

CONTENTS.

CHAPTER	PAGE
XXVII.—FALCONBRIDGE PARTS WITH HIS MOTHER'S RING	134
XXVIII.—THE LETTER	138
XXIX.—THE THREADS OF THE WOOF	142
XXX.—THE ARREST	148
XXXI.—LIGHTFOOT	152
XXXII.—HOW CAPTAIN WAGNER OVERTHREW HIS ADVERSARY	155
XXXIII.—THE WIZARD OF THE MASSINUTTON	161
XXXIV.—THE PRISONER AND THE JUDGE	169
XXXV.—THE RESEMBLANCE	176
XXXVI.—CAMPAIGN OF GENERAL LONGKNIFE	182
XXXVII.—THE EARL AND FALCONBRIDGE	191
XXXVIII.—THE PORTRAIT	196
XXXIX.—THE OLYMPIAN IRE OF CAPTAIN LONGKNIFE	199
XL.—THE BEGINNING OF THE END	203
XLI.—PROGRESS	209
XLII.—IN THE MOUNTAIN	214
XLIII.—HOW AN ANIMAL CHANGED THE DESTINIES OF THREE HUMAN BEINGS	218
XLIV.—IN WHICH CAPTAIN WAGNER REQUESTS MONSIEUR JAMBOT TO PULL HIS NOSE	223
XLV.—THE LAMIA	231
XLVI.—HOW FALCONBRIDGE KINDLED A FIRE TO SEE BY	235
XLVII.—PRELIMINARIES	242
XLVIII.—THE ARRANGEMENT	247
XLIX.—THE COMBAT	251
L.—HOW FALCONBRIDGE RECOVERED HIS MOTHER'S RING	258
LI.—THE APOLOGY	267
LII.—THE COURIER	373
LIII.—THE BALL IN THE RIGHT SHOULDER	278
LIV.—THE ORIGINALS OF THE PORTRAIT	286
LV.—WHAT THE PACKAGE TORN BY THE BEAR CONTAINED	291
LVI.—CONCLUSION OF THE EARL'S NARRATIVE	298
LVII.—THE CONFLAGRATION	305
LVIII.—THE SEARCH	311
LIX.—AT THE HOUSE IN THE MOUNTAIN	313
LX.—THE DEVIL'S GARDEN	317
LXI.—THE HALF-BREED	320
LXII.—THE TRAIL	327
LXIII.—LIGHTFOOT AND CANNIE	332
LXIV.—THE SLAVE AND HIS MISTRESS	341
LXV.—CALIBAN AND MIRANDA	348

CONTENTS.

CHAPTER	PAGE
LXVI.—LIGHT SHINING IN THE DARKNESS	355
LXVII.—THE RIVAL OF THE HALF-BREED	358
LXVIII.—THE MARCH OF THE HUNTERS	360
LXIX.—THE SON OF WAR EAGLE	364
LXX.—THE CONFESSION	368
LXXI.—THE FLIGHT	372
LXXII.—THE BORDERER AND THE HALF-BREED	376
LXXIII.—THE YOUNG INDIAN	385
LXXIV.—THE YOUNG CAVALIER	388
LXXV.—THE DAUGHTER OF THE STARS	394
LXXVI.—THE HEART OF LORD FAIRFAX	399
LXXVII.—THE HEART OF GEORGE	401

FAIRFAX;

OR,

THE MASTER OF GREENWAY COURT.

I.

THREE CAVALIERS.

ON an evening of October, in the year 1748, the slopes of the Blue Ridge at Ashby's Gap were all ablaze with the red light of the sinking sun.

At this hour of hours, in the month of months, two horsemen coming from the east, ascended the steep road above the present village of Paris, and ere long reached the summit of the mountain.

What they saw before them, looking westward from that point, was worthy of attention from the most indifferent. Through the foliage-embowered walls of the mountain pass, the eye embraced a wondrous spectacle.

Southward, the ramparts of the great Blue Ridge rolled away like waves of the ocean, disappearing in a delicate mist. Beyond the Shenandoah stretched a limitless prairie, starred with brilliant flowers, which the fall winds gently agitated, making the expanse resemble a vast lake, whose waves were of every color of the rainbow. In the dim distance, on the far horizon, rose the azure battlements of the Great North Mountain: and in front, the Massinutton soared aloft—its huge blue outline standing out, clear cut, against the crimson curtain of the sunset.

Never did artist, in his dreams of supernal glory, imagine anything more lovely than this landscape. The richest colors seemed exhausted to make up the picture. Forest and prairie, river and mountain, shone in blue and gold and crimson :—the rosy mist of autumn drooped above the landscape like a dream :—the enchanting Valley of the Shenandoah lay before the eyes of the travellers like some land of Faëry or bright realm of Arcady.

One was young, the other had reached middle age. Let us draw their outlines with a few strokes of the pen. The first was a boy of sixteen : tall, straight, and full of life. His hair was brown and curling, his complexion ruddy, his lips smiling. He wore a jaunty little cocked hat; elegant top boots; kneebreeches of buckskin; a broadskirted coat, and white ruffles; in his hand he carried a small rifle, and behind his saddle were strapped the instruments of a surveyor. The laughing boy rode a handsome little sorrel, and his smile, his carriage, his gestures, all indicated youth and joy and hope.

His companion was no longer young, and a grim smile lit up the bold features, vividly contrasting with the enthusiasm of the boy. The worthy was tall of stature, huge of limb, a gigantic war machine, armed to the teeth and ready for combat. Under the drooping hat flashed a pair of dark eyes beneath shaggy brows; the sarcastic lips were hidden by a heavy black moustache which swept down into the huge beard; and behind this moustache shone a row of sharp white teeth which resembled those of a bear rather than a man. His dress was rough, travel-stained, and chiefly of leather; from his well-worn belt depended an enormous broadsword, which clattered against his heavy boots—and the warlike personage bestrode a charger, mighty of limb, and as rough and powerful in appearance as himself.

The two figures remained for a moment stationary, gazing

at the landscape; then the elder touched his horse, and moved on.

"Come, my young friend," he said, in a species of growl, "the sun's getting low yonder, and we had better push on and cross the Shenandoah before dark."

"Yes, yes, Captain," returned the boy, "but I could look at this scene forever—see the beautiful colors of the leaves, and hear the wind in the pines!"

He who had been thus addressed, smiled grimly.

"Listen to him!" he growled: "sentiment in the backwood, i'faith! Keep it for the ladies, Master George!—it's thrown away on Captain Julius Wagner, otherwise called Captain Bloody Longknife, or the Devil take me!"

"Pshaw, Captain!" laughed the boy, "that is all affectation. You are known to be romantic—to be a favorite with the ladies! As well deny that you are the prince of frontier-fighters."

A grim smile curled the huge moustache, and with his finger the worthy pushed up that appendage until it stood out almost horizontal.

"My young friend," was the sarcastic reply, "you are flattering. I reply to your pleasing observation by saying that my fortune, both as an admirer of the fair sex, and a defender of the border, has been truly disgusting—more especially the latter. Glorious! the life of a soldier! Humph! to wear your life out fighting, and then die, some day, in an unremembered skirmish!—to have an end put to you by a stray bullet from the rifle of a rascally Injun;—to be huddled into a hole to everybody's satisfaction, who will get promotion by your death!—there's fame, there's glory, there's good fortune!"

And the Captain's lip curled elaborately.

"But you have done your duty!" said the ardent boy; "that at least remains. And are you not Captain Wagner, the Valiant?"

"Oh yes! Captain Wagner the Valiant, without a clean

shirt! Captain Wagner the Valiant, in leather breeches! Captain Wagner the Valiant, in an old seedy buff coat, and boots with holes, and rusty old spurs, that jingle, by my faith, like the armor of Mars, that Egyptian hero I have heard of! Yes, that's all Captain Wagner is fit for—seedy coat, boots in holes, rusty spurs, and fighting Injuns! Worse even than that! I am becoming a mere courier, a travelling horse, a miserable hack—I would be a dandy!"

"A dandy!" laughed George.

"Yes, young one, a dandy, like what I have seen yonder at Belhaven, i'faith! A nicely curled fop, with silk gloves, a jewelled snuff-box, and a sweet little simper in my voice—then I'd please the fair sex. Oh that Wagner was a dandy—Wagner the savage! Oh that the shaggy old bear, with his growling voice, and long sharp teeth, could be changed into a kitten, sleek and glossy, to gently pur-r-r-r-r!—and be taken up into the female lap, and smoothed down the back, and made a pet of!"

George replied with a laugh much gayer than before.

"I really believe you have had bad luck lately, Captain! Is it possible that "——

"All things are possible in this miserable world, my young friend; but I decline any statement upon this interesting topic."

"Oh, now I remember! I heard that the handsome Mrs. Butterton "——

"Don't call names, George, my friend, and let us change the subject. I am getting hungry, or the Devil take me; and yonder I see the Shenandoah between us and supper. The water's up and booming or I'll eat my head!"

And pushing on they approached the river, which roared on angrily beneath the huge white-armed sycamores, growing on the steep bank, and extending their boughs above the current.

All at once, as George and his companion reached the bank, their attention was attracted by a white object in the middle of the stream, which the fading light illumined—and this object was seen to be the head of a horse, above which rose a pair of shoulders, and a hat decorated with a black feather.

"A good swimmer," muttered Wagner; "who the devil can he be?—but we'll soon see. Come, Injun-hater, take to water!"

And spurring his black charger into the angry current, Captain Wagner began to swim with the phlegm of an old traveller—George following in his wake upon his little sorrel. The snorting animals ploughed their way through the rapid current; placed their feet upon the opposite bank; and with vigorous bounds reached dry land again. The rider of the white horse had already emerged from the stream, and was awaiting them.

He was a young man of twenty-three or four, erect, slender, and what is called "aristocratic" in face, bearing, and expression. The frank and smiling countenance was lit up by a species of joyous pride—that sunshine beaming in the sky of youth—and it was plain from the young man's dress, as from the carriage of his person, that he belonged to the class then known as "the Gentry." His brown coat was heavily embroidered; his delicate ruffles as white as snow, and his fair top boots, defining the small and slender feet, of the finest leather. At his side, he wore a handsome sword in a black leather belt; behind the saddle was his valise, of the same material, and his hands were cased in yellow gauntlets, reaching nearly to the elbow. One of those hands now reined in, with careless grace, the spirited thoroughbred, dripping from the stream; with the other he made a salute full of friendly courtesy to Captain Wagner and George.

"Give you good day, gentlemen," he said, in a clear and sonorous voice. "As we are travelling in the same direction, perhaps you can direct me on my way. Where are we at this moment?"

"I'll tell you in a few words, my friend," returned Wagner. "You are now in the Great Valley of Virginia, otherwise, the Shenandoah Valley, not a long way from that assemblage of huts called Winchester; what is better, considering supper, you are near Greenway Court, the residence of Thomas Lord Fairfax, baron of Cameron, and so forth, and so forth—a friend of mine, who will not let you go further to-night, comrade."

"Good! I came to see his lordship."

"Well, you have only to follow us. My name is Wagner, and my young friend is called Mr. George."

The stranger saluted with a motion full of grace and frankness.

"You are by no means a stranger to me, Captain," he replied, "and I am truly glad to make your acquaintance— also yours, Mr. George. My own name is Falconbridge— very much at your service."

"Good, good!" said the Captain, twirling his moustache. "I like these little complimentary speeches: they sweeten this miserable life! Well, comrade—and observe, I must decidedly have taken a fancy to you, as I call you 'comrade' all the time—a few miles from here is the white post his lordship has stuck up to direct travellers to Greenway. I never see that post but the long arms seem to stretch out toward me, and a voice says, 'Come on, Wagner, supper is smoking!'"

With these words, the worthy put spur to his horse, and set forward, his companions following and conversing. In fifteen minutes, George had completely fallen in love with the young man, whose smiles and accents, full of winning simplicity, won his heart. From that moment to the end of the drama, these two hearts were to beat in unison.

Captain Wagner was meanwhile pushing on, through the tall grass of the prairie, over which stretched a narrow road, his mind absorbed in deep reflection on the subject of supper. The last rays of sunset streaming over the great, flowery expanse, failed to attract his attention ; he moved on steadily ; then a grunt was heard from the worthy, and his finger pointed to a white post, glimmering in the twilight.

From this, a good road led to Greenway Court, scarce a mile away. They followed the road; a clump of oaks rose all at once before them, and a long, low mansion, in front of which some locusts grew. The travellers had reached Greenway Court, the residence of Lord Fairfax.

II.

GREENWAY COURT.

GREENWAY COURT was a long, stone building, with an extensive portico, and the roof was overshadowed by the boughs of lofty locust trees. At each end rose a slender chimney; between, upon the summit of the roof, were seen two belfries; beneath, three or four dormer windows were brushed by the October foliage.

At fifty paces from the mansion, and connected with it by a winding path, across the sward, a low stone cabin nestled under a great tree—and here Lord Fairfax, sitting in state, with his court of deer-hounds, had delivered the title deeds of nearly all that portion of Virginia.

The grounds of the mansion were encircled by a rude fence, and to this fence Captain Wagner proceeded to attach his horse, in which he was imitated by his companions.

They were not, however, the first comers. Near at hand were seen two animals, tethered in the same manner; one, a plain, substantial cob; the other a slender-legged filly, covered with a cloth, which evidently concealed a woman's saddle.

Captain Wagner gazed intently for an instant, at the two animals, which seemed familiar to him; pulled his moustache upward with his finger, nodded confidentially, and then went with long strides toward the house, his companions following.

The main room, which the Borderer now entered, was peculiar. It was an apartment hung around with guns, blunderbuses, antlers, portraits, fishing nets, and long tapering rods. The walls were rough and rudely plastered

—the furniture oaken, with the exception of two or three high-backed, carven chairs of mahogany, then very rare; and on some shelves in one corner, near a buffet of oak, a number of old volumes in brown leather binding were visible, much worn and soiled. Among these was a fine embossed copy of the "Spectator," lately printed in London, to which the owner of the mansion had contributed some papers, written perhaps in the study of his friend, Joseph Addison.

It will thus be seen that the apartment was a striking exhibition of the commingling of two things—refinement, and rudeness, of two types, the court and the backwoods. This characteristic was further apparent in the jumble of silver plate, and cheap gaily-colored crockery on the buffet: and finally, the muzzle of a rifle standing in the corner had forced itself between the leaves of one of those volumes in which serene Mr. Addison discussed the last refinements of the luxurious society of England.

This was the apartment which the travellers entered—to whose broad fire-place, with its crackling sticks, they drew near.

Lord Fairfax was not visible, but two other personages were seated before the fire, illuminated by the last beams of sunset streaming through the western window. The first was a gentleman past middle age, plainly clad, and with nothing striking in his appearance. The other personage, a young girl, whose figure was eminently noticeable. She was apparently about twenty, with dark hair, dark eyes and radiant complexion. Her bare arms, from which she had thrown the sleeves of her riding cloak, were models of symmetry, and her figure was extremely graceful. She was clad richly for the border, and wore many rings upon her tapering fingers, but no one for a moment gave a thought to her costume. The remarkable face attracted all eyes. It was a singular face—the eyes dark and liquid, full of softness and fire; the lips red and moist, and adapted to express all emotions; the brow lofty and snow white; the poise and carriage of the head, and equally of the person, fascinating. This was the appearance of the young woman whom the stranger gazed at with surprise and admiration.

Captain Wagner greeted the occupants of the apartment with the air of an old acquaintance, acquitting himself of the task of introduction with much easy unconcern, except that a keen observer might have imagined from the rude frontiersman's manner that the lady was no favorite with him.

This, however, was not seen by George or Falconbridge; at least they did not bow the less low, or smile the less courteously.

"See," said the Captain, stroking his beard and smiling amiably, "see what pleasant people we meet at the end of our journey, instead of my Lord Fairfax, who, I don't mind saying, is sometimes, nevertheless, an agreeable companion. Faith! I know my good luck, friend Argal, and would rather be here than out yonder in the backwoods with some surly rascal, who crouches over a wet fire and grudges you your seat on the log, and your part of the blanket! And then the smoke!" continued the Borderer, bending over the blaze, and snuffing up the clouds of white smoke; "faith! it reminds me of my childhood—our chimney smoked!"

George smiled and sat down opposite the soldier; the stranger had already taken his seat near the young lady, and had entered into conversation with her.

"Well, friend Argal," said the Captain to the gentleman who held in his hand a package of papers which he had been examining, "what news on the border? Any Injuns, eh?"

"Yes, Captain," said Mr. Argal, courteously, "reports are rife about them."

"Reports?"

"They say that there is imminent danger of an inroad soon."

"Humph!" replied the Borderer,—"'they say' is a great

liar, I need not tell you, sir. But let us not frighten the fair sex. I hope Miss Bertha is well?"

And the soldier, with a movement in which a close observer might have descried a singular coldness, turned to the young girl.

She simply inclined her head, and went on conversing with the stranger; toward him her air was very different. It was full of a winning grace, a fascinating favor.

The Borderer did not seem to notice all this, but a vague sound from his stalwart chest indicated some concealed sentiment. This, however, he suppressed in a moment, and turning to Mr. Argal, he said:

"I don't see my Lord Fairfax. Where is he, my dear friend?"

"He is gone a-'unting, sir," said a grave and respectful voice behind the soldier, "a-'unting, if you please, sir."

"Ah! here's old John!" cried the Borderer; "glad to see you, my friend. Faith, give me your hand!"

And the Captain cordially pressed the hand of the old servant. Old John was Lord Fairfax's body servant, and wore his master's livery with the exception of the coat, which was one of the earl's—heavily laced and ornamented.

He took the offered hand of the soldier with deep respect, and then drew back quietly, overwhelmed with the honor.

"He's gone a-hunting has he—the good earl! eh? Well, when will he return, John?"

"I rayther expect him to-night, sir," said John.

"Good!—then you are not certain?"

"No, sir; very often he is gone a day or two, sir."

And John stood respectfully awaiting further questions.

"Did he expect me to-day?"

"I think rayther, sir."

"Very well, get me supper and beds for my friends."

Old John was in his element again; his master's hospitality was put in requisition.

"D'rectly, sir—yes, sir," he said, going toward the sideboard. "Plenty o' beds, sir, for you and your honor's friends—d'rectly, sir!"

But Mr. Argal stopped him as he was going out.

"Bring up our horses first, John," he said, "I have waited as long as possible to see his lordship. It is already night, Bertha."

Bertha placed one hand upon her breast, and uttered a little cough.

"Yes, sir," she said, "I wish we had gone sooner. I am afraid"——

And the young girl was interrupted by a violent fit of coughing.

"What! you have a very bad attack of cold," said her father. "I did not observe it before."

"Yes, sir," returned the young girl, placing her hand upon her throat, and contracting her beautiful brows, as though she were suffering pain; "yes, sir, I have felt it coming on all day, but managed to suppress it until now. It pains me very much:" here she paused to cough again; "but if you desire it, I will"——

A more violent fit here seized the young lady, and she coughed until she was completely exhausted, leaning back in her chair for support.

Mr. Argal looked very much annoyed.

"Permit me to say, sir," said Falconbridge, "that exposure to the night air will aggravate Miss Argal's indisposition. If possible she should remain here until"——

Another fit of coughing.

"But I cannot—it will be extremely inconvenient: besides the house here is limited in size, and"——

"Don't fear, your honor," here interposed old John, who had entered with a hissing urn and a pile of plates the moment before. "Don't fear, sir; plenty of room, sir. We have two spare chambers, and several beds in them, sir; my master would never hear of your going, sir."

Mr. Argal hesitated, evidently annoyed.

"Getting very cold, sir," added the hospitable John, respectfully, "and if it's not presumin', sir, the young lady, sir, is "——

Here the young lady coughed distressingly.

"I'll go if you wish, father," she said, in an artless, uncomplaining voice; "but my breast feels very badly. I don't suppose it will make me very sick—if you want to go, sir "——

"Well, well, daughter, we will remain," said the old gentleman. "If you are really unwell, all the business in the world shall not make me you take you out. See to our horses, John," he added, "and as you say there are chambers, make one of the women prepare a bed for my daughter."

"Yes, sir—d'rectly, sir."

And old John, having set the table with the ease of a practiced hand, hurried out, and was heard giving orders in a magisterial tone to the negroes of the establishment.

Captain Wagner remained silent, gazing into the fire; his huge shoulders bending forward, as was habitual with him, and his sword striking heavily from time to time against the floor as he moved.

George was looking over a map of the region, which he had taken from the shelves; Falconbridge and Miss Argal had resumed their conversation.

The young lady's cough had disappeared.

Then old John entered, marshalling in a smoking supper, borne by youthful Africans; and the savory odor seemed to diffuse an emotion of pleasing satisfaction through the mind of Captain Wagner.

They all supped comfortably, and the Borderer was still eating when they had finished.

"Faith, I'm always hungry!" he said; "more beef, friend John."

"Yes, sir—d'rectly, sir."

And old John carved rapidly.

"More everything!" said the Captain. "I've just commenced, or the devil take it."

More of everything was supplied, and at last the soldier rose, stretching himself, and yawning.

"Nearly bed-time, I think!" he said. "Come, George! give up my couch "——

"Your couch, Captain?"

"Yes, that leather chair! Vacate! I sleep here by the fire; I know nothing of beds!"

George smiled, and resigned his broad, sloping-backed chair.

"You and the rest can take the big room," continued the Captain; "this young lady the small apartment. Faith! I know Greenway Court by heart!"

And the Captain, having first piled some more wood upon the fire, stretched himself comfortably in the leathern chair, and closed his eyes.

III.

HOW CAPTAIN WAGNER BECAME UNEASY IN HIS SLEEP.

IN five minutes the Borderer was snoring with an unction which brought a smile to the faces of his companions. He had closed his eyes with the words, "Take care, my dear friends, I hear very well in my sleep—therefore don't speak ill of me;" but this seemed quite an idle boast. The Captain presented the appearance of a frontier Goliath, worn out by fatigue, or somniferous from the extent of his last meal.

"Come, Bertha," said Mr. Argal, rising, "we must set out very early, and it would be advisable to retire, I think. I see old John at the door waiting for us."

"Yes, sir—when you're ready, sir—everything right, sir,' came respectfully from the door, which opened on a flight of stairs, "right hand for the gentlemen—the other room is ready for Miss Argal."

"Please send the maid to show me the way," said the young lady, with a smile, "good-night, father, I will follow in a moment."

The old gentleman nodded, and kissing her on the forehead, went out, followed by George.

Falconbridge rose.

"Stay and entertain me for a moment," she said, smiling "until my maid comes."

He sat down quickly: so quickly that any one would have understood from the movement, how gladly he complied with the request.

The door closed upon Mr. Argal and George. Then

commenced a conversation, at first upon indifferent subjects in the ordinary key, but gradually becoming more confidential, if the word may be used, and carried on in lower tones. To a curious observer, the spectacle would have possessed a profound and absorbing interest—for it was that of a woman of dazzling beauty, and immense *finesse*, marshalling all her dangerous powers against the heart of a frank and truthful gentleman, into whose breast the shadow of suspicion never had for a moment entered. The glances which she cast upon him were dazzling, electric ; he felt his cheeks flush, and his pulses throb.

"Then you do not think me unmaidenly ?" came in a low murmur from the crimson lips.

"Because you express your satisfaction at my coming ?" said Falconbridge; "how can you ask such a question ?"

"I feared you might; I am so unfortunate, in never concealing what I feel. Frankly, then, I hope you will come and see me—we are almost buried in the woods."

"I surely shall. I am too happy to be able to contribute to your amusement."

"No, do not say my amusement "——

She stopped, blushing deeply.

"Do not look at me," she murmured, turning away, "I am so foolish "——

"Your room is ready, miss," said the maid, opening the door.

"Wait for me in the chamber," was Miss Argal's reply. "I will come up in a moment. It is very early, is it not ?" she added, turning with a languishing smile to Falconbridge, as the maid disappeared.

"Very," he replied, "and if you'll not regard me as presumptuous, I will say that I have little desire to exchange your society for my own thoughts or dreams."

"Of what do you dream ?" she said, smiling archly, and throwing at him one of those fascinating glances which possessed such a singular attraction.

"Oh! of many things. Of my lowland home—of the strange land to which I go, for I have come to see about some property in the wilderness which I am entitled to, by a grant from Lord Fairfax."

"Are your dreams never filled with brighter images?"

"With brighter images? Ah! you mean with the forms of ladies fair!" he laughed; "no, no, I have never loved."

"Then your heart is cold?"

"Oh, no! I think 'tis a warm one."

The young lady sighed deeply.

"Why do you sigh so?" he asked.

She played with the ribbon around her waist, and looked in silence at the floor.

"Only my foolish thoughts," she murmured; "I thought —what a treasure it would be to me—a heart that had never loved"——

As she spoke she suffered the hand which played with the ribbon to fall beside her. The hand of Falconbridge was hanging down, and the two came in collision. Mastered by a sudden and wild impulse, and forgetting every rule of etiquette, he imprisoned the snowy hand in his own, and raised it to his lips. The young lady blushed, but did not withdraw it. For an instant the eyes of the two persons met and exchanged a long, and absorbing look:—the young man's were filled with an ardent admiration, the young lady's with a languishing sweetness.

"I must go now," she murmured, slowly withdrawing her hand. "Good-night!"

And with a last look, she opened the door just as the maid placed her hand on the knob. Had the young lady heard her step descending the stairs?

Falconbridge sat down, and leaning his head upon his hand, gazed into the dying fire. Nothing disturbed the silence but the heavy breathing of the soldier, who, stretched in his great leathern chair, had never once moved during the colloquy.

"Strange!" murmured Falconbridge; "strange young girl! I scarcely fathom her character, or understand her singular demeanor. They tell me that I have sound intelligence, that I read men—but, pshaw! I am quite at sea with this young girl. What a dazzling, superb beauty! Well, well—this is folly!"

And he gazed again in silence into the fire. For more than half an hour he remained thus motionless—reflecting. Then turning his head, with a deep sigh, and a wistful smile he gazed at the form of the sleeping giant in the leathern chair.

"A brave man, and with a warm, strong heart under all that roughness, I see plainly!" he murmured. "How great a contrast to this beautiful young creature, does he present! A strange world—yes, very strange—strangest of all that I am here!"

And he leaned back in his chair, and smiled. The dying fire-light lit up his youthful face, rich costume, and brilliant eyes, making him resemble some picture of the Middle Age. He remained thus, leaning back for a few moments, and then rose.

"Well, well," he said, "all this will have its course —but I soon pass—enough for one day."

And saluting the sleeping soldier with the smiling words, "Happy dreams, companion!" he left the room, and retired to his chamber.

No sooner had the door closed than the eyes of Captain Wagner slowly opened, and he looked in the direction of the door, muttering. Then his heavy moustache curled slowly toward his ears, and under the mass appeared his large, sharp teeth. He sat up and looked at the fire.

"Some people would say that I have done what is dishonest and unsoldierly," he muttered, kicking the brands of the fire together, "let 'em! I was asleep and I woke," he added, gloomily. "I believe the sound of that voice woke me."

His eyes were raised toward the ceiling, and a strange expression filled them, making them burn under their shaggy brows.

"Good, good! it's well I'm here," he muttered, "and I'll act a comrade's pàrt by him, or the devil take it—but not too much! A noble fellow! He shall not be tricked!"

The Captain muttered something more to himself; and then stopping suddenly, listened.

"There, I am at my folly again," he growled. "I'm a dog and can't sleep—I am dreaming!"

But in spite of this he rose, and went to the front window. It was secured by the heavy shutter, through which a streak of moonlight was visible.

The Borderer seemed uneasy; he walked to the other window; stooped down, and for an instant seemed almost to be smelling at it: and this idea appeared to cross his mind, for he laughed, and returned to his place before the fire.

"I'm a fool," he said, "but I swear I felt uneasy: I must decidedly get over this! I'm never at rest—why can't I sleep?"

The fire began to burn clearly again, and give out a pleasing warmth. The Borderer held his hands over the blaze for a moment, then lay back in his chair; and placing his huge boots upon the broad-topped andirons, began to snore almost immediately.

The fire caught a fresh stick and licked it merrily, and blazed aloft, but the Borderer slept on in spite of the full light it poured upon him.

IV.

HOW CAPTAIN LONGKNIFE SAW WITHOUT SEEING, AND WHAT FOLLOWED.

THE long hours of the night passed on, and no sound was heard throughout the slumbering mansion but the subdued tick of an old clock in the passage, and the heavy breathing of the soldier. At times he would stir in his sleep, and the heavy sabre would rattle against the floor; but this noise would soon shudder and die away in the remote apartments, and again all would be silent.

Without, the moonlight slept upon the wild and solemn scene of forest and prairie, and nothing disturbed the quiet of the chill October night, but the cry of wild birds, or the stealthy footsteps of the mysterious inhabitants of the forest, abroad now, while their enemies were sleeping. At times, the chill wind would sweep over the tall prairie, and a sobbing sound would rise, then die away; and over all poured the solemn moonlight, which seemed to brood upon the wild scene like a dream.

A piercing eye, however, might have descried more than one flitting form under the lofty forest; an acute ear have discerned sounds which belonged neither to the bear, the panther, nor the wind. Other eyes than those of wild beasts were directed toward the silent mansion, which raised its walls thus on the outskirts of civilization, disputing the sovereignty of the great woods:—and those burning glances were measuring its strength and weakness, the capacity of its inmates for a mortal struggle.

The huge Borderer breathed heavily in his chair, and resembled some gigantic statue come down from its pedestal, and taking its rest while mortals slept. From time to time the flitting and bubbling fire would burn out brightly, and reveal the recumbent figure in its full proportions:—but it already flickered and promised soon to die away. The cool air already began to invade the apartment, and the soldier turned uneasily.

At the same moment, the window opening into the passage stealthily creaked, and suddenly a thread of moonlight silvered the floor.

Then the shutter was opened still more, the window cautiously raised, and a head appeared at the aperture. It was the head of an Indian boy, with long, straight, black hair, sparkling eyes, and swarthy cheeks.

The head remained perfectly motionless for about five minutes; only the restless and ever-moving eyes roved from side to side.

At the end of this time the window was wholly raised—the Indian drew his body up, and falling upon his feet noiselessly, stood within the house.

Motionless as before, he reconnoitered. The door of the great room in which the Borderer slept, was half open, and creeping stealthily toward it, the Indian looked in. At sight of the warlike sleeper, he recoiled two paces, and looked behind him fearfully, in order to be sure that the means of escape remained. The window remained up; and the sight of the opening seemed to reassure the spy.

He again approached the door—opened it a few inches wider, and looked curiously in, as though to take note of any other persons in the apartment. His eye then dwelt upon Captain Wagner, and he placed his hand upon his girdle, from which hung a hatchet.

As he did so, the Borderer opened his eyes, and looked him full in the face.

The Indian, with one stealthy bound arrived at the window, and was about to pass through, when he suddenly checked himself. No noise had come from the sleeper, hence he had not really waked; doubtless it was a presentiment, the eye fixed upon his face which had waked him, or rather disturbed him in his sleep.

The dull eye of the Indian boy glittered, and he drew back into the deep shadow, out of the gleam of the fire. With a muttered "ough!" he touched the forefinger of his left hand with that of his right, apparently counting.

Then his roving eye turned on all sides, and he looked up the short, steep stairs:—his foot rested on the first step. The step was of firm oak and did not creak. The Indian mounted another step, and so, stealthily, and pausing each moment to listen, arrived at the top.

His first movement was to creep to the window opening upon the roof—one of the dormer windows, of which we have spoken—and raise it. From the roof of the house to that of the long porch, was but a step. Thence he could easily glide down.

Two or three dusky forms appeared for a moment in the moonlight, and then vanished beneath the solemn trees of the forest.

The spy placed his hand upon the knob of Miss Argal's door, and slowly and noiselessly turned it. The door opened without sound.

The moonlight streamed full upon the bed, but threw the features of the sleeper into shadow. It was evidently the aim of the Indian, however, to ascertain the numerical strength in men, of the house: and he crept stealthily, like a young panther, toward the bed.

Before he could bend down close enough to see, however; before his black eye and hot breath had approached her cheek, the young girl started up, and uttered a piercing shriek, which rang through the house like a cry of death.

The Indian seized his hatchet, and catching her by the wrist, endeavored to raise the weapon and strike her. It had become twisted in his belt, and before he could extricate it, a noise in the opposite room caught his quick ear, and he arrived by a single leap at the window.

At the same moment, the opposite door was thrown violently open, and Falconbridge came forth quickly, fully dressed, and hurried toward the room.

The young girl, who had risen in her night-robe, ran toward him, threw her arms round him, and sobbing, "Oh, father! father!" buried her head in his bosom.

All had taken place in a moment; but that had been time enough for the soldier to rouse himself.

He now appeared at the bottom of the steps, bearing in his hand a flaming torch, from the fire; and mounted with a bound which shook the flooring.

"What's this? What's this? Speak!" he cried.

The lady clung closer to Falconbridge, burying her face more deeply in his bosom.

"Oh, father! father!" was all which she uttered.

Mr. Argal and George appeared at the door half dressed, and uttering wondering exclamations.

"How, daughter?—what? how?—the meaning of this extraordinary scene? and that noise?"

"I don't know what it means," said Captain Wagner, with a sort of ironical gloom, "but the devil eat me, if I ever saw anything as striking as that picture in all my life before.

And the Borderer, with a curl of his moustache, extended the huge arm bearing the torch, toward Falconbridge and the lady.

"Most extraordinary!" cried the bewildered gentleman; "why, Bertha, something has frightened you! Look up! are you aware, daughter"——

The young girl raised her head, and started, or pretended to start, violently at sight of Falconbridge. No one observed the sarcastic curl of the Captain's lip.

"Oh, father!" she cried, hastily retreating into her room, and drawing her drapery quickly around her soldiers, "Oh, it was so dreadful!"

"What!—dreadful?"

"Oh, yes sir—an Indian came to my bedside, and caught my wrist, and tried to kill me—oh, sir?"

And the young girl was heard falling into a chair, and sobbing faintly.

"An Indian in your room? you are dreaming, daughter!"

"No, sir!" said Captain Wagner, gloomily, "your daughter did not dream it!—in my sleep I dreamed, I thought—wretched animal that I am, to lie there like a hog—but see!"

And stooping quickly, the Borderer pounced upon a porcupine quill.

"Here!" he said, "here is the proof! This is from an Injun moccasin! And that window! Friends, I for one am no fool!"

And the Captain hurled his torch upon the floor, and trod upon it with his iron heel.

"To your tree!" he cried, "Injuns!"

At the same instant a flight of arrows whistled through the air, and passing within a few inches of the soldier's head, buried themselves, quivering in the beam of the staircase.

"Bah! no rifles!" cried the Captain. "But they're on us!" he cried, arriving at the bottom of the stairs by a single leap, "to arms!"

As he spoke, a terrific war-whoop rang through the forest, and a dozen Indians darted from the shadow, and threw themselves upon the house.

Captain Wagner reached the door just as it yielded to the powerful pressure of the assailants.

Having no time to draw his sword, the gigantic Borderer seized one of the carved chairs, and whirling it like a straw around his head, struck the foremost Indian a blow so terrible, that it literally drove him through the crowd behind him, maimed and bloody.

Set on fire by the sight of blood, and devoured with his old fury of battle, the Borderer, without waiting for his companions, rushed into the midst of the assailants, whirling his broken weapon around his head, and bearing all before him.

The Indians endeavored in vain to strike him—his gigantic stature and sweep of arm bore them down:—they unconsciously drew back.

The movement brought the Borderer into the moonlight, which streamed full upon his face and person.

- The Indians uttered a yell of rage and fear.

"Longknife!" burst from the crowd, and they retreated before the soldier with almost superstitious awe.

As they did so, Falconbridge, Mr. Argal and George rushed from the house, to the Captain's succor, and behind them appeared the affrighted domestics with pale faces, and uttering exclamations.

The Indians, spite of their numbers, lost heart—retreated toward the forest—and with cries of rage dived into its gloomy depths, and fled, followed by the chance-aimed balls of their enemies.

Captain Wagner drew back, bending down, panting, and knitting his brows.

"I counsel a return to the house, friends!" he said, "you'll lose nothing; all's done!"

And he turned toward the door. Directly in his path lay the Indian he had struck upon the head—stunned, bleeding, and insensible.

"Take the black devil in; he's not dead!" said the soldier to the servants, "and secure every window!"

The Indian was borne into the house; every one followed, and doors and windows were secured.

"A very pretty little scrimmage," said the soldier, curling his huge moustache and throwing some sticks upon the fire, "ough! you copper colored devil!"

And he pushed the body of the Indian with his foot.

The Captain looked at him more closely.

2*

"Playing dead," he said, contemptuously.

"Oh no! he's dead," said George, "look! that brand has rolled against his foot!"

"Bah! that's all you know, master George," said the Captain.

And bending over the Indian, the soldier kicked away the brand, and said "speak!"

The Indian remained motionless.

"Well if you're dead, my friend, I'll have your scalp!"

And the Captain seized the Indian violently by the lock of hair upon the top of his head.

The eyes opened and he made a violent, though feeble effort to spring up. In an instant the Borderer was upon his breast and his hands were securely tied.

"Now speak, you copper-colored devil, or you are a dead man! Speak in the Delaware! I know you, and understand your lingo!"

And bending down, the Borderer uttered some words in the tongue of the Delaware.

It was some time before the soldier could extract anything from the Indian. At last he muttered a few words.

The Captain rose satisfied.

"Not a regular inroad," he said, "only a wandering party. I gathered that from the lies he tells me. Now my friends be good enough to put this worthy in the cellar and double lock the door, first tying his hands securely. My part is over, and I'll sleep."

His direction was obeyed, and very soon the Indian captive was safe in the vault beneath, where Lord Fairfax kept his liquors.

No one retired again. By common consent the affrighted domestics huddled together in one corner of the apartment—and the visitors arranged easy-chairs in the most convenient manner for sleeping. Soon every one sank into uneasy slumber—except Captain Wagner. That worthy's repose, in his great chair before the fire, was as deep as before.

From time to time, he would growl and grunt it is true; but this was habitual with him.

There were two other exceptions to the above statement. Falconbridge and Miss Argal slept neither easily nor uneasily. They conversed in a low tone in one corner of the room :—when the first rays of dawn entered the apartment, they were still conversing in the same low murmurs.

V.

THE ESCAPE.

THE morning brought light and cheerfulness. The sleepers aroused themselves; Miss Argal retired for a time, to make her toilet, and soon all had re-assembled in the large apartment where a plentiful breakfast was smoking upon the hospitable board.

"Suppose we have the Injun rascal up," said Captain Wagner. "I think the sight of his copper-colored mug will give me a better appetite."

And every one acquiescing in this suggestion, the Borderer directed several of the servants to lead up the prisoner. They promptly left the apartment, and Wagner turned to Falconbridge.

"Do you know, my dear comrade," he said, "that I think you are the pearl of gallants?"

"Pray, how?" asked the young man, smiling.

"Why, you came so promptly to Miss Argal's assistance last night, that you shamed us all, companion."

Falconbridge smiled again, and said:

"I deserve no praise, Captain. I had not retired. I was sitting at the window thinking, as I often do—a bad habit I confess—when Miss Argal screamed. To go to her assistance was surely natural."

"Dooms natural!" said the Captain, pushing up his black moustache; "and Miss Bertha needed you."

"I—thought—it was—father," replied the young lady coloring.

"Good, good! We're not expected to see in the dark," was the Borderer's sardonic answer; "and when Injuns are about, a woman may run into the arms of the first fighter she sees—faith, 'twas a pretty picture!"

A suppressed flash of the young lady's eye seemed to indicate that she discovered in these words something more than they expressed: but otherwise she betrayed no emotion.

"Well, well," added the Borderer, "let us think of the rascal we caught. I'm mistaken if we don't get out of him the real meaning of this little scrimmage in the dark—which I think was a wandering party only, that is safe a score of miles away by now in the Southwest Mountains."

Old John appeared at the door, as the words were uttered—his face elongated, his eyes full of meaning.

"Where's the copper-colored rattle-snake—the serpent?" cried Wagner.

"Gone, sir! clean gone!" said the old body servant, holding up both hands.

Captain Wagner rose with sudden energy, and hastened to the cellar, followed by his companions.

"Gone, as I'm a man!" he cried, twisting his moustache. "Look! Falconbridge, he got through there, the snake!"

And the speaker pointed to a low window from which two rusty iron bars had been wrested by main force.

"He managed to get his hands loose, and by this time is at the end of the world. I'm a hog not to see better to his tying up!"

And having thus unburdened his mind, the Captain slowly retired from the cellar, shaking his head, and returned to the breakfast-room. The sight of the smoking meal seemed to restore his equanimity; and his huge nostrils evidently experienced the utmost pleasure in snuffing up the savory odor of the rich broils and hashes.

"Faith! something yet remains!" was the philosophic remark of the worthy; "life is not gloomy when a man can eat as I am going to. Come friends, let us get to work!"

And first regaling himself with a huge gulp from the pungent "dram" which old John had concocted, the Borderer applied himself with energy to the business before him. It was a spectacle full of interest to see the piles of edibles disappear before him. Not until almost everything had vanished did the Captain lean back in his chair, like a son of Anak, twist his moustache, and open his lips for the purpose of conversation.

The movements of the entire party were discussed, and very soon every one had determined upon his plans of the day. There was not the least danger of any attack from the Indians, said the Captain, in broad day, out of the woods: but his intention was to scour the surrounding country, and pick up every detail. George declared he would go with him.

"And I," said Falconbridge, "shall accompany Miss Argal as far as her home, if she will permit me."

"I shall be very glad," said the young lady, looking at him with her strangely fascinating glance. Then casting down her eyes, she added, "but pray do not let me inconvenience you."

"'Tis none, I assure you," he replied. "Captain Wagner has spoken to me of a certain 'Van Doring's Ordinary' in the same direction, and here I purpose stopping until I arrange some business with my Lord Fairfax."

With these words, Falconbridge offered his hand to the young lady to assist her in mounting her horse, which stood ready at the steps. The young girl's hand was ungloved like his own, and—could he be mistaken?—did the soft, slender fingers press and cling to his own, as if she would retain the hand of the youth? His eyes filled with sudden light, and mounting his glossy white throughbred, he cantered off joyfully by the side of the young lady: Mr. Argal following more leisurely upon his cob.

"What a noble face!" said George, looking after them. "Do you know, Captain, that I can't help loving him?"

"Who? Falconbridge?"

"Yes—though I've known him less than a day."

"Well, you're right. 'Tis as fine a head as ever I saw on human shoulders. There's only one fault I can see in it—not enough of gray hairs."

"Gray hairs!"

"Yes, my young friend; he's too grand and true and unsuspecting. All that won't answer in this miserable world, that's full of snakes, Injuns, rascals, and deception. Don't ask me what I mean—I never mean anything. Let us rather take a drink of this fine October air, that is better by far than twenty year old Jamaica, or I'm a dandy!"

And the Borderer inhaled the breezy atmosphere, drinking in life at every pore. His eye wandered over the great landscape of prairie, forest, mountain, and river, variegated by the shadows of vast floating clouds; and his whole face glowed with pleasure.

"His lordship's got a splendid country here, friend George," he said : "I envy him the look he's taking at it now."

"Lord Fairfax?"

"Yes, he's in the mountains yonder, 'unting, as the worthy John says—is this good Baron of Cameron, and Earl of Fairfax. When we shall see him, the devil only knows. He's a perfect Nimrod, a wild Injun on the trail of game, a real iron fellow, or I'm a dandy. I expect him back at Christmas —not before!"

A sonorous neigh arrested the Captain's remarks, and two servants led up "Injunhater" and George's sorrel. They were soon in the saddle, and the Borderer paused only to give old John his parting injunctions.

"Tell my Lord Fairfax, if he comes back before dinner, that I'm coming too—Injuns and wild beasts to the contrary notwithstanding. Also friend George, who rides with me. And hark you, John, have up some of that old Jamaica that we know about—and one of the old hams, a round of beef, some fowls, and other trifles. You know I'm one of the family—good day, my friend."

And leaving old John bowing hospitably and respectfully, the companions set forward.

We shall not accompany them, as nothing in the shape of an adventure befell them. After a wide circuit around the Greenway Court domain, they came to the conclusion that the wandering party of Indians had hastily fled from the region into the western mountains. They accordingly returned to Greenway to dinner, and rest. The Earl had not made his appearance—nor had Falconbridge.

VI.

CAPTAIN LONGKNIFE'S PRIVATE MATTERS.

ON the next morning, Captain Wagner and George were again in the saddle—but this time they had determined to take different routes. The young man wished to explore the wonders of the prairie toward the South; the Borderer's design was to visit his friends at the Ordinary which Falconbridge had selected for a stopping-place.

"I'll go swill some Jamaica with Van Doring," said the worthy Captain, "and you, George?——toward the Fort Mountain?"

"Yes! It seems to draw me, it is so beautiful!"

"Good! how your eyes do sparkle! Youth! youth! what a fine thing it is: like a fresh horse with a full feed! But look out for the Injuns."

"I'm not afraid."

"I see that plainly, and you've got a proud-looking head there, George, my son. Don't let 'em scalp you. I assure you, on my honor, it will ruin your appearance for life."

And saluting with his hand, the gigantic warrior set forward on his heavy black charger toward Van Doring's.

The Ordinary was but a few miles from Greenway, and the partisan, advancing rapidly through the tall grass of the prairie, and beneath the drooping boughs of the forest, was not long in reaching his destination.

It was one of those large, oddly-fashioned taverns which are still found at Virginia cross roads. This one was the half-way house, so to speak, between the Lowland and the Frontier. It was constructed of hewn logs, the interstices of which were filled with rough plaster; in front extended a long rude porch; before the door was a horse rack and drinking trough.

As Captain Wagner drew near he perceived standing at the door a sort of covered wagon, which seemed to have arrived but a few moments before. He was looking at it carelessly, when all at once Falconbridge issued from the tavern, and courteously offered his hand to a buxom dame who was on the point of getting out of the vehicle.

"La! thank you, sir," said a simpering and complaisant voice, which made Captain Wagner suddenly start: but this start was of so ambiguous a character that it was not plain whether the soldier's emotion sprang from surprise, pleasure, or dissatisfaction. But immediately the Captain threw himself from Injunhater, whose bridle a stable boy received; and before the lady, with Falconbridge's assistance in front, and that of a travelling companion behind, could emerge from the vehicle, the gallant Captain had received into his own the hand yet unappropriated, and kissed it with chivalric courtesy and devout respect.

Falconbridge turned his head and saw his companion.

"Good-morrow, Captain," he said with a smile.

The buxom lady, finding her hand in contact with a bearded lip, and pressed by palms of martial strength, uttered a little affected cry and raised her modestly downcast eyes.

"Captain Wagner!" she said, with an exhibition of great surprise: "Captain Wagner!"

"At your service a thousand times, madam," said the Borderer, "now and ever, or may the devil—hum! How do I find you here, madam?"

The portly dame descended from her vehicle, smiling on the Captain and the Stranger, and sending backward a Parthian glance at every moment to her companion who had not yet descended. Her eyes were well adapted to this species of employment, as they were bright and cheerful, and her whole face was equally good-humored.

She was, or seemed to be, about thirty-five, and was clad in a fashion rather more gaudy than tasteful.

Her companion was a little dried-up Frenchman, dressed in a worn-out Court suit of the fashion of the time, and having on his head a cocked hat. He seemed to be in an agony of perplexity whether to drop the reins, a band-box and a shawl which he held in his right hand, or an old black violin which he carried carefully in his left.

The lady ran forward with quite girlish vivacity to greet an old fat German, who at the moment emerged from the Ordinary; and then with a shower of backward glances more bright than ever, which glances were directed towards Captain Wagner and his companion, entered the tavern, closely followed by her shawl-carrying, much perplexed French body-guard. Having reached the landlord's side, she clasped the old German so tightly that he found it utterly impossible to greet Wagner in any other manner than with the two sonorous words—"Well, Gaptain!"

The Captain stood for a moment looking after her, with an expression of amazement seldom seen upon his martial features.

For once in his life he seemed to be taken completely by surprise; and hesitated before he followed the enemy.

"Who would have dreamed it!" he said, pushing up his shaggy moustache; "she was Miss—beautiful Miss—Van Doring before espousing the lamented Butterton down yonder!"

And a sort of chuckle shook the stalwart breast of the Borderer.

"Well, well! Luck has declared for me!" he muttered. "I'm losing time."

"Lose a moment more with me, Captain," said Falconbridge ; and laying his hand upon the Borderer's shoulder he added, "What a noble morning!"

The Borderer shook the hand of the young man cordially, and said:

"Glorious! comrade : really amazing is this splendid morning—and faith! on my word! I think you suit it!"

"I?—how is that?"

"Why, you are as bright and jolly as the sunshine."

Falconbridge laughed, stretched himself, and yawned.

"I am fresh enough," he replied, "and you seem not at all fatigued."

"Fatigued! I believe you, comrade. A pretty thing for an old dog like myself, that has grown to the saddle,—whose legs are getting crooked, faith ! on that account—to talk about fatigue! But let us dismiss the subject of legs. You are stopping here?"

"Yes, till I see Lord Fairfax."

"Well, you'll have a pleasant lady guest."

"This lady? What is her name?"

The Captain looked cunning, and hesitated before answering this query.

"Come," added Falconbridge, "am I not to know who the lady is—her simple name?"

"I doubt whether it would be politic for me to tell you, comrade," said the Captain, shaking his head.

Falconbridge laughed.

"Politic? How so?"

"I would have necessarily to enlarge upon her character, her loveliness, her advantages, as the miserable cant is—her desirabilities : her thousand claims to regard, respect and admiration!"

"Ah?" laughed the young man ; "well, why not?"

The Captain shook his head.

"You're a dooms good looking fellow," he said.

"Oh!"—

"The truth, comrade ; and if you add to this the fact that

you seem to have much time on your hands at present—by which I mean that your business does not seem pressing—the motive for my caution will be plain."

"The motive, eh?"

"You might fall in love with this fair widow Butterton—my pleasant acquaintance down in the town of Belhaven, which I'm told they are going to dub Alexandria, where I came from. See, now, I've let the whole thing slip out."

And Captain Wagner pretended to regard his conduct with supreme contempt. Falconbridge only laughed and said:

"I believe you are in love, eh, Captain? Well, I wish you good luck."

His companion groaned.

"There's no such thing for me, comrade. I'm defeated, repulsed, driven off ignominiously!"

"You have paid your addresses to the fair widow and failed?"

"Something like it. I really believe that you have guessed the state of things to a hair. I thought from the first, Falconbridge, that you were a man of discrimination."

"And this is really so?" laughed the young man, amused by the Borderer's lugubrious expression; you have really proposed and been discarded?"

"Precisely, my friend, precisely: you have guessed rightly. Yes! I was overcome, subjugated, compelled to lay down my arms: ignominiously, miserably,—I, who have lived in the midst of battles, who have heard the cohorns roaring from year's end to year's end—the muskets rattling here, on the border, everywhere; I who have married twice, and each time paragons of women! I thought I knew the sex tolerably well, and I was mistaken. Vain thought for any man to imagine he has found the key of woman! Open one lock, another, then another, the next one baffles all your skill, defies all your cunning—which word I use in its ancient and commendable sense—laughs at all your exertions, if, indeed, locks ever laugh. And now I was that benighted individual; I thought I knew their wards, and springs, and windings, and turnings: I was mistaken; and here I am a mortified and humbled man, or if not that, a beaten man at least, or may the—hum! no swearing!"

"Come, Captain," replied Falconbridge, who with difficulty refrained from laughing, so melancholy were the tones of the soldier's voice, "better luck next time! You have a fine opportunity to make up your losses."

"I find I have, indeed."

"Avail yourself of it."

"I will," said the Borderer, with great cheerfulness.

"As to finding a rival in me, you need not have any fears on that point, Captain," said Falconbridge, laughing. "I'm on the wing—I soon pass. In a month I will not only be gone, but forgotten."

"Faith! no."

"No, what?"

"You'll not be forgotten. For I'll remember you, comrade, as one of the most gallant-looking fellows I ever knew."

Falconbridge laughed again and held out his hand.

"You are determined to make me a partisan of yours, Captain," he said.

"No, not at all! I like you, my dear comrade, and I can't conceal my thought. If I'm angry I growl; if I'm pleased I laugh—I conceal nothing because I can't, faith! No: don't fear Captain Longknife, who, whatever may be his faults—and he has a few—is not the man to flatter. If you fear anybody, let it be the man or the woman who smiles on you, and holds out a friendly hand, while the other is under his or her cloak, clutching the knife that will stab you!"

And the Borderer for a moment looked gloomy.

As to Falconbridge, he laughed gaily at this ominous speech, and playing with his rich swordhilt said carelessly:

"I'm not afraid, and I think two can play at the cutting

game! Nevertheless, thanks, Captain, for the interest you feel. I am going now to a different sort of combat—to encounter perhaps a more dangerous enemy."

And Falconbridge with a laugh looked westward.

"I know you are," said Wagner, gazing at his companion wistfully.

"There comes Sir John, as fresh as a dew drop."

"A fine animal : and you are going, I don't doubt "—

"To see the fair Miss Bertha? Yes, indeed. What a splendid beauty!"

"Yes, very splendid : remember what I said just now."

"What did you say?"

"I said beware of smiles; distrust the hand thrust into your own ; take care of the knife!"

And refusing to say another word, the Captain with a sullen movement of his head went into the house, his forehead bent thoughtfully toward the ground and overshadowed.

Falconbridge stood looking at him for a moment in silence, and then laughing silently, nodded his head upward and downward with the muttered words :

"Yes, yes! a queer genius—a great dreamer! The 'smile,' the 'knife'—'take care of them!' Oh yes! he jests with me; but he's a good comrade and I won't complain. Good morning, good Sir John! A fair sunshine for us, and I hope you are refreshed. Ho! comrade!"

And the young man vaulted into the saddle laughing. He gathered up the reins, threw a coin to the respectful hostler, and set forward gaily toward the west.

"What an oddity, the Captain!" he added, " with his knives and warnings! Forward, Sir John! we are expected!"

And he put spur to the fine animal, who set forward more rapidly than before.

VII.

THE CAPTAIN RENEWS THE ATTACK.

CAPTAIN WAGNER entered the Ordinary shaking his head mysteriously, but his reflections were all at once banished by the sight of the fair Mrs. Butterton, who was seated gracefully upon a cane-bottomed chair, conversing. The Captain joined in the conversation with an easy air, and soon the visit of the lady to the Valley became the topic. The explanation was simple. The settlers of the region, Lord Fairfax at the head of them, had determined to organize a county government; and the question at the moment was, the locality of the county-seat. For this honor, the two microscopic villages of Stephensburg and Winchester were candidates; and as Mrs. Butterton chanced to possess a number of lots in and about Winchester, she was naturally desirous that their value should be enhanced by the selection of that place for the seat of government.

The fair widow concluded her sensible explanation by taking from a reticule, which hung jauntily upon her arm, a number of documents, which she gracefully handed to the Borderer.

Captain Wagner looked at the papers and pondered; then pushing up his martial moustache, he said to the widow:

"I admire your business talent, my dear madam; what a wife you would make! what an admirable wife! I shall recommend my friends to come and make themselves agreeable."

"La! Captain, you are jesting," said the lady, covering her face affectedly with her fan.

"Jesting? Jest on such a subject—never!"

"You are a sad joker!"

"Not with you."

"Why not with me?"

"I know not, my dear madam, except it be on account of that high respect I have for you."

"Flatterer!"

"That friendship, that regard—that, I may say, hum—that, yes, that "—

Captain Wagner finished the sentence with a look which spoke volumes. The widow fairly blushed.

"What are you talking about, daughter and Gaptain?" said the old German, coming up, "not fell out, I hope."

"Oh, far from it, father!" said Mrs. Butterton, laughing.

"She is a great rattle-drap at times, Gaptain," continued the landlord, "and full of all sorts of notions. Here is Mounseer Jambo, for instance—come here to deach dancing."

"He is a fine artist, father," said Mrs. Butterton.

"Hum!" said Captain Wagner, "he seems to be your particular friend."

"Oh, yes—he is a very gallant gentleman."

Captain Wagner scowled at Monsieur Auguste Hypolite Jambot, and that gentleman chancing at the moment to raise his eyes, was nearly struck motionless by the look. Indeed, Captain Wagner was a disagreeable man to have for an enemy, so large of limb, and terrible in arms was he; and his scowl was one of horrible expressiveness. He looked sword, pistol and blunderbuss at the very least.

"I have no doubt that Monsieur Jambot is gallant, madam," said he; "this he has proved by condescending to accompany you hither."

"Come, you look at Monsieur Auguste as if you did not like him," said Mrs. Butterton.

"Not like him, madam?" said Captain Wagner, bringing

down his great, gloved hand on the table; "that's true! I do not like Frenchmen."

"And I," said Monsieur Jambot, rising and bristling up at these words, "I do not like, no, I have no liking for *capitaines*, begar!"

Captain Wagner touched his sword instinctively, but reflecting that a quarrel, and combat with so diminutive a gentleman, and on so slight a provocation, was out of the question, withdrew his hand, and only scowled again on Monsieur Jambot.

Having thus terminated the conversation as far as the dancing-master was concerned, Captain Wagner turned, with great good humor and cheerfulness, to Mrs. Butterton, who had counterfeited excessive trepidation: but who, seeing matters thus amicably arranged, was again all smiles.

"My dear madam," said he, "the sight of you to-day has rejoiced me—and you were right in telling me your business. I shall assist you in that business: I will, madam!"

"La! thank you, Captain," said the lady.

"I will, madam," said Captain Wagner, solemnly. "I pledge you my word that Winchester shall, on your account, be the seat of Justice of the county of Frederick."

The widow regarded Captain Wagner with a tender glance;—not so much in return for his promised services—to do her justice be it said,—as in requital of his devotedness.

"For your sake," said the Captain, in a tone inaudible to the rest of the company, "I would do far more."

"You are very disinterested, Captain," murmured the lady.

"Disinterested? Not so, faith!" said the Borderer; "remember what I say!"

And having overwhelmed the fair widow by this unmistakable avowal, Captain Longknife directed another scowl, far more terrible than the former ones, at Monsieur Jambot, who was still tuning his fiddle; and turned the conversation upon indifferent topics.

The lady smiled, the old German smoked, the dancing-master meditated a solo, or frowned with lofty dignity at his rival.

Thus some hours passed, and then the Captain, pleading business with Lord Fairfax, took his departure.

It is unnecessary for us to say, that like a stalwart soldier, the huge Enceladus had returned unterrified to the attack, with better knowledge of the enemy he assaulted, and a fixed determination to be victor in the struggle.

VIII.

HOW GEORGE WAS LED BY PROVIDENCE.

LET us now return to George, who, as the reader will find, met with more adventures in his ride than he expected.

The boy stood watching Captain Wagner until that worthy and his ebon steed were swallowed by the bright October foliage; and then mounting his handsome sorrel, left Greenway Court, and—happy, laughing, joyous with that rare roseate joy of youth and inexperience, and confidence—went forth toward the South, over the swaying, splendid prairie, and through the brilliant forest.

Poor words!—for what words can describe the forests of the Shenandoah Valley in October?—what painter, even, though he stood in stature above Titian, and the masters of all time, could place upon the canvas the resplendent glories of this noble season? Not a mere thoughtless rhapsody is this—for in the heart of him who writes, a thousand Autumn scenes live, like memories of youth, beautiful and brilliant with the glories of the "jocund prime" of existence!—so beautiful that, remembering them now, in days not so bright, he is thankful for the treasure given him, and living in his recollections, cares not for the present.

George was still in that brilliant land of youth—with senses open to its glories and delights; and so he went on joyfully, and gladly, through the golden morning, drinking in at every pore, the splendors of the Autumn.

It was one of those mornings which seem to come like a blessing on the earth: when the azure sky, piled up with snowy clouds, droops down upon a world of beauty; when the cool breath of joyful winds sweeps across hill and valley, with a murmurous laughter, as of myriads of merry goblins, let loose for a holiday, and reveling in their freedom. The variegated foliage of the waving forest, like the banners of every nation met in leaguer around the battlements of the noble mountains, shone in the clear sunlight, and the rich prairie waved its gorgeous flowers from end to end of the great valley.

To George, the Autumn did not present an aspect of mournfulness or decay: rather of full-handed, ripe, and matured beauty. His eye dwelt with delight upon the forest, with its magical colors; his roving and bright glances penetrated the white, delicate mist which, clearly relieved against the mountain, lay, like a milky cloud along the winding river:—the boy's heart filled with youthful joy and romance.

As he approached the mountain, the blue gradually changed to green; the undefined shadowy giants stood out in bolder relief, with rocky shoulders, and belts of haughty pines;—and then, after an hour's rapid riding straight on, he had approached so near, that it seemed to him an easy thing to push his horse up the slope, and gain the inviting summit. George had, however, yet to learn that nothing is more deceptive than the apparent distance between the beholder and the great towering sentinel of Nature. He was yet a considerable distance from the mountain, and in his path lay an obstacle not to be despised—the tree-fringed river.

As George drew near the river, and went along under the bright foliage of the lofty trees, a thousand woodland sights and sounds were around him. On the prairie the landscape was wild and undisturbed; he had heard no sound, but the far resounding cry of the crane as he rose from some streamlet's bed; had seen nothing but such air-wanderers as swept the blue sky on long stately wings, far up among the clouds:—for the most part all was still, and calm, and vast, as undisturbed as the landscape untouched as yet by the foot of man.

But now all was changed; the forest seemed instinct with life, and joy, and beauty. Long vines fell in bright festoons from the trees, and if these vines did not exhale the delicate perfume with which they flooded the forests in May mornings, they still were beautiful with their flaunting garlands, and fantastic outlines.

The pines were full of whisperings, as though the mountain wind would never have done telling them its secrets. The oaks, yellow and tall. The dogwood brilliant with its crimson clustering berries. The alder-tree, like saffron. and the hickory, yellow, but still strong, and graceful as a youthful giant—all were full of life and motion, and the voice of birds.

At distant openings the young man caught sight of more than one flying deer, and on the far mountain-side he saw distinctly a herd of huge elk galloping, as is their wont, into the verdurous, undiscovered depths of the deep glens.

As he approached the sloping bank of the river, an otter showed his brown nose, and bead-like eyes, then dived, making circles as he disappeared in the bright water; and at the noise a flock of wild geese, who had been feeding in the tall flags, rose up with a shrill clanging scream, and soared away, far into the bright clouds, on snowy wings, toward the South.

George reined up his horse and gazed with delighted eyes on the tranquil stream, whose surface, scarce broken into ripples by the gentle wind, mirrored the drooping boughs of the crimson and golden-leafed trees, and white floating clouds. The woodland sights and sounds delighted him— the freshness and wild grace of the fair nook with its green grass, and tree-trunks and fresh water, charmed him;—never had he seen so beautiful a landscape.

As he sat quietly in his saddle, gazing at the bright water, from which, at intervals, the "fall fish" leaped into the air;

his attention was attracted by a figure upon the opposite side of the river, which at this point was not very wide. This figure was that of a girl of about fifteen, who was evidently gathering flowers.

For the purpose of reaching the water-blossoms, growing far down in the shady nooks, near the surface of the stream, she stooped very carelessly over—so carelessly at times, that George, who, unseen himself amid the foliage, was watching her, feared every moment that her foot would slip, and she would be precipitated into the stream. But the little maiden took her way along the steep and dangerous bank with the care and skill of one practiced in roadside wandering; and her basket was soon full of fall flowers, which she paused to gaze at with evident satisfaction.

The boy looked at her for a moment, as she stood in the sunlight—glad to have seen this fresh woodland picture. He then turned the head of his horse, dismissed the little maiden from his mind with a careless conjecture as to her presence in that wild scene, and gazing at the clouds, was about to continue his way. As he touched his horse with the spur, a cry suddenly resounded in his ears—a cry of alarm and helplessness—and wheeling round, he saw at one rapid glance that his fears had been realized.

The little maiden had boldly ventured out upon a large, moss-covered log, at the end of which grew a magnificent cluster of yellow primroses; and this log having turned, she had lost her footing.

When George saw her she was just losing her balance; and her cry of terror scarcely reached his ears, when she dropped her basket, and fell into the stream.

George was one of those persons who never hesitate or lose their presence of mind—whom no sudden surprise affects.

The girl had scarcely touched the water before the boy, with a violent stroke of the spur, had driven his horse into the river, and was swimming vigorously and rapidly toward her.

IX.

HOW GEORGE MADE THE ACQUAINTANCE OF CANNIE.

THE girl seemed to feel that a friend was coming to her rescue, for her head was turned even in the midst of her struggle against the watery death which threatened her, toward the boy.

Her garments at first afforded her some support, and George thought he could easily reach her; but this hope began to disappear, and his trembling lips and flushed face showed his desperate anxiety. His eyes burned, and leaning forward on his animal, he devoured the sinking form with his looks, and struck the animal with his hand to hasten its speed.

Before he had arrived within twenty yards of the young girl, the water began rapidly to fill her clothing, and thus to add its own weight to the weight of her body. She gradually sank lower and lower; her long, chestnut hair rested on the water, and the waves toyed with it.

Nothing but the bright face was now visible; the small, bare arms were raised above the water; and a cry for help issued from the child's lips. George felt his throat choke; his eyes seemed to be starting from his head; his hands trembled like a leaf. Again a faint cry came from the child's lips—again the small arms beat the water; but the effort only hastened her fate. A wave passed over her head while George was still ten feet from her, panting, overcome with horror and despair.

Then she was gone! snatched from him! suffocated within his very sight! He uttered a groan of despair. But suddenly he seemed to feel that one course was left him; he might still save her. He threw himself from the saddle into the stream; passed over the space which separated them with half a dozen strokes, and came to her side. A curl of hair, before he was conscious of it, glided into his hand, and the next moment the girl was in his arms, her pale face lay upon his shoulder, and he swam with his almost lifeless burden to the shore.

George raised her in his arms, as though she had been an infant, and bore her to a grassy bank. Here, he used every means to restore her to consciousness, and at the end of ten minutes had the inexpressible satisfaction of seeing her open her eyes.

"Oh, sir! I was nearly drowned, was I not?" she murmured.

"Yes, indeed you were," said George, gazing kindly on the little face.

"Did you save me?" said the girl.

"I believe I did," said George, smiling, to keep up her spirits; "you fell into the water, and"——

"Oh, yes! I remember all now—oh, me!"

And with a shudder, the girl closed her eyes, overcome by the recollection.

"Don't think about it any more," said the boy; "it will agitate you. And you ought not to keep these wet clothes on—you ought to go home at once. And I must ask you your name, and where you live."

The girl sighed, and said, faintly:

"My name is Cannie Powell, and we live up in the Fort Mountain, sir."

"Very far?"

"Oh, no, not very, sir."

"Don't call me sir," said George, smiling; "I'm only a boy, and it seems so constrained; my name is George."

The lips of the girl moved as though she were impressing the name forever upon her memory.

3*

"You ought to go home at once now," he said, "I will go and catch my horse, and we will return together."

The girl's cheeks colored, and she murmured:

"You are very kind! But I ought not to—you were going "——

"Nowhere! nowhere in the world; if I had been, I know my duty as a gentleman."

And George raised his head with simplicity; and casting a last look toward Cannie, went to search for his horse. The intelligent animal had not wandered far. Emerging from the water, after being abandoned by his master, he had quietly commenced feeding on the long grass—and now allowed himself to be recaptured easily.

George led him back to the spot where the girl sat, and throwing one stirrup over the saddle, helped her to mount, in spite of many protestations that she could easily walk. The boy only smiled, and with the air of an elderly protector, led the animal by the bridle, along the narrow road, through the rugged gorge. To the music of the brawling Passage Creek they thus entered the Valley of the Fort.

Glancing often back at his little charge, the youth now took in every detail of her face and figure. Long chestnut hair fell in moist, rich curls around a delicate face, with large, hazel eyes, rosy cheeks, and lips full of a grave sweetness and simplicity. There was something fresh and pure in every trait of the countenance, and the slender form possessed a childish grace and attraction. She was not clad like the daughter of a woodman, and this fact had very soon attracted George's attention. The fabric of her dress was almost rich, although greatly worn; traces of embroidery were visible upon the skirt; and around her neck the girl wore a string of very beautiful pearls. Her small feet were cased, it is true, in rough, high-reaching shoes; but her white stockings were of the finest silk; and her hands had evidently never been acquainted with toil.

These singular peculiarities of the girl's dress attracted, as we have said, the attention of her companion; but he did not dwell on them as strongly as he would have done, had he lived longer in the wild country which they were traversing, whose inhabitants still wore such rude costumes. He was looking at the sweet face which riveted his eyes, and he gazed at her so intently that the girl colored under his look. George saw that the blush was occasioned by his glance, and immediately looked away, and commenced talking—the girl replying with her grave sweetness, in which he found a singular charm.

They thus took their way along the wooded road, and soon disappeared behind the huge trees.

Had George chanced to look back as the road turned a great mossy rock, he would have seen something to startle him. As the two forms disappeared, the red leaves of an immense oak slightly rustled—a swarthy face peered carefully out—and the next moment an Indian, who had lain close at full length on one of the great limbs, dropped noiselessly to the ground. He was a young man, apparently about twenty-three, with a slender figure, bare to the waist. His nervous limbs were cased in fringed leggings of doeskin; his feet in moccasins, profusely decorated with the quills of the porcupine—and above his forehead nodded a plume of bright-colored feathers, the badge of a chief. In his bearing there was something noble and impressive; and as he stood for a moment leaning with crossed arms, bare like his chest, upon a long cedar bow, he presented an appearance eminently attractive for its wild and graceful beauty.

The young Indian looked gravely in the direction taken by George and Cannie—threw a quick glance toward the sky—then murmuring something in a low voice, which was very musical and sad, set forward with the rapid pace of a hunter, on the path which they had followed. He saw them mount the winding road, and approach a little mountain dwelling. Then, as if satisfied that further watching was useless, he sighed, plunged into the forest again, and was lost in the shadow of the autumn foliage.

X.

A SINGULAR PERSONAGE.

AROUND the small house upon the side of the mountain, the finest tints of autumn seemed to cluster. The great oaks were like pyramids of crimson; the tufted pines, resembling the tall tropic palms, which wave their gigantic plumes in the breezes of the Indian ocean, rose clear and beautiful against the sky—and over all fell the rosy haze of autumn like a happy dream.

The house was of logs, rough-hewn, and with clap-boards for a roof; the windows small, and evidently constructed with an eye to defence; the stone chimney in the rear leaned, as it were, against a huge mass of rock, fringed with close-set shrubbery. Flowers of autumn were in bloom beside the low door—and the whole mansion had about it an indefinable air, which seemed to indicate the presence of a woman or a child. George assisted Cannie to the ground, and fixing the bridle of his horse to a bough, followed her into the house. The room which they entered was simply furnished, but scrupulously neat; some books were lying on the rude shelf used as a mantel-piece; and the whole apartment was very cheerful and attractive.

As Cannie entered, an old man came to meet her; and the eyes of this personage were fixed upon her companion with an intentness which was for the moment not at all agreeable. They seemed to look through him, and that, without the least effort, and in an instant.

Then the expression of the old man's face changed; he greeted the boy with collected courtesy; and when Cannie, in a broken and agitated voice, spoke of her accident and rescue, the old man's expression changed more and more, and with a slight color in his pale cheeks, he held out his hand, and grasped that of George with the warmest gratitude.

George scanned the figure of his host; and this scrutiny evidently resulted in a manner similar to that former one in regard to the child. The old man was evidently no rude backwoodsman; his countenance and eyes wore the unmistakable stamp of the student, and the man of intellectual cultivation; and even in his dress the same difference was discernible. He was clad in a suit which had once been rich, and still exhibited traces, beneath a thousand stains and rents, of its former splendor. Upon one of the thin fingers, sparkled a diamond ring, and a pair of large, gold-cased glasses covered his eyes, rolling beneath their heavy white eyebrows.

As Cannie related, in her grave, sweet voice, the events of the morning, George read in the eyes of the old man a depth of tenderness, which he had never before seen in the face of mortal. When she told how George had saved her life, the wan cheeks flushed, and holding out, as we have said, his thin, white hand, the strange host inclosed the youth's in a grasp, which resembled the pressure of steel springs.

"You have saved two lives, sir," he said, with a singular nobility of tone; "thanks, thanks! And now, my child," he added, turning to Cannie, "go change your dress, or you will be ill."

The girl obeyed, and disappeared for a quarter of an hour, during which time the singular host spoke calmly on a variety of subjects. There was an air of collected strength and composure about the speaker, which puzzled George more and more—for he felt that he was in the presence of a superior man. In the midst of the conversation, Cannie re-appeared, with a primrose in her hair, and a smile on her lips

—far more beautiful, George thought, than before. She joined simply in the conversation—and an hour fled by imperceptibly, during which the youth found himself more and more absorbed in the process of gazing at Cannie. Then remembering his agreement with Captain Wagner, he arose, and in spite of the most courteous urging, declared he must depart.

"I really must return, sir," he said; "they will expect me at Greenway Court."

"At Greenway Court!" said his host, with an unmistakable start; "are you staying at Greenway Court?"

And the piercing eyes seemed to dive into his own, as though their owner wished to read his very soul.

"Yes, I came to the Valley but a day or two since," replied the young man, "and stopped at Lord Fairfax's. What surprises you, sir?"

"Nothing, nothing, my young friend—it is nothing!"

And withdrawing, as it were, into himself, the speaker controlled every exhibition of emotion. But George afterwards remembered the quick start—and understood why the utterance of the simple words produced an effect so singular.

With the promise that he would come very soon again, to know if Cannie had recovered from her accident, he at last departed—the grave, sweet face of the girl going with him—her smile seeming to light him on his way. A thousand speculations chased each other through his bewildered mind; he tried in vain to imagine who his eccentric host could be. But he was completely at fault. He gave up finally in despair; and turned with a sort of delightful relief to the image of the grave little maiden.

He was still absorbed in his thoughts of her, when the silence of the lonely road was suddenly broken. The notes of a bugle rang out clear from the mountain side—the echoes chased each other from cliff to cliff—and then a great trampling and baying was heard near at hand, and a huge stag, pursued by a score of hounds, bounded into the gorge, and fell bleeding to the earth, almost at the young man's feet.

XI.

THE WILD HUNTSMAN.

THE trampling which George had heard all at once became louder; a hoarse voice hallooed to the dogs; and in an instant a tall huntsman, mounted on a fiery animal of great size and muscle, thundered from a narrow bridle-path into the open space.

The stag had fallen, but, half raised upon one knee, was goring the dogs with his huge antlers. They strove to clutch him by the throat, but he foiled them, one and all, and several of them had already received bad wounds when the huntsman reached the spot. The sight seemed to arouse a wild ferocity in him. His cheeks flushed crimson, his eyes glared, and leaping from his horse, he drew his *couteau de chasse*, and threw himself into the midst of the dogs.

The stag made a last desperate effort. He seemed to feel that all was over. The dangerous antlers were lowered to pierce the hunter's breast—but all was in vain. The nervous hand grasping the sharp hunting-knife, darted forward —the blood spouted forth—and the stag fell to the earth, his throat cut nearly through and through.

The hunter rose, and calmly wiped the blood from his knife on his sleeve. Then he turned to the youth. George had thus an opportunity to scan his appearance. He was a man of middle age, with a tall, gaunt figure, penetrating eyes, and lips which seemed to indicate a temperament rather melancholy and cynical, than happy. He wore a brown peruke, and otter-skin cap, with a buck's tail stuck in it, and tall boots with heavy spurs. The remainder of his costume was rich, but discolored by rain and sun. The coat had once been profusely laced, and the orange silk waistcoat still showed traces of gold embroidery ; but the suit, like its wearer, appeared to have "seen better days." The hunter had carelessly wiped the blade of his fine French *couteau de chasse* on his cuff, and now scanned with great calmness his companion.

"A stag of ten, sir," he said, in a quiet, deep voice ; " you were fortunate to be in at the death."

"It is bloody sport," returned the young man, "but wonderfully exciting. What will you do with the carcass of the deer, sir?"

"Carry it home with me," returned the huntsman.

And whistling to his horse, which came slowly to his side, he raised the ponderous body, and threw it across the front of the saddle. Then mounting, he said:

"You were going in this direction—were you not, sir ?"

George replied in the affirmative ; and followed by the dogs, of whom many limped painfully, they took their way straight toward the river.

"A day for an emperor!" said the stranger in a deep voice. Then all at once smiling grimly, he looked at the young man and added : "but that may seem an improper distinction to you—you appear to be a Virginian, and the Virginians are all republicans."

"I am a loyal subject of his Majesty, George II.," returned the boy, " but God made the sunshine for all alike— did he not, sir ?"

A grim smile seemed to deepen on the stranger's face.

"No doubt, no doubt," was the half indifferent reply, "but the lion has more right to the forest than the jackal—if not to the sunshine. You see, sir, that his is the divine right of kings, and his court of tigers, leopards and panthers, have their privileges of nobility."

George looked puzzled. The strange huntsman seemed to aim at provoking discussion ; but it was difficult to reply to him.

"You dissent," continued the grim speaker, "but you don't reply to me. Come, say now, my chance friend—is not all this proper? Should not the lion rule the forest—the eagle the air? Should not the beautiful tigers and cougars be above foxes—hyenas?"

"Oh, assuredly!" said George, "but kings and nobles are not lions or eagles always—great lords are very often foxes I have heard. And tell me, is it just, sir, that because the fox bites the heel of the huntsman, as in the fable, and saves the life of the lion—is it just that the lion should declare the foxes throughout all time superior to the higher class of animals?"

"Good, good!" said the stranger, "you strike hard at hereditary privilege. You are a republican—you would overturn *class* ?

"I would raise up worth!" said George with animation; "I would have the strong and pure, instead of the weak and corrupt, at the head of affairs. I think when God gives integrity and powerful brain to a man, he should hold the reins of power, rather than his inferiors, though his origin be as obscure as a peasant's. Is not that entirely rational, sir?"

"Hum! hum!" said the stranger with his former smile, "I was not wrong in declaring you a republican—but that's no matter. What care *we* for kings or nobles in the wilds here? Here's the river."

And with these laconic words the huntsman pushed his horse into the water; and, half fording, half swimming, soon reached the opposite bank. George was there as quickly, and they again set forward—soon issuing from the forest into the waving prairie, whose myriads of brilliant flowers were glittering in the rich light of the sinking sun.

All at once two figures on horseback appeared a quarter of a mile in advance of them; and these figures plainly descried them, and awaited their approach.

XII.

THE DRAMA COMMENCES.

GEORGE recognized Falconbridge and Miss Argal. He rode his white thoroughbred, she her little filly—and standing in the tall grass which reached nearly to the backs of their horses, they presented, in the golden flood of sunlight, a richly picturesque appearance.

"I am very glad to see you," said Falconbridge, pushing forward and shaking George's hand, with a gay smile : then bowing courteously to the stranger, he added, "give you good day, sir."

The hunter inclined coolly ; but something in the face of the young man, or his tone of voice, seemed to affect him strangely. His penetrating gaze riveted itself upon the proud, laughing features of Falconbridge, and a shadow passed over his brow, like that from a floating cloud.

"It is strange !" the grim lips murmured ; "what a singular resemblance !"

Falconbridge did not observe the expression or the tone. He had turned to George, and began to explain how the young lady and himself, in riding out, had lost their way. His manner, when he addressed or looked at her, had changed greatly. There was something ardent and impassioned in his gaze as it rested on her face ; and the lady was not backward in returning it with looks almost as significant of her feelings. By some fatality this emotion seemed suddenly to have ripened in both hearts—thenceforth it was plain that the young lady was the fate of Falconbridge—his fate for weal or wo.

"And Miss Argal," said George, when Falconbridge had told how they had circled at random over the prairie, "was she frightened?"

"Oh no! she has behaved like a heroine, in spite of her utter ignorance of the road back to her home."

"I can't think where we are," said the young lady, with one of her pretty smiles. But for some vague reason George felt as if this declaration were not true. There was an imperceptible constraint in her manner as she spoke; and his truthful instinct told him that there was deception of some sort beneath her apparent candor. He did not reply, but turning to his companion said:

"We are not far from Greenway Court, I believe, sir."

"Some distance," returned the huntsman coolly, "but the path is well beaten."

And with a courteous but cold inclination to the young lady, he set forward, followed by the party. The sun ran in a stream of rich purple light across the hills, and far away beyond the mountains; the golden cloud ships slowly floated off into the distance and were lost: and as the shades of night descended and the stars came out, they reached the old mansion of Greenway.

The tall huntsman tied his bridle to the bough of a tree, lifted the carcass of the deer to the ground, and turned toward the porch. As he did so, old John appeared upon the threshold, and bowing low, respectfully approached.

"Dismount if you please, Miss Argal," said the hunter, with grave courtesy, "and honor my poor house with your presence."

"Lord Fairfax!" exclaimed George, "I might have known that you were Lord Fairfax—but my mind was busy with other thoughts!"

And something like a blush came to the cheeks of the boy. The Earl smiled, and pressing the young man's hand, said in a friendly tone:

"I am glad you did not know me—had you recognized one

of those 'foxes' you spoke of, you would have expressed yourself, perhaps, less honestly."

And with courteous gesture, Lord Fairfax marshalled his guests before him into the mansion.

The first object which greeted all eyes, was the huge form of Captain Wagner stretched in his favorite leathern chair : he was sound asleep, and his snoring resembled distant thunder. It was an amusing picture. His cocked hat had fallen on the floor, and half covered a pipe which had escaped from the soldier's hand. A half emptied cup of Jamaica rum at his elbow proved that the sleeper had been also occupied by the task of drinking after dinner. The long sword in its leathern scabbard had gotten between the athletic legs of the Captain, and at every chance movement rattled fiercely against the rowels of his spurs, or the iron heels of his large horseman's boots.

"Captain Wagner!" exclaimed the Earl, "so he's here!"

The Borderer stirred in his sleep, and the words "fairest lady!" escaped from his heavy froth-soiled moustache. Whether it arose from the nature of his dreams, or from the vicinity of that lithe and beautiful form, we cannot undertake to say : but it is certain that when Captain Wagner was awakened by the loud voice of Lord Fairfax, his conduct seemed to indicate anything but dreams of ladies. He started up, seized his sword, and overturning the flagon of Jamaica with his elbow, threw himself forward, crying "Injuns! or the devil take me!"

The grim melancholy smile George had already observed, passed over the face of Lord Fairfax, and he sat down, courteously motioning to his guests to be seated also. Then turning to the soldier, who was rubbing his eyes :

"Well, Captain Longknife," he said grimly, "sleeping on duty I see. When did you arrive?"

The Captain bowed with great composure, and picked up his hat.

"You, my lord," he said, "are responsible for this nap I

have taken, and if I have slept on my post, you see I was ready at a moment's notice."

"True; you came near splitting me and my friends here."

"That would have been too bad," said the Captain, "to split so noble a seigneur as the baron of Cameron; such brave companions as friend Falconbridge and George, or so peerless a dame as Miss Argal."

With which words Captain Wagner executed a stiff inclination toward the lady in question.

"Thanks, sir," said Miss Argal in her self-possessed voice.

"I hope in my absence you procured everything you wished, Captain," said Lord Fairfax; "old John"——

"Is a trump, or I'm a dandy, my dear sir," interrupted the Borderer. "Did I find all I wanted? I believe you! I'm an old campaigner, and feeling entirely at home had everybody running, of course."

"Right, right," said Lord Fairfax, smiling; "now, with your permission, we'll have supper, as I'm hungry."

"My permission!" cried the Captain, "you are jesting! You could not please me better; I am dying for something to eat, my dear friend!"

Old John, who was standing respectfully in a corner, opened his eyes at this statement, in a way that expressed volumes—but he was far too hospitable to allude to the Captain's performances at dinner. At a sign from his master he busied himself at once to get supper—and soon it was smoking upon the board.

Neither Falconbridge nor Miss Argal seemed in a hurry to depart; and when after the meal Lord Fairfax urged the young lady to remain all night, to avoid the chill air, she consented with very little difficulty. George unconsciously asked himself if young ladies in his neighborhood ever remained away thus from home, and treated the feelings of their relatives with such slight ceremony: but as Falconbridge, beyond a slight movement of surprise, indicated no opinion, the youth thought he was unreasonable, and blamed himself for his growing dislike to the young lady.

She kept her fine eyes cast down bashfully, the greater part of the time, only raising them occasionally to throw toward Falconbridge one of those glances full of subtle fascination, which made her so dangerous. It thus happened that she did not observe the steady look which Lord Fairfax bent upon her face. This look, full of admiration, and so striking in one who seemed to care very little for aught around him, took in every detail of the surpassingly beautiful woman's appearance:—the gently arched brows, the ripe red lips, the rounded chin, and the snowy throat, against which the dark curls were clearly relieved, making the white skin more dazzling from the contrast. Miss Argal did not observe that absorbing look; her marvellous acuteness would have discerned in it more than it expressed. He soon turned away, and commenced talking with Captain Wagner, and George; and thus the hours fled, and bed-time came. A maid announced that the young lady's apartment was prepared; and Lord Fairfax, rising, conducted her to the door, which he courteously opened, and ushered her through with a ceremonious inclination. She inclined her head gracefully in turn, and with a quick glance from the corners of her eyes toward Falconbridge, disappeared.

"What a very beautiful face this young lady has!" said the Earl, indifferently, "who is she?"

"The daughter of your neighbor Argal," said the Captain; "the new settler up there toward Stephensburg."

"The lady is a friend of yours, I believe, sir," said the Earl, turning courteously to Falconbridge. "I do not know that I have seen you in our neighborhood before."

"That is easily explained, my lord," returned Falconbridge, with the same easy courtesy. "I have but just reached this region. I have come hither to gather information as to the condition of a large tract of land which I own on the South Branch, by grant some years since, from your lordship's agent there. As to Miss Argal, I think I may style myself her friend, though our acquaintance has been short."

Lord Fairfax bowed and said:

"To-morrow I shall endeavor to afford you the information you desire, Mr. Falconbridge, and to cut out a task for you, George, my young Republican."

"Oh, then you've been debating!" said the Captain, with a yawn.

"Yes, and George is a leveller—but no matter. I care for nobody's politics. As long as he surveys accurately, and you, Captain, drive off the Indians, I'm content. And now, gentlemen, I must bid you good-night. I am really weary. Your apartments are all prepared."

With these words the Earl inclined his head, and rang a little silver bell, which speedily brought old John to the apartment. In half an hour, the whole mansion was silent. Were all sleeping?

XIII.

HOW FALCONBRIDGE HAD A STRANGE DREAM.

FALCONBRIDGE had a singular dream. He imagined that about two hours after midnight, his door opened; a heavy step stealthily approached his couch, which was flooded by the pallid rays of the great soaring moon; and a tall form bent down, and looked long and in silence upon his face.

What the mysterious figure was like, he could not tell, as the shoulders and head were wrapped in a heavy mantle, completely concealing the sex and character of the visitant. All that he plainly perceived, was a pair of burning eyes between the folds of the mantle—dark stars, as it were, which glittered as they shone upon him with a lurid lustre.

The figure remained thus motionless beside his couch, lost in the deep shadow, and silently scanning the sleeper, who was full in the moonlight, for what seemed to Falconbridge, an interminable time. Mastered by a vague influence, which he could not throw off, the young man lay still, asking himself if he were really asleep and dreaming this—or half awake, and looking upon a real form. He could not determine the question in his mind, and remained thus, lying supine and powerless before the vision, in the condition of a sleep-walker, or one in a trance.

To the first sensation of surprise and vague discomfort at the presence of the singular visitor, ere long succeeded a deep curiosity to discover what would be the next action of the figure. The eyes seemed to have burned down upon his face for centuries, but at some time they must be withdrawn. Falconbridge waited, therefore, and was not disappointed in his expectation.

The mysterious figure slowly assumed an upright position; a deep sigh seemed to issue from its bosom; and with head bent over its shoulder, and drooping form, it slowly returned toward the door through which it had entered.

The absence of the strange, glowing eyes seemed to give the dreamer courage. No longer paralyzed, as it were, by the magnetic glance, Falconbridge started from his couch, and grasping his sword, which lay upon the table, near his bed, bounded to the door.

He thought he saw it open and close upon the figure.

His sword pierced the solid wood—the clash echoing through the mansion with a strange, weird sound.

Falconbridge tore open the door, and issued forth upon the landing of the staircase. Nothing was to be seen. The pale moonlight slept upon the rude banisters, and the oaken floor, but no form was visible.

He rubbed his eyes, and returning to the apartment, wrenched his sword from the wood in which the point had been buried.

Had he dreamed? Could it really have been his fancy?

"I swear I saw it!" he muttered, wiping the cold perspiration from his brow, and returning to his couch; "it bent over me, and looked into my face!"

With these words he deposited his sword again upon the table, and lay down. He remained for an hour or more awake, watching for the return of the figure, but nothing disturbed the lonely silence. At last he fell asleep, murmuring; and slumbered undisturbed, until the sunlight streamed into his chamber through the eastern window, and waked him.

XIV.

THE NEXT MORNING.

"YOU must have eaten a heavy supper, sir," said Lord Fairfax coldly, as at breakfast the young man related his strange vision; "Greenway Court is not ancient enough to possess a ghost, and your dreams took a singular direction."

"True, my lord," returned Falconbridge, thoughtfully, "but I could almost swear I was not asleep."

"Not asleep!" said the Earl, with grave surprise.

"At least I think so. But plainly, I am mistaken. Yet 'tis strange! I seem to have seen really those lurid eyes full of pain and yearning—unhappy eyes!"

And Falconbridge leaned back in his chair and sighed.

"There, comrade!" said Captain Wagner, with his mouth full, "stop that groaning, or you'll make me melancholy. Luckily my appetite is proof against everything—but come, laugh!"

Falconbridge smiled. The sonorous voice of the soldier aroused him; and his constitutional spirits gradually returned.

"You are right, Captain," he said; "this is idle, and I am carried away by sickly fancies. And yet I could have sworn! but enough. I fear I've terrified you by my ghost!" he added, turning with a brilliant smile to Miss Argal; "I trust your own dreams were more pleasant.

"Very pleasant," was the low reply; and George caught in its passage, a quick glance, which seemed to say, "I dreamed of you."

The breakfast soon afterward terminated; and Falconbridge requested the Earl to have his horse and Miss

Argal's brought up. The young lady replied to his lordship's hospitable invitation to remain, that she feared her father was uneasy on her account; and this excuse was conclusive.

So they departed; Falconbridge making an appointment with the Earl to visit him on the next day; and soon afterward George, too, mounted his horse and left Greenway.

Was it to look at the country, or make surveys? If so, the youth evidently preferred the region of the Fort Mountain; for in an hour or two he had crossed the river, and was galloping along the road to the house of Cannie.

XV.

HOW LORD FAIRFAX INFORMED THE CAPTAIN OF A FAMILY PROPHECY.

LORD FAIRFAX and the Captain were thus left alone together.

The worthy Borderer lit his pipe, and stretching himself in his favorite leathern chair, prepared to listen or to converse.

The Earl sat opposite in one of the carved-backed seats; and, resting one arm upon a small table, prepared for business. Two great deer-hounds lay at his feet, and altogether he presented, in his rich costume of blue velvet, slashed and ornamented with embroidery, an extremely picturesque appearance, though the listless and melancholy expression of his features seemed to indicate that his feelings were far from cheerful.

On the table, beneath the hand of the Earl, lay a rudely-drawn map of the frontier, and beside it were a number of roughly-folded letters, and an inkstand, from which a long eagle's quill rose, like a bulrush bowed by the wind.

As to Captain Wagner, that worthy was clad as usual in his rough travelling dress, and heavy boots. One would have imagined that the soldier never doffed these vestments, so wholly a part of him did they seem; and it would have astonished his acquaintances to have seen the huge sword anywhere else than in its natural position, suspended from the great broad belt, and between the athletic legs.

Lord Fairfax leaned back in his chair, and passed his hand wearily over his brow. His features wore their ordinary expression of gloomy, almost harsh repose, but from time to time the grim, melancholy smile flitted over them.

"Thus, you see, Captain," he said, at length, "that I want assistance. The audacious attack upon my house here which you have just related, proves that I was not wrong in sending for you to come and help me. You think that this was only a prowling band, and of no strength—mere pillagers from the recesses of the mountains, come down on a momentary foray, as we say in Scotland; you may be right —I do not dispute it—in fact I agree with you. But that the appearance of Indians, in any numbers, east of the North Mountain, is a thing to take heed of, I need not tell you. Besides, I have other information which I have laid before you, to which you have listened attentively, and beyond doubt carefully considered. It comes to me in right of my office. I am Lord Lieutenant, or, as they say here, County Lieutenant of Frederick and the adjoining shires, and this information proves to me, that a great Indian attack may be expected at any moment. I am not sure that this day will pass in peace; that a runner will not, in an hour from this time, burst into my presence to announce an attack upon my manors on the South Branch."

"Not improbable," said the Captain, smoothing his moustache, thoughtfully.

"Thus I have sent for you," continued Lord Fairfax, "and I thank you for your promptness. You have grown hard in these encounters, and I know your military genius perfectly well."

"Thanks, my lord."

"Look," continued the Earl, pointing to the map; "all these lands are, as you know, a part of my grant from the Crown; this is the South Branch of the Potomac, and you see these crosses. You know better than I do myself that they are houses of settlers. I do not wish these Indian devils to ruin my lands, to scare off settlers. I shall never return to England at that rate."

"Does your lordship think of going back?"

"Assuredly," said Lord Fairfax, with a grim look; "I do not expect to live all my days here in the wilderness."

"I thought this was your chosen home."

"You have thought wrongly, then. As soon as I have collected money enough to re-purchase Denton, I shall return."

"Denton, my lord?"

"The paternal estate."

"How was it sold?"

"By my rascally guardians; the entail was cut off while I was a minor, and thus the prophecy of old Lord Thomas, the founder of our house, was fulfilled—but I shall disappoint him yet."

These words were uttered gloomily, but with a dark flush upon the swarthy features of the Earl.

"What prophecy does your lordship allude to, pray?" asked the Captain.

"Have you never heard it?"

"Never."

"Listen, then; the story is not long. The house of Fairfax had for its founder and head, Sir Thomas Fairfax, who became, for services to the Crown, Earl of Fairfax, and Baron of Cameron, somewhere about the year 1600. He was a sagacious man, and held great sway in Yorkshire, where lies Denton—*my* Denton it shall be again if there is money enough in the province of Virginia to re-purchase it! You do not understand, Captain Wagner, the feeling a man has toward a place which not only his earliest years have been passed in, but in which his house has lived for centuries. I love Denton, its park, its chase, its hills, and flats and forests; the old dining-room, the fencing gallery, the dogs and horses—yes, the very rustle of the great oaks around the door! Well, sir, that estate, as I said, was taken from me, the entail was cut off by my guardians, who, I firmly believe, were bribed to betray my interests. And so the prophecy was fulfilled. But I have not told you what that was. I have said that the founder of the Earldom was Sir Thomas Fairfax, and he was the grandfather of the Parliamentary General, the "Tom Fairfax," of the civil war, whom you have doubtless heard of—whose wife was present at the mock trial of King Charles, and created so much confusion by crying that her husband was too politic to be there. But I digress. The character of his grandson, the young general, had often caused Sir Thomas anxiety, and so clear-sighted was the old first earl, that he foresaw that this young man would ruin the house of Fairfax. This was put regularly upon record. Charles Fairfax, son of the first Earl, wrote it down. The old gentleman, walking in his great parlor at Denton, about the year 1640—a century ago—was much troubled. He said that something told him that General Tom, and his descendants of the same name, would bring the house of Fairfax to an end. It was fulfilled. General Fairfax alienated his family estate to marry into a powerful house. A century afterward, I felt the effect of his act, and Denton escaped from my hands—I am here."

The Earl paused and looked coldly through the window.

"And this exiled your lordship?" asked the Captain, with sympathy; "this act of your guardians?"

"That and other things," replied Lord Fairfax, a dark shadow passing over his brow. "My life has been unfortunate and tragic; Fate has sported with me, and woven a wild mesh to entangle me; I have been mastered in the struggle, and struck me down. But I'll not yield! Let a million prophecies be hurled against me—let Fate do her worst! I'll struggle and contend with her till I die!"

The Earl set his teeth close and was silent.

"That is right, my lord," said Captain Wagner, approvingly: "no brave man knocks under. I do not myself, believe in prophecies, nor any such flummery—and even am a disbeliever in witchcraft."

"I have had doubts myself, on the subject of this latter, and no longer place as much confidence in astrology either, as I did formerly," said the Earl, coldly. "A great seer in Italy informed me that I would recover Denton, and hence my struggling thus in the teeth of fate. I will struggle so to the end—and I will collect every pistole in this colony, but I will have it back."

"You have a tolerable grant of land from his Majesty, here, my lord, in place of the said Denton," replied Captain Wagner; "why not be content?"

"I am not content, because I am in fact a landless man. I tell you, Captain Wagner, that as long as the oaks of Denton are not mine—the old walls, the chase—everything—I'll not rest."

"Well, all that is natural, my lord."

"Certainly. And now you will understand me perfectly. I own a fourth of Virginia, and I wish to sell it."

"Zounds!" said the Captain, "it's a glorious bit of land to be in the market. I'd like to buy it."

The Earl smiled gloomily.

"You may at least help me to make it attractive to settlers, by grants to whom I aim at realizing what I need to re-purchase Denton."

"An empire for a plantation!" said the Captain; "but every man to his humor. Your lordship is the best judge of your own wishes—now, I'd take Virginia—but that's nothing. I don't deny that there are drawbacks in the shape of bloody savages, but we'll grind 'em, or I'll eat my own head!"

XVI.

HOW CAPTAIN WAGNER DECLARED WAR ON HIS PRIVATE ACCOUNT AGAINST LORD FAIRFAX.

THE stalwart Borderer uttered these words with so much energy and expression, that Lord Fairfax was diverted from his gloomy thoughts, and smiled. It was the old grim smile, habitual with him; but this even was more pleasant than the gloomy shadow which lay before upon his lips and forehead.

"Captain," he said, with his sardonic expression, "permit me to say that your invention in respect of oaths is truly wonderful."

"Many thanks, my lord," returned the Captain, evidently pleased and flattered; "I *have* a small genius in that line which my friends have complimented. But after all 'tis a bad habit! a bad habit!"

And the worthy looked modestly down, with an expression of mock self-depreciation which was a treat to the author of the papers in the "Spectator."

"I agree with you, Captain," replied the Earl, coolly, "but 'tis nothing to our present purpose. You have spoken of the Indians in time. When I touch on the subject of Denton, and the wrong done to me, I am never in my right mind. What do you counsel? speak plainly and without paraphrases. I require the assistance of a man who knows the habits of these devils, and who can plan. I don't care to acknowledge that I am a mere nothing in council as Tom, the General, was before me. I am irresolute—have a morbid inertness clinging to my mind; it is only in the chase that my nerves are strung, my brain clear and vigorous."

"I have seen as much in your lordship," said Captain

Wagner. "You are irresolute, but would be an excellent officer for a cavalry charge.

"Speak plainly," said the Earl, indifferently, "but when you have finished with me, come to the threatened Indian attack. I know nothing of these matters. Come, your counsel! I have laid before you the particulars."

"My counsel is easily given, or the devil take me," said the Captain. "'Sdeath, my lord, I know these Injun rascals; they hold pawpawing days the year round, and will be on you like an avalanche some morning; you should prepare. Send runners to the South Branch, with instructions to assemble the men with all the pistols, cohorns, muskets, rifles and carbines to be found: entrust commissions to them for persons I will designate. Such men as Martin, Miller, Howard, Walker, and Rutledge—direct the levies to be trained in bush-fighting, in loading while running at full speed, and in everything connected with a combat, and the instruments of the said combat, down to the cutting off the necks of the balls of the rifles. You have no time in an attack to unbreech and extract the ball—consequently a rifle is done up, or the devil take me. I will repeat to your lordship all the particulars, and you shall write them down, and entrust them—with the commissions you have the right as County Lieutenant to issue—to the runners. As to myself, I shall remain here, partly on private affairs," said the Captain, curling his moustache, "and partly because my services may be needed here more than yonder. It is not out of probability, even, that these devils will make their swoop upon Cedar Cheek, and this portion of the manor, from the mountains yonder toward the Northwest. Let 'em come!"

"That is a wild country, is it not?"

"The ruins of an overturned world, grown over with grass and trees, and inhabited by panthers and Injuns," said Captain Wagner, succinctly.

"Pardy," said the Earl, with his grim look; "I think we may expect them from that quarter."

"Therefore I shall remain here, my lord. Zounds! I will

have an opportunity, even here, of breaking some skulls, I warrant you : I hope so at least ; my hand is getting out of practice. Since I have stopped dragging at scalplocks and eating buffalo hump I have felt badly. Give me an attack soon, or by the devil's horns, I will rust to death!"

The stern smile came back to the Earl's face. He liked to hear the sonorous voice, the martial oaths even, of the rude soldier: they were but additional proofs that the instrument which gave forth such sounds must be robust and strong. The Earl needed Captain Wagner; he had estimated his own character—its strength and weakness—with perfect exactness. Brave, impetuous, even wholly fearless when aroused, he was yet morbidly irresolute when unmoved—could not bring himself to any determination—had scarcely power to decide upon the most obvious courses. He would often spend long, weary, miserable hours thus, in his great dining-room, his head resting on his hand, his thoughts wandering back to the past, or forward to the future; and would only rouse himself at last to dash off to the forest, there to drown his morbid feelings in the excitements of the chase, as other men do in the stimulant of wine. Thus the sight of Captain Wagner was always welcome to the Earl; he was glad to hear the loud voice, the rattle of spurs, the clatter of the sword; they kept him from thinking. He needed a counsellor, too, as has been seen, and thus the soldier stood high in the Earl's regards.

"Well, remain!" he said, in reply to the Captain's last words, "I shall have need for you in other matters, not so warlike."

"In what, pray, my lord?"

"They speak of a trial for witchcraft here soon."

"Who?"

"These gentlemen justices of Frederick, or rather one of them, a Mr. Gideon Hastyluck."

"I know him. A crop-eared rascal!" said the Captain; "zounds! one itches to kick him—this Master Hastyluck, or Haste-thee-Luke, as he was formerly called. But who on the earth is to be charged with witchcraft?"

"An old settler here in the Fort Mountain."

"His name?"

"Powell," said the Earl.

"Old Powell? what folly! A more peaceful man I never knew."

"Well, I take no part in the affair; let the gentlemen justices follow their own ideas."

"They have none, my lord; they really have not, many of them, capacity to follow their noses, even."

"I am sorry therefor, inasmuch as I shall have to submit to them, very soon, a proposition in which I am interested."

"What is that?"

"I wish the county seat of Frederick County to be Stephensburg, over here."

"Well, my lord," said the Captain, collecting his forces.

"Well, there are gentlemen who desire that Winchester should be selected."

"And ladies too, pardy!"

"What, Captain?"

"Nothing, my lord; I only said that there were ladies who wished Winchester to be chosen."

"Indeed! why?"

"Who have property there."

"I regret it; but I cannot yield; my interests all point to Stephensburg."

"Let us argue that point, my lord," said the Captain; "I know that Stephensburg, from its position, as "——

"Enough, Captain," said the Earl, indifferently; "spare your logic, I have determined to have the county seat at Stephensburg, if my influence can compass it."

"Good! then it only remains for me, in due and honorable form, to declare war on my private account against your lordship in this affair."

"You?" said Fairfax.

"Myself."

"*You* wish Winchester to be selected?"

"Yes, indeed, my lord."

"Why?"

"For private reasons."

"Ah! a lady is concerned; I have heard of your gallantry very often, Captain. A lady!"

"I do not deny it, my lord," said the Captain.

"Well, I am sorry to say that I cannot oblige yourself and your fair friend in this matter. I have determined on Stephensburg."

"And I, my lord," said Captain Wagner, "have determined on Winchester. Zounds! with all possible respect for your earlship, Winchester shall be the county seat."

The melancholy smile flitted over Fairfax's face.

"How will you compass it?" he said, "I have a majority of the justices already in my favor."

"How large a majority, pray, my lord?"

The Earl smiled again.

"You seem to forget that you have declared war," he said, "but this moment. I will afford an enemy no information, whatsoever."

"Ah, that is just, or may the devil take me—right, right! I must do my own nosing-out, I see—and faith, as your lordship has so much the start of me, I will commence at once."

"And I promise not to bear the least grudge, Captain, if you succeed, since we are fairly pitted, arms in hand."

"Except that my sword is shattered to the hilt, when I enter the contest; yours whole and sharp."

"It is the fortune of war: so much the more glory if you overcome me.

"Very well, my lord. I promise you to give you a hard fight, and from this moment I sound the trumpet," said the Captain, rising.

"Where are you going?" said the Earl.

"I decline to reply," returned the Captain, cunningly; "I follow your excellency."

"Not a bad hit, upon my honor; you are invaluable to me, Captain; you alone of all my friends make me laugh. Go then: but let us empty a cup before your departure."

"Willingly, my lord."

And so Captain Wagner tarried and emptied a fair flaggon of Jamaica—wine he cared not for—to his own success. Then assuring his lordship that on the next day, the instructions for the border settlers would be ready for him, the Captain mounted his horse, and took the road to Ordinary.

XVII.

MONSIEUR JAMBOT'S DEATH'S HEAD.

IN the main apartment of Mynheer Van Doring's Ordinary, the fair Mrs. Butterton is dancing a galliard to the music of Monsieur Auguste Hypolite Jambot's fiddle.
That gentleman is clad in a picturesque coat with barrel cuffs turned back to the elbows, a blue satin waistcoat fitting tightly to his thin, slight figure, and pumps adorned, in place of buckles, with immense rosettes of red ribbon. Monsieur Jambot is thus very picturesque—but the widow is resplendent. She is dressed in all the colors of the rainbow; she wears rings, breastpins and bracelets without number; and when she lifts her skirt gracefully in the animated dance, the other hand balanced akimbo on her side, she makes a full display of a pair of substantial ankles cased in real silk stockings, and large, serviceable feet plunged in slippers of immense elegance.

The dance comes to an end, and the fair widow fans herself, saying:

"How did I get through, Monsieur?"

"Elegant! elegant!" cried Monsieur Jambot, "but nex' time you shall step not so quick, not so jig, *ma chère madame!*"

"Not so *what?*" asked the fair widow, laughing.

"Ah, my poor head!" said Monsieur Jambot, ceasing for a moment to tune his violin, in order to press his forehead with a theatrical air; "my poor head—I no understand *l'Anglais;* I mean you step out too—what you call him—*vite,* too quick, too spirited: *voilà le mot!*"

"Well, let us try again."

"Same, madame?"

"Oh, yes! are you tired of it?"

"Ah, *non, non*—I could not be tired of you when you dance."

"You are very gallant, Monsieur."

"*C'est vrai!*"

"Well, then, play for me again. Do you like that tune?"

"'Tis beautiful."

"I think so too. So you are willing to try again?"

"*Ravi!*"

And Monsieur Jambot struck up a lively air, and Mistress Butterton tripped gaily down the room to the quick music, her arms akimbo, her wrist bent and resting on her side, her eyes sparkling, her red-heeled shoes merrily clattering on the brightly scoured floor.

"*Ah, c'est grand!*" cried Monsieur Jambot; "you might dance the *contre dance* before his *Majesté* Louis le Grand himself."

"I'm glad to hear it," said Mrs. Butterton, fanning herself, and casting a languishing glance upon her companion—it was to keep herself in practice—"I am glad you think so: for I shall go to a number of frolics before returning to Belhaven, and I wish to show the folks up here the difference between the town and the country. I must not dance any more jig tunes, for they dance them very well here: now a minuet is so much better: *that* is a court dance!"

"A royal dance, madame! But *parole d'honneur*, you dance minuet most elegant."

"Oh, you jest!"

"Jest? never!"

"Shall we try one, then?"

"*Oui, madame:* I will play and dance also."

When Monsieur Jambot danced the minuet he became, for the time, a different person, so loftily did he hold his powdered head, with so graceful and stately an amenity did he move on the points of his high-heeled shoes to the slow, gliding music. This change now passed over his countenance and manner. He held his violin as a monarch does his sceptre; he took up, then laid down his cocked hat, as an emperor would his crown; his whole person became at once stiff and supple, erect and inclined. The lady was not behind-hand. She drew herself up in a stately way, assumed a gracious and condescending smile, and raised gracefully her long skirt, ready to step forward at the first notes of the violin.

Monsieur Jambot commenced with a low prelude, full of elegance. The instrument, which had at first shook from its strings a bright shower of laughing and sparkling notes in the gay gavotte, keeping perfect time to the rattle of the lady's slippers on the floor of the apartment, now changed its tone completely, as if ashamed of such inane gaiety and unseemly mirth. It now gave forth a slow, ceremonious strain, such as was fit and proper for great lords and ladies in princely hall assembled, to bow and courtesy to each other by: even for kings to incline their royal heads to in a graceful, royal way, leading out princesses in gilded, picture-walled saloons.

As to Monsieur Jambot, he seemed to be perfectly happy; he could play and dance very well at the same time, and on this occasion he excelled himself. He glided, he ambled, he simpered, he bowed, his very eyes seemed to be full of music, and to be ready to dissolve away in fluttering delight. Those eyes were fixed upon the fair widow, and they expressed, in a way quite unmistakable, the condition of the owner's heart—the state of his feelings. It was very plain, from those languishing, and admiring glances, that Monsieur Jambot was a victim to the *belle passion*, as he called it; and would rather prefer to die for her than otherwise.

Not to do injustice to the fair widow's discrimination, we will add that she understood both the look and the state of Monsieur Jambot's feelings perfectly well. She was well assured that he was one of her most ardent adorers, and that he aspired to her hand; but whether this hand was to be reduced into possession by the dancing-master, or by Captain Wagner, the reader will discover in due time.

And now they approached each other in the graceful dance, bowing, smiling, and rolling their eyes—in which latter exercise we must say Monsieur Jambot very far excelled his fair friend—and the music seemed to sigh forth a species of luxurious delight. The lady, with her skirt raised with one hand, the other hand, or rather the wrist thereof, resting on her side—executed profuse bows, and so to the triumphant fiddle of Monsieur Jambot, the dance went on its way in triumph.

He wound up the minuet with a graceful flourish, improvised for the occasion, and full of beauty; and in the excitement of the moment, sank upon his knees before the fair lady, grasping her plump hand, which hand he pressed rapturously to his lips. The lady stood calmly fanning herself with her disengaged hand, and looking at her admirer with a roguish twinkle in her eyes.

The parties were arranged in this elegant and striking tableau, when suddenly the widow turned abruptly, and Monsieur Jambot rose angrily, brushing his knees. These movements were caused by a very simple circumstance, a circumstance which assuredly, in the ordinary course of human events, was not calculated to overwhelm one, or cause any profound astonishment. Not to keep the reader longer in ignorance, the lady and her admirer had been startled by the arrival of a third personage, and this arrival was announced by the form of words :

"Snout of the dragon! what do I see! Kneeling, or the devil fly away with me!"

And Captain Wagner, the hoof-strokes of whose horse had been drowned by the music of the violin, stalked into the room—a dreadful frown upon his brow, his martial spurs jingling as he strode, his heavy sword half drawn, and clattering portentously against his legs, cased in their heavy boots.

XVIII.

HOW CAPTAIN WAGNER PREDICTED HIS FUTURE FAME.

MONSIEUR JAMBOT drew himself up, and exclaimed in a theatrical tone:
"*Malediction!*"
"What is that you say, sir?" said Captain Wagner, sternly. "I do not understand your barbarous lingo, though Mistress Butterton seems to comprehend it perfectly, or the devil seize me!"

And Captain Wagner threw upon the fair widow a look which nearly took away her breath. She scarcely knew what to reply, and found all her presence of mind unequal to the task of repelling the valiant Captain, and asserting her own right of action. She finally decided to burst into tears.

"You are a cruel man! that you are, Captain," she sobbed, "to speak to me in that way—that you are!"

The Captain was proof against tears; he knew the sex, as he often said, and was not to be moved by such trifles.

"I was not addressing you, madam," he said, frowning, "but this gentleman, who used toward me the highly injurious term, *malediction*. In the whole course of my life, madam, I have never been called a malediction by any one before, and I now inform Mr. Jambo, that whatever may be the fashion in his own frog-eating country, in this country when one man calls another a malediction, it is a declaration of mortal enmity—in which light I receive it!"

"*Sacre!*" groaned Monsieur Jambot, between his clenched teeth, "*ce maudit capitaine!* I will fight him—I will abolish him from ze face of zis earth!"

"Abolish me!" cried Captain Wagner, indignatly; "may the devil take me, but we shall see. I have heard that you teach fencing, Mr. Jambo, as well as capering; well, draw your sword, pardy, or I will nail you, Monsieur, to that table!"

Monsieur Jambot jumped back, for Captain Wagner's sword flashed forth like lightning from its scabbard.

"Your sword! your sword!" cried the Captain.

Monsieur Jambot was no coward; and now thoroughly aroused by the presence and insults of his hated rival, he executed two steps, professionally speaking, to the mantelpiece, and took down a good rapier which hung there among pepper-pods, balls of twine, and ears of corn; with which he turned and faced his adversary.

"Begar!" he cried, in a great rage, "we shall see what we shall see!"

But before the Captain could put himself into position, a loud screech was heard, and Mrs. Butterton rushed between them with tears and sobs.

"Oh, for mercy's sake!" she cried, "oh, no fighting—oh, you must not! Captain—Mr. Jambot—you shall not! Put up your swords—this moment!—or—or—I shall—faint—my smelling-bottle—in—my—room—Monsieur—Jam!—Cap!"——

With which faintly-uttered words the lady closed her eyes; then her form swayed backward and forward, her head drooped, her feet bent beneath her, and just as Monsieur Jambot, with all the gallantry of the Frenchman and the lover, rushed from the room to bring the smelling-bottle, she yielded to "nerves," and sank back into the sturdy arms of the valiant Captain.

"Oh, how could you!" she said, languidly opening her eyes a moment afterward, and drawing back.

"A thousand apologies, my dearest madam—I have done wrong—forgive me!" groaned her admirer.

"Oh, Captain!" murmured the lady.

"But to see your beautiful hand pressed to another's lips! —to see another kneeling to you, which individual you might in another moment have raised from his knees—May the fiend seize me, madam!" cried Captain Wagner, "but I will yet have my revenge on that perfidious rival—revenge, revenge!"

The lady drew back pettishly.

"You care nothing for me," she sobbed, "I am angry, sir, and I won't be treated so, sir. You treat me too badly—that you do."

"Tears!" cried Captain Wagner, tearing his hair, "tears caused by me!"

"Yes, sir, by you."

"By me—the most devoted of your admirers—of your—yes, of your"——

"Enemies—yes, the most bitter enemy I have."

"Madam!"

"You would kill my friends, because they are my friends."

"No, no."

"You would fight Monsieur Jambot."

"He is a good swordsman, I know well."

"And if he is?"

"He might run through the midriff me myself—the most faithful of adorers; but that would be nothing," added Captain Wagner, gloomily; "a broken heart and a clay-cold corpse go well together."

"Whose heart is broken, sir?"

"Mine, madam, by your coldness—your unkindness."

"Captain," sighed the lady.

"You turn all my virtues into faults, or may the devil take me!"

"Oh," remonstrated the lady.

"If I show jealousy, you laugh at me; if I wish to drive off other—yes, other rivals, madam, you quarrel with me."

"I have not quarrelled."

"You feign not to perceive that I am the most devoted of"——

The lady turned aside her head: the Captain pressed to his lips the hand which was abandoned to him: the other covered her face. Just at this moment, Monsieur Jambot re-entered, and stood transfixed with horror.

As Captain Wagner, in his profound wrath and astonishment, had cried out violently: "Snout of the Dragon!'— so now, Monsieur Jambot, with rage quite as profound, saluted his adversary with the words:

"*Milles diables!* what do I see?"

The Captain twirled his moustache.

"You see me," he said, curtly.

"And who are you, *sacre?*"

"Captain Julius Wagner, at your service, sir."

"Captain Waggeneur, you shall answer to me zis!" cried Monsieur Jambot.

"Answer what?"

"For your insult to me," replied the Frenchman, adroitly avoiding a commital of himself.

"I will answer anything," said the Captain. But perceiving the eyes of the fair widow fixed beseechingly upon him: "still," he continued, "I am not aware, Monsieur Jambot, that I have insulted you half so grossly as you have me?"

"*Comment!*"

"Did you not characterize me as a *malediction?* answer me that."

"But," said the lady, delighted to see the two adversaries gradually cooling and speaking in more amicable tones, "that is not an insult, I am sure, Captain. *Malediction* is —I don't know exactly what—but it is not an insult."

"If that is the case, madam, and Monsieur Jambo has not insulted me by this *malediction*, I am ready to end our quarrel."

Monsieur Jambot bowed with ceremony.

"It shall end," he said, coldly.

"Good!" continued the Captain, "and now, madam, let me proceed to business. I am here purely on business."

Monsieur Jambot hearing these words, understood that it would not be polite for him to remain: so taking his fiddle from the floor, and restoring the rapier to its place, he betook himself to the porch, where, seated on the wooden bench, he discoursed sweet music, soft enough to penetrate the very heart of his mistress.

"Business, Captain?" asked the lady, seating herself near the table.

"Business, madam," said Captain Wagner, taking out a paper, upon which were written, in huge, sprawling letters with a pencil, a number of names; "your business."

And he seated himself on the opposite side of the narrow table, spreading out the paper between them.

"My business?"

"Yes, madam—that which brought you to the Valley."

"Oh, my lots?"

"In Winchester—yes."

"I now recollect your kind offer of assistance. La! Captain, you put yourself to a heap of trouble."

And the lady gently agitated her fan of swan's feathers, gazing thereon.

"Trouble? no, nothing is trouble for which we expect to be munificently paid, pardy!"

The lady cast down her eyes with a blush.

"Thus, then, it is," said the Captain, leaning over the table, and caressing his martial moustache, as with his enormous hand he pointed out the names written on the paper in a double row, "thus it is. At the next meeting of the Honorable Justices of the County of Frederick—which county, by the horns of the devil!—excuse me, madam—should be a kingdom, for it reaches from the Blue Ridge here to the Mississippi—at the next meeting of the Court here, madam, the county seat, as you well know, will be determined on. It will be either Stephensburg over there, or Winchester"——

"Yes, Captain."

"And your interest," said the Captain, in a business tone, "points to Winchester?"

"Yes, indeed—I have some excellent lots there, as I have before told you."

"Good! well, I have determined, as I informed you, madam, that Winchester shall be the place."

"La! Captain!—but how can you—there is Lord Fairfax, a sweet nobleman, I am sure, but he is determined to have Stephensburg chosen."

"Whether Lord Fairfax is a sweet nobleman or not, my dear madam, is not the question: nor which of these two places he inclines to. I have time before court-day, and I will use it in your favor."

"Oh, thank you—you are very good."

"No: by no means: as I said before, my reward will come from you. But that is beside the question. I procured from your worthy father, whom I met on the road coming hither, these names of the justices. You will perceive that they are very nearly balanced equally—for and against Winchester. Two names, you see, are marked *Doubtful.* They are those of Argal and Hastyluck."

The Captain leaned over the table, as did the lady: they were a great contrast: he with his dark, martial face, black moustache, and grotesque humor in the eyes, buried under their shaggy brows; she with her fair, plump face, and red lips, and affected simper. Their eyes met, and an odd smile passed over the features of each.

"I will bring over Argal and Hastyluck," said Captain Wagner, watching his companion like a dog with head lowered, "and Winchester will be chosen."

"In spite of Lord Fairfax?"

"Yes, indeed; in spite of everything!"

"You are so kind!"

"Ha, ha!"

"You are the most disinterested person in the world."

"No, I am selfish."

"La! Captain."

"And in proof of it I shall claim the reward for my services."

The lady blushed, casting down her eyes.

"Will you grant me what I ask, should I succeed?"

"Oh, Captain," murmured his companion, with a fluttering heart.

"If it is reasonable?"

"If—it—is reasonable—y—es."

"Good!" cried Captain Wagner, rising, and bringing his fist down on the table, like a battering ram, "then Winchester shall, from this time, be the county-seat, and shall grow wealthy, and increase in population and in size, and in importance and in glory! Yes, I have determined upon that! Stephensburg shall have its foolish ambition overturned; for the more I ponder upon the matter, the more proper does it seem that Winchester—where your lots are, my dearest madam—should be the capital town of this great county. I rejoice, not only for my own present sake and yours, that such will be the event: but I see with pride that brilliant future, when the name of Captain Julius Wagner will be-loved and respected by thousands now unborn: when they will possibly erect statues to him here in this beautiful land; and where—who knows?—some one of that idle and disreputable, but still useful class called authors, shall write out an account of my services in this matter, and print them with types such as are used for books, and so inform the world of my patriotism!—yes, of my chivalry, my devotedness, my—hum! I think I see that bright day coming, and I shall leave in my will a sum of money with which my children, or grandchildren—if I have any, which heaven grant!—shall pay one of those scribblers, or Grubstreets, as I have heard them called, to write about my life.

And therein, madam, your virtues will shine] therein you will be rendered, from your connection with myself, immortal!—therein we will go down to posterity hand in hand, as I trust we shall do, even—hum?— my horse there!" cried the Captain, breaking off in the middle of his eloquent speech.

"I am going," he added; "and now rest in peace, madam. Your interests are mine."

With which speech Captain Wagner took his leave.

XIX.

OLD · MEMORIES.

WHILE these scenes were occuring at the Ordinary, the master of Greenway Court, leaned back in his tall carved chair, absorbed in gloomy thought.

His pale face indicated some concealed emotion—his lips were contracted sorrowfully, and the long eyelashes rested on his pallid cheek. He remained long thus buried in thought; and then wearily rose erect in his seat and sighed.

"Strange! very strange!" the Earl muttered, "that fatal likeness! Never have I seen reproduced in human face a more perfect resemblance to another! Falconbridge? Falconbridge? Whence does he come? Pshaw! why should I wish to find out? 'Tis one of those fancies which seize on men at times: and yet I swear, as I bent over him, when something drove me in the dead of night to his chamber, I could have taken my oath that the face was the very same—eyes, lips and everything! How like, too, the courage which made him spring up and pursue me! There I recognize the likeness again, as in the form—in the spirit as in the outward lineaments. Strange world!—strange life!"

And for some moments the Earl remained silent, his breast shaken with sighs; his lips quivering. Then he seemed to realize the folly of his emotion: and by a great effort controlled himself.

"What madness!" he murmured, "thus to yield to the ghost of the past, and shake like Hamlet at a shadow! I'll be stronger and colder. He will come to-day or to-morrow, and I must not excite attention by my manner. I must govern myself. Yes—the past must be buried : it is gone. Why rake in the ashes for burnt out hopes and memories? I am thousands of leagues from the scenes of other days —let me not recall them ; let them sleep!"

And rising, the Earl put on his hat and gloves, and followed by his stag-hounds, wandered forth to the prairie, still pondering, and pursuing his secret thoughts.

XX.

FIRST LOVE.

GEORGE pushed his horse gaily up the mountain road, and ere long reached the spur upon which was situated the cabin of his singular host of the day before.

As he approached it he observed above the great rock in rear, a light cloud of smoke which puzzled him greatly. It plainly did not issue from the chimney of the house; and as no outbuildings were attached to the cabin, the smoke could not be that of the kitchen. Still, there it was: an unmistakable cloud, rising slowly it seemed from the very fissure of the great mass of rock, and gently floating away among the fir trees.

George was still occupied with this singular phenomenon, when all at once a form appeared at the door of the house which routed all his speculations, and gave him something else to think about.

It was the figure of Cannie: and in an instant the youth had thrown himself from his horse, and held in his own one of the soft hands of the girl, which she abandoned to him with her old air of grave sweetness and simplicity. There was much less constraint in her air now, however, than at first. She had evidently become acquainted with George: and thus her greeting was more familiar and unceremonious.

"I'm so glad you have come!" she said simply, "I did not expect to see you so soon."

"I thought you might be sick from your wetting," he replied with a smile, as he looked into the pure sweet face.

Cannie smiled in return.

"Oh no!" she said, "I am very well, I think, though I certainly have caught cold—but I am subject to colds."

With which she coughed slightly; and led the way into the house.

"I don't see your father," said George, "is he absent?"

"He is my grandfather," returned Cannie, in her low, musical voice; "and he is not far—shall I call him?"

"Oh no! unless you're already very tired of me—Cannie."

George uttered the girl's name with a slight tremor in his voice; and the tell-tale blood rushed to his cheek as he gazed at her. Cannie exhibited no similar emotion—indeed seemed, rather, very much pleased at this absence of ceremony.

"I beg your pardon for my familiarity," said George, blushing. "I scarcely knew I was speaking so—calling you plain 'Cannie.'"

"Beg my pardon?" said the girl, in a tone of surprise, "why should you? I wish you always to call me Cannie, if you please. We are friends—and you know that you saved my life."

The words were uttered very simply and sweetly,—so sweetly indeed that George heard the tones of her voice many hours afterwards. His confusion disappeared entirely ere long: and proposing to Cannie a stroll on the mountain side—a proposition to which she at once assented—the boy and the girl were very soon rambling beneath the magnificent foliage of the autumn forest.

Bright hours full of magical tints and odors!—filled with so much romance and delight! They became a portion of his memory and heart: and long afterwards, far away in other scenes of hardship and pain, he remembered them, and sighed for his bright boyhood. They wandered away along the mountain side thus, with no aim in their wanderings, no consciousness of the sentiment that was ripening in their hearts. George only knew that Cannie was there at his side with her pure sweet face, and kind good eyes; her lips full of cheerful, loving smiles; her voice like soft music in his ears. When she rested on his arm in crossing some mountain rivulet, or gave him her hand to mount to the summit of a rock, George felt, he knew not why, a singular beating of the heart, and his cheeks flushed without the least reason.

Bright days of youth!—brighter thoughts of the heart! They are flowers that bloom but once, and then die. What remains is the wiry stalk and bald head. It may contain the seed, but the odor and the bloom, where are they?

So George and Cannie wandered away for hours: and the golden autumn day sank into their hearts, and filled them with its magical delight. When they came back home, they were silent, and happy. It seemed but a moment since they had left the house.

In the main room they encountered the old man.

"Grandpapa," said Cannie, "here is George."

The old man returned the young man's greeting with easy courtesy. They then commenced conversing, Cannie joining easily in their talk.

In the midst of one of the speaker's sentences, George observed a glittering object lying on the floor. It was a *carolus*, as the gold coin was then called, and George picked it up. To his astonishment it was atmost hot: and his look, as he held it out, betrayed his wonder. His host took it with a sardonic smile, which George afterwards remembered.

"It is a coin I have just been experimenting on," said the old man; "I dropped it and forgot to pick it up. I am a savant, or chymist, Master George, you must understand. I experiment on gold and silver. You no doubt saw the smoke from my furnace up there—and so let us turn to something more interesting."

With these words the speaker calmly put the coin in his pocket, and changed the topic with the ease and grace of a thorough man of the world. George had never heard such brilliant and profound talk from any one ; and for more than an hour he sat listening with delight to the absorbing monologue of the stranger.

It was not until evening that the youth took his departure; and then it was with a promise that he would come again.

"Remember I am lonely," said Cannie, smiling and giving him her hand, "as grandpapa is often busy. Come back soon!"

George required no urging, and all the way back to Greenway, heard her voice.

XXI.

CAPTAIN WAGNER GOES TO CALL ON HIS FRIENDS.

WHEN Captain Wagner undertook to perform anything, he was accustomed to set about it with a rapidity and energy almost fatal, in the very beginning, to an opponent of sluggish disposition.

The Captain had come to the Valley of Virginia at the bidding of Lord Fairfax, to assist that nobleman with his counsel in the troublous days which were plainly lowering on the border: and in so doing, the soldier had only acted in conformity with his views of duty, and his war-instincts. As the Indian attack was evidently delayed for the time, however, as no breeze brought to the huge ears of the frontiersman the rumor of battle, as he was doomed to inactivity for the moment, and was not needed by his lordship—under this state of things it seemed to the Captain that his most rational employment would be a diligent application of his energies to the cause of Mrs. Butterton, with the prospective view of inducing that lady to become Mrs. Wagner, into which changed state she would doubtless carry with her, her thousand "desirabilities."

These reflections had occurred to the soldier at his first interview, and we have been present at his formal declaration of war against Thomas, Lord Fairfax, Baron of Cameron, and Lord Lieutenant of Frederick and the shires adjacent.

The Captain, after leaving Mrs. Butterton as we have seen him do, immediately set about his task.

He instituted inquiries upon all sides; procured a full list of the justices, with the greater part of whom he was perfectly well acquainted; and with this basis of operations, and the comfortable assurance that there was quite a formidable party against Stephensburg and Lord Fairfax, and consequently in favor of Winchester and Mrs. Butterton, cheerfully took to the high road, and commenced his rounds.

It is not the purpose of this history to follow the valiant Captain and great negotiator in his campaign, or to repeat in detail the various and ever-ready arguments which he used to impress his friends with the importance of selecting the village of Winchester for the county-seat. Perhaps we lose a most favorable opportunity of showing the tremendous energy and conspicuous ingenuity of Captain Longknife, by passing thus over a series of scenes in which he was impressive and indefatigable—but, unfortunately, we are not now writing the history of Winchester.

It is enough, then, to say that the Captain returned to the Ordinary, three or four days afterwards, with a countenance in which might easily have been discerned an expression of much pride and triumph.

"Faith, madam!" he said, bending down and pressing gallantly to his lips the plump hand of Mistress Butterton, who smiled, and murmured, "La, Captain!" and covered her face with her fan, "faith, madam! I begin to think that I ought to have undertaken more in your behalf—to have the county-seat moved to Belhaven, or, as these new-fangled folks begin to call it, Alexandria, or even to Williamsburg, or the village of Richmond, or any other town in which you may have property! Be easy on the subject, my dear madam, for this very morning I am going to finish everything. I'm going to see Argal, and that rascal Hastyluck, and I want company. Where's your gallant acquaintance, Falconbridge, our mutual friend?"

The lady smiled, and with an innocent air, said:

"I think he has gone before you, Captain."

"Gone before?"

"To Mr. Argal's."

And the lady laughed.

"Rather to Miss Argal's," said the Captain, frowning, and looking thoughtful.

"Yes."

"He's in love!"

"Is he?"

"Dead in love! What a foolish fellow!"

"Hem!" said Mrs. Butterton, gently, and with a dangerous look, "do you think that is very foolish, Captain?"

"It would not be in your case, beautiful and"——.

"Oh, Captain!"

"May the!—well, that's wrong: but I will maintain, with fire and sword, the good sense of the individual who falls in love with you!—that is," added the Captain, guardedly, "I will cut the throats of all persons, or individuals, who presume to do anything of the sort."

With which somewhat inconsistent declaration, Captain Wagner again kissed the hand he held in his huge paw, pushed up his black moustache with his finger, as was habitual with him, and issuing forth, mounted his horse, and took his way toward Mr. Argal's.

XXII.

THE CAPTAIN REVELS IN THE CREATIONS OF HIS FANCY.

"FALCONBRIDGE!—Madam Bertha!" muttered the soldier, gloomily, as he went onward, "infatuated! Really, nothing is more astonishing than this passion, or indeed madness, as one may call it, which invades a man's heart when his locks are still black, his moustache untouched by gray. But this is not an infallible test, since I, myself, am not at all gray. But then, I, myself," continued the Captain, philosophically carrying on a logical fencing with himself, as with another person, "I, myself, possibly am in love. In love! what romance and folly, and all that! Still the fair lady yonder is not unworthy of the affection of a soldier, and a man of intelligence—a good, sensible, fair, wealthy, and very engaging widow! If that don't satisfy an individual in search of matrimony, nothing can. I'll have her!—may the devil eat me whole but I'll have her! On! Injun-hater, on!" •

And the Captain dug his spurs into the huge sides of the snorting animal, and went onward like a moving mountain.

He soon reached Mr. Argal's—dismounted—and entered. It was a plain and rudely-constructed house, with few comforts about it, and scarcely discernible at the distance of fifty yards, so dense was the clump of trees in which it stood.

The Captain was met on the threshold by Mr. Argal, who politely welcomed him, and led him into the house, where dinner was being placed upon the table. The Captain snuffed up the rich odor of the repast, plain as it was, and a mild expression diffused itself over his martial countenance. Dinner must have been invented by the earliest inhabitants of the globe, Captain Wagner often said, and he hailed it as one of the greatest discoveries which had ever adorned science. To say the truth, the soldier had an equally exalted opinion of the individual, or individuals, who discovered breakfast, supper, intermediate meals, and all descriptions of eating.

After satisfying himself that his material wants would be amply supplied, Captain Wagner looked around him to see where Falconbridge could be—as to Miss Argal, he never felt a very great anxiety to see her: for which the honest Captain probably had a good reason. They were neither of them visible, but soon made their appearance, the arm of the young girl resting upon that of her companion, and her bright eyes turned to him. Falconbridge grasped the hand of the Captain with hearty pleasure, and declared himself delighted to see him: to which the Captain replied in the same tone. Then, after some conversation, the party sat down to dinner. The Captain ate with great gusto, and emptied more than one fair cup of wine, or—more accurately speaking, Jamaica rum. In those days wines were not much affected, especially upon the border; the mellow rum of Jamaica was the favorite beverage; and, as we have said, this was Captain Wagner's chosen drink.

At the termination of the repast, and when all rose and walked out in the fine October evening, the Captain found himself in excellent condition for the attack upon Mr. Argal.

He was speedily left alone with that individual; for Falconbridge and the young lady accidentally wandered off toward the prairie, a glimpse of which appeared through a glade in the woods, toward the south; and the Captain's eloquence had thus full scope and room to move in, without fear of interruption.

The difficulty experienced by the very best stenographers

in reporting the utterances of great orators, is proverbial and undisputed. We find ourselves in this predicament in relation to the harangue of Captain Wagner on this occasion. Full of his subject, in a talkative and eloquent mood, and with an important end to attain, the Captain's oration was really remarkable. It was also sprinkled with the newest and most impressive flowers of speech, of that description which the soldier was accustomed to use in decorating his utterances—and the originality and beauty of these newly-coined forms of expression riveted the attention of his smiling and amused auditor. As to his eulogium upon the town of Winchester, it was almost sublime in its eloquence and enthusiasm.

"A magnificent situation!" cried the Captain, pushing up his moustache; "the pearl of towns, the paragon of villages! Like Rome and other cities of Asia, which grew up from small beginnings. Winchester, my dear friend, is destined to rule the world! But perhaps that is too strong —I wish to confine myself strictly within the most reasonable bounds—I will be moderate, and say that Winchester is destined to be the capital of Virginia! I expect to see his Excellency, Governor Gooch, take up his residence there, and leave forever that abominable county town, called Williamsburg—I expect everything; and nothing is too good for that noble village! Who knows but his Majesty, George II., attracted by the wide-spread fame of the place, may some day set out from London on a visit to Winchester, and delight the hearts of his faithful subjects of Virginia with a sight of his royal and divine physiognomy! I think I see myself his herald and king at arms, riding before the royal chariot, through Loudoun Street, on Injunhater, and crying to the crowd: "Make way, my friends! his Majesty is coming!' This, sir, is the future of Winchester—and is anything so splendid to be descried in the future of Stephensburg—a mere assemblage of huts, and unworthy of the least attention? You are laughing at me, my dear friend, and you think I am not impartial. Well, maybe I'm not—and this is all my jesting. But recollect, my dear friend, what I say—recollect what Wagner said when it is fulfilled:—in one year from this time, there'll be a splendid wagon road from Winchester to the ferry, on the Potomac, and the town will have its jail, and court-house of the finest logs!"

Having uttered these words with deep solemnity, Captain Wagner paused a moment, and revolved the remaining points of his subject not yet touched upon.

We need not follow the conversation further; it is enough to say that when Falconbridge and Miss Argal made their appearance again, Captain Wagner had received from his companion a promise to vote for Winchester—a matter, he said, of no importance to him, and rather in accordance with his previous convictions of what would be most advisable.

"And now, Captain," said Mr. Argal, "is there any more intelligence of Indians?"

"You heard the rumors: but that's little. I think, my dear friend, that we shall hear from the South Branch before long. Body o' me! you can't trust those rascals, because you don't see or hear them:—you can't, on that account, be sure that they're not at your very doors: and this young lady might have been carried away yonder in a moment, in spite of the presence of her gallant."

"Bah! Captain!" said Falconbridge, as he drew near, smiling, "you can't frighten me."

"I wouldn't attempt it, comrade. Such men as we are don't get frightened. But Injuns are Injuns!"

"Well, let them come," said Falconbridge, laughing; "we are equal to them in strength."

"And the women?"

"Ah!"

"And the children?"

"You are right—I forgot them, boy that I am."

"In case the Injuns show their noses, companion," replied the Captain, "I undertake to say that you will not possibly be able to forget the said women and children."

"How, Captain?"

"They have a way of squalling—an awful noise it is, or may the fiend seize me!"

"I couldn't bear that," said Falconbridge; "I never could endure the thought that a woman or a child was suffering. I would close my ears to it, if I could not strike!"

"Well, you may, perhaps, have to close your ears, companion, before the arrival of the blood-thirsty rascals."

"What do you mean, Captain?"

"I mean that Mr. Gideon Hastyluck speaks of having old Powell, up yonder, and his daughter, whose name is Cannie —a sweet child—burned as witches, at the next assizes."

"Burned?"

"Yes."

"A man?"——

"And his daughter."

"You jest, Captain!"

"I'm in dead earnest!"

"For witchcraft?"

"Precisely."

"Why, it is barbarous!—worse than the bloodiest murder: a man and his daughter burned for witchcraft!"

"Then you do not believe in witchcraft, comrade, eh?"

"I believe nothing, and disbelieve nothing."

"Very well," said the Captain, "that is just my case— only if that fellow, Hastyluck, makes me angry, I will cut off both his ears. Sufficient unto the day is the evil thereof. Let us dismiss the subject, and it's in very good time, as I see the sun setting yonder, and a storm brewing. Comrade," he said, turning to Falconbridge, "will you go?"

There was so much sternness and gloom in Captain Wagner's voice, as he uttered these latter words, that Falconbridge, for a moment, remained silent, gazing with astonishment at him. Then his eyes turned suddenly toward the lady—her hand had pressed his arm, that was all: she was looking with a smile at the evening sky.

"No, my dear Captain," he said; "I think I'll prolong my visit a little. When I am in agreeable company, I am loth to leave it."

"Good, good!" said Captain Wagner, indifferently, but gazing with a wistful look at the open, careless face of Falconbridge, "I can understand that. But I am not a youngster, and I really must go."

He turned his eyes as he spoke toward Miss Argal; and his rapid glance took in every detail of her figure—her head bent down—her glossy curls half covering her cheeks—her rosy lips half parted and moist—her brilliant eyes veiled by the long and dusky lashes, but raised from time to time toward her companion: all this Captain Wagner saw, and the frown grew deeper.

He said nothing, however, and refusing to accept Mr. Argal's invitation to remain all night, went and mounted his horse, and set forward.

Falconbridge remained half an hour longer; and then seeing the storm rapidly rising, also took his departure—but not so sullenly as Captain Wagner.

He went on, at full gallop, gaily through the darkness which lightning from time to time illuminated: and his countenance clearly indicated of whom he was thinking.

The dazzling beauty of the woman whom he had just left, had intoxicated the young man; and he went on with the carelessness of a lover, or a madman, without heeding the lightning or the storm.

A brighter flash than he had yet witnessed, lit up the road, and he saw a tall, dark horseman before him, who could be no other than Captain Wagner—and so, upon a nearer approach, it proved. The Captain had ridden at a measured pace; Falconbridge had galloped furiously; and thus they had encountered each other.

XXIII.

CAPTAIN WAGNER DISCOURSES ON THE NATURE OF PANTHERS.

CAPTAIN WAGNER quietly returned Falconbridge's salute; and touching his horse with the spur, galloped on by his side without speaking.

"Well, my dear Captain," said his companion, "you did not expect to see me?"

"No, I did not," said the soldier.

"Why?"

"Because you were with a woman."

"Pshaw!" cried Falconbridge: "you think me a mere lady's man."

"No—but how did you succeed in getting away?" asked the Captain.

"Succeed in getting away?"

"Yes, pardy! It seems there is much to attract you yonder."

"Is anything more natural than that I should wish to get to the Ordinary before the storm? See! that flash! and the thunder! I doubt whether, even at the rapid pace we are now going, we shall arrive without a drenching."

Captain Wagner made no reply, and the two horses continued to devour the space with their long gallop, which was so regular that but one footfall could be heard. At last the Captain turned, and said, abruptly:

"Comrade, you are from the Lowlands, down yonder, are you not?"

"Yes, from Tide-water. Why do you ask?"

"Oh, mere curiosity; fine animals you have down there—your horse for instance."

"Yes, he's of the purest blood—out of Mariana by Bothwell—a racer."

"I believe you; he is eating the road like wildfire—worse than a rabbit at a head of cabbage. But there is one very beautiful animal which I have never yet seen in the Low Country, and though the breed of horses there is superior, I believe, to the mountain nags, I think we are ahead of you in"——

"In what, Captain?"

"Panthers," said the Captain, concisely.

"Panthers? I have never seen one."

"Are you sure?"

"Certainly."

"Quite sure?"

"Absolutely—there are none on Tide-water."

"That does not matter, comrade—not in the least."

"How so?"

"You may have seen them since your arrival in this fine country of the Valley, or the devil eat me!"

"I have not, however."

"Do you know a panther when you see it?"

"No."

"How, then, can you say you have encountered none? Answer that, pardy! companion!"

Falconbridge endeavored to make out the expression of the Captain's face through the darkness. What could this persistence of the soldier in one subject, a subject of no interest to him, signify?

"Well, have it as you will, Captain," he said, smiling, "perhaps I may have seen these animals—describe one to me."

"Ah!" replied Wagner, "at last you are becoming curious! Well, I will do as you wish. Listen, then, to the description of a panther."

"I listen."

The soldier was silent, and seemed to be struggling with

himself—debating in the depths of his acute and vigorous brain whether it were advisable or not to follow a certain course. But Falconbridge did not perceive the singular expression of the Captain's face, or indeed, hear his dubious mutterings; the darkness shrouded completely his companion's person—the hoof-strokes of the horse drowned his growl. The expression of the soldier's countenance would have afforded his companion much food for thought. That expression was both stern and pitying, gloomy and satirical.

The Captain remained thus silent for some time.

"But your description of a panther, Captain," repeated Falconbridge.

"Well, in the first place," said the soldier, "eyes both soft and fiery—that is to say, as tender-looking as the leaf of a flower in bloom, and at the same time as brilliant as a flame of fire."

"Indeed!"

"Yes! extraordinary eyes, wondrous eyes; both human and inhuman, attractive and repulsive, but far more fascinating than menacing, or the devil take me! It is only at certain times that these eyes menace you, and then they blaze!"

"Ah!" said Falconbridge, "then you have seen both expressions?"

"Yes, often! a wondrous pair of optics, that draw you toward them, however firm you may be, as the sun draws, I am told, the fixed stars, pardy!"

Falconbridge laughed at this illustration.

"Well," he said, "continue."

"Next the voice is not less wonderful."

"The voice?"

"Certainly."

"Of a panther? Has a panther a voice, Captain—a voice?"

"Nothing less! Have you never read of the strange *cry-*

ing of a child, which hunters have heard in the deep forests in their expeditions?"

"Ah, yes! I now recollect"——

"Well, that is one of the tones of the panther's voice. You understand," continued the soldier with a cold sneer— "a ferocious, blood-thirsty animal, worse than a tiger, or a rattlesnake, cries like a little fatling baby for its amusement?"

"Strange, indeed!"

"But this voice, which can sigh, and wail, and murmur like a baby's, can also send terror to the strongest heart!"

"Yes."

"To proceed, then, with my description of this fine animal."

"Captain—your voice! the tones of it! how singularly you speak! but pardon me."

"Oh, my voice, it is true, can't compare with a panther's; but, nevertheless, I have the advantage in one particular. I have never yet seen the panther who could ease his feelings with a good round 'devil take me!' But let me finish. Next to the eyes and the voice come the velvet covering, the graceful movement, the beautiful, sharp teeth, and the sharper claws; but here again is an astonishing thing; with these teeth the fine panther, male or female, actually smiles"——

"Smiles? Captain, you mean more than you say! There is a covert meaning in this description my mind struggles to make out!"

"Covert? How is that—it is as accurate a description as possible; no fiction, no imagination, or may the devil fly away with me!"

"Proceed!" murmured Falconbridge.

"I was saying that as the panther, with its fine voice, could not only make you shudder, but also fill you with pity as for a poor little crying child, so with its fine teeth it cannot only tear you to pieces, but just as easily persuade you that its nature is all tenderness and love—by smiling understand—a soft, gentle, fascinating smile! I have seen it, or the devil take me!"

"Captain, Captain!" murmured Falconbridge, passing his hand over his forehead."

"Then the claws," continued the soldier, paying no attention to this interruption, "they are gifted with the singular power of drawing themselves in, and burying themselves beneath the velvety hair, you understand"——

"Yes!"

"Then when they are so drawn back, you touch nothing but a soft, velvet cushion, which natural historians have most ungallantly called *a paw*—I say ungallantly, because all this time I have been speaking of the female panther, or perhaps I may say pantheress. You have a beautiful, soft cushion before you, a pretty thing to toy and play with—nothing more—no claws any where visible; you comprehend?"

"Perfectly!"

"But if you happen to excite the slumbering ferocity of the fine lady panther, why this beautiful, soft palm will turn into a bundle of iron springs, the sharp claws will dart forth like magic; and the bright teeth which you admired so much will come to the assistance of the claws; and there! you find the consequences of intimacy with a pantheress! When your friend, uneasy at your absence, comes to search for you, he finds a mangled body, half-devoured, and emptied of every drop of blood; panthers like blood!"

"Captain—Captain Wagner!" murmured Falconbridge, "speak to me as a friend—speak to me in plain words—you mean"——

"That I do not like panthers, male or female," said Captain Wagner, sullenly; "they are too tender and cruel, too beautiful and fatal with their undulating bodies, their graceful limbs, their soft, velvety covering, their smiles, their sighs, their fascinating glances!"

"Captain! Captain!"

"They smile too sweetly and bite too ferociously! They caress too softly the victim before tearing him to pieces, and lapping with a smile his heart's blood! Would you have me like the animal when I know it so well!"

Falconbridge was silent for a moment, evidently overcome by this terrible allegory. At last he said, with much agitation:

"Captain! friend! why have you spoken with such cruel enmity of Miss Argal?"

"I have spoken of no one," said the Captain gloomily; "I have not mentioned Miss Argal's name! I have spoken of an animal which I should fear mortally, were not my muscles of force sufficient to catch that animal in my arms, were she to spring upon me, and there crush her!"

Falconbridge, plunged in disturbed thought, made no reply. They galloped on for a quarter of a mile in silence, and then the moon came out between the lurid clouds. The storm had passed away toward the south.

Captain Wagner, chancing to look at his companion, saw that he was very pale, and that his forehead was covered with a cold sweat. The words of the soldier seemed to have paralyzed him, for he remained perfectly silent—with eyes full of wonder, fixed far away upon the distance.

Not a word more was uttered by either of the companions until they reached the Ordinary, and here they separated, and retired to their beds.

With Falconbridge the night was a vigil of wonder and incredulity.

XXIV.

REFLECTIONS OF CAPTAIN LONGKNIFE.

SOME days after the scenes which we have tried to make pass before the eyes of the reader, Captain Wagner, who had been uninterruptedly engaged in conferences with the Earl, bethought him of paying some attention to his private affairs. Accordingly, one morning before the sun had risen he donned his warlike accoutrements, mounted "Injunhater," and set out for the Ordinary.

The sun soon appeared above the brow of the mountain, and scattered the river mist before him. The landscape waked up, the birds began to sing, and not to be behind them, the Captain shouted lustily an old border ballad, with an ardor which was superior to its musical execution.

"The fact is," he said in a confidential tone, after finishing the chorus, "the fact is, I was not intended to delight the world by the sweet tones of my voice. Astonishing, but dooms true! It's not given to everybody to excel in all things, and this is one of my failings. On, Injunhater!"

And the worthy touched his great black animal with the spur, and cantered along gaily, presenting, as he moved through the burnishing sunlight, an exceedingly striking and martial appearance.

"A fine morning, by the snout of the dragon!" continued the Captain, looking round with satisfaction on the expanse of forest and prairie. "I should like to feel for once like Fairfax yonder, that the world belonged to me—that I was master. But wherefore? Am I not better off by far than this good baron of Cameron? First, I am a common individual—and these lords must have such a weary time! Then I laugh, and the baron only sighs! He eats little or nothing, and at this moment I could devour a raw buffalo, or I'm a dandy! To end the whole matter I'm going to see my wife—I'm going to breakfast with my intended! A noble woman, a real fairy, though she's so fat. But who cares? I rather like fat people! They laugh where lean ones groan; I'll have this one! If I don't I'll eat my head!"

And the Captain seemed inspired by the reflection and pushed on more rapidly. Then as he gazed in the direction of the Ordinary his brow clouded—he was thinking of Falconbridge.

"A noble fellow!" he muttered,—"a heart of oak—an honest boy! And he's going to his doom as sure as my name's Wagner. Well, I've done all I can, and more than I have liked—things must go on their way. He has had full warning, and though my breast aches at the thought that he's going to bleed, I am done with it. Woman, woman! why can't we male things stay away from them? We die for them—which is better than living for 'em sometimes! We laugh at 'em, sneer at 'em, curl our moustaches with a high-handed air, and then we go kneel down, and make fools of ourselves. Why did they enter the world ever? What is it that draws us so toward 'em?"

The Captain knit his brows as he saw the tavern before him, and after some moments of silence, muttered grimly:

"Woman! woman! wherever you turn in this miserable world, you're sure to find a woman!—and an individual of the masculine sex not far off!"

6

XXV.

HOW THE TOWN OF STEPHENSBURG, OTHERWISE NEWTOWN, WAS SOLD FOR A FLAGON OF PUNCH.

HE Captain proceeded toward the Ordinary without further reflections, or at least utterance, and was soon entering the door of the main apartment.

A disagreeable picture awaited him. The handsome widow was leaning familiarly upon Monsieur Jambot's shoulder, and conversing confidentially with that gentleman. Whether she had heard the sonorous neigh of Injunhater, and arranged for his rider's benefit this pleasing little tableau—or whether the idea of making her admirer jealous had never entered the mind of the lady, we cannot say. But she certainly exhibited great surprise and confusion. Monsieur Jambot only scowled.

On this trying occasion Captain Wagner acted with that consummate knowledge of the female character which his friends declared made him so dangerous. He squeezed Monsieur Jambot's lily white hand with the warmest and most fraternal regard—greeted Mrs. Butterton politely but with easy indifference—and then turning his back in a careless way, proceeded to converse with Mynheer Van Doring, taking no further notice either of the Frenchman or the lady.

The result of this stratagem was soon apparent. Mrs. Butterton pouted, tossed her fair head, and abandoned the vicinity of Monsieur Jambot, whose teeth began to grind against each other.

Captain Wagner did not move. He was perfectly absorbed in his conversation with the fat landlord.

The lady lightly touched his shoulder:—he turned indifferently.

"Why do you treat me so unfriendly, Captain?" said the lady; "all because I was looking at that music?"

"Unfriendly, madam!" ejaculated the Captain, "I am not unfriendly—but I know too well what is expected of a soldier in the presence of the fair sex. As you were conversing with Monsieur Jambot, I was too polite to interrupt you."

And the Captain raised his head with martial dignity and hauteur, with which was mingled a proud misery.

Mrs. Butterton put her handkerchief to her eyes and sobbed. The Captain set his teeth together, and summoned all his resolution.

Another sob issued from the handkerchief. Monsieur Jambot rose to his feet with ferocious rapidity. In a moment his little dress-sword was drawn, and he had confronted the Captain, whom he charged, in a voice hoarse with rage, with making *Madame* " grieve."

Captain Wagner drew his sabre, courteously saluted, and took his position with the coolness of an old swordsman. It was then that Mrs. Butterton threw herself between them with sobs and tears, beseeching them to be friends—for her sake, for the sake of goodness gracious—and on other grounds.

"For the sake of a lady," returned Captain Wagner, coldly, "I am prepared to do anything. But blood will come of this, or the devil take it! Blood, sir!"

And the Captain struck ferociously, the hilt of his sword, which weapon he slowly returned to its scabbard. Monsieur Jambot declared his entire willingness to fight all the *Capitaines* in the world, singly, or together—and then with his hands superbly placed upon his hips, and his hat cocked fiercely, sauntered carelessly from the apartment.

Then commenced a terrible scene between the Captain and Mrs. Butterton. We forbear to relate the particulars.

The lady was the pleader—the soldier was the dignified listener. For a long time he remained obdurate—in the end he melted. When Mrs. Butterton brought him Jamaica with her own fair hands, and provided all else which he wished, with smiles breaking through tears, the Captain fairly succumbed. He took the chubby hand and kissed it gallantly—declared he was more her devoted slave than ever—and then busied himself in mingling his morning dram, for which he possessed a recipe known only to himself.

"Really, my dear madam," said the worthy, now completely mollified by the sight of breakfast coming in, "you are the. paragon of your sex. You resemble the goddess Diana, or I'm a dandy!—Diana rising from the sea; for which reason she was called *Diana Urainy*. You are her very image!"

"La, Captain!" said the lady with a simper, "you are really too flattering!"

At the same moment, a loud and harsh voice on the stairway was heard calling.

"Who's that, in the devil's name?" said the Borderer.

"Oh, only Major Hastyluck, who slept here last night."

"I'll wager my head against a sixpence that he didn't see the way to bed, madam."

And the Captain's black moustache curled until his long white teeth resembled icicles pendent from the eaves of a house.

"I fear he was—intoxicated," was Mrs. Butterton's reply with a smile; "how shocking!"

"Oh, dreadful, awful, really deplorable, my dear madam, and what's he calling for?—there again! like the growl of a bear, or I'm a dandy!"

In fact Major Hastyluck was calling violently to old Hans, the waiter.

"Goming, sir," said Hans quietly: and ascending leisurely, he was heard conversing with the Major. Soon he reappeared, announcing that Major Hastyluck was impatient for his morning draught, and all at once a brilliant thought struck the Captain. He had secured the votes of precisely one half of the justices, for the establishment of the county-seat at Winchester—and Major Hastyluck's vote would decide all. The reflection stimulated the worthy to a tremendous exertion of politeness. This was no less than to send up to the official gentleman, the flagon of delightful punch which he had just brewed, with every ingredient, and in the highest perfection.

"Take that up, Hans, my hogshead," said the soldier, handing him the cup, "and present it to the Major with the respects of Captain Wagner."

Hans obeyed, and very soon descended again, with the request, on the part of the Major, that Captain Wagner would brew him another supply. To this task the Captain, who had meanwhile attended to his own wants, addressed himself immediately—and very soon after the justice made his appearance. He was a little weasen man, with a dried up physiogomy, of a fiery red hue, and carried himself with an immense affectation of dignity and superiority.

"My dear Major!" cried the Captain, "I am really delighted to see you—you arrive at a moment when my heart is open, just as breakfast is coming. How is your health?"

"Hum!—hah!—thank you, Captain Wagner, pretty well, pretty well. You are lately arrived, sir?"

"Precisely—from Belhaven, on the Potomac, down there."

"A thriving place."

"Yes, but by no means equal to Winchester, or I'm a dandy!"

"Hum!—perhaps—hum!"

And with these oracular words, Major Hastyluck sat down to breakfast, slightly staggering as he did so. His appetite once satisfied, he rose with the same oracular expression and air. The Captain soon followed, and lighting a corncob pipe with a reed stem, which he took from the mantelpiece, he addressed himself to business.

"How did you like that beverage I sent you, my dear Major?" said the Captain, sending forth clouds of foamy smoke; "was it a scorcher—as mild as milk, and as strong as a yoke of oxen, eh?"

"It was a pleasant draught," returned the Justice; "I will freely say, *more* pleasant than any which I have tasted for many years—ahem!"

"The fact is, I make it by a recipe known only to myself, and my respected grandmother—*formerly* known by that excellent lady, I mean—and as she has now, alas! paid the debt of nature, you understand, I am the sole depositary of the recipe."

This announcement seemed to excite unusual interest in breast of the Major. He assumed a coaxing expression, and said in a wheedling voice, almost wholly divested of his habitual pomposity:

"Is it a very great secret, Captain?"

"Secret!" cried the soldier; "I believe you! I promised my venerable grandmother that no one should ever worm it out of me."

"That is unlucky. I'd give a great deal to have it, Captain."

"Understand me," added the Borderer, curling his moustache, and assuming a serious expression, "there was one condition to my promise: that those individuals who proved themselves my true friends should participate with me."

"Ah, indeed! Well, I trust that you regard me as one of those—hum!"

"That depends upon circumstances, my dear Major. You can easily convince me, however. Prove yourself my friend—vote for Winchester for the county-seat."

"Winchester? Why, what interest have you there, Captain?"

"What interest? Can you ask? Are you ignorant, my dear friend, that I possess large and valuable estates immediately in that vicinity? I and my friends, General Adam Stephen, and Colonel Carter, are the real owners of all this region, or the devil take it! We let Fairfax live yonder as a favor—and to make a long story short, I want the county-seat at Winchester."

The Major shook his little withered head doubtfully.

"Very well, my dear comrade," returned the Captain; "I don't need your vote as yet—but I warn you that you have lost the only chance of getting my recipe."

The Major groaned.

"Will nothing else do, Captain?"

"Nothing."

"And if I were to make the bargain," he added, looking round guardedly, "would it be confidential?"

"Confidential? I wouldn't breathe it to myself."

"Then it's a bargain!" returned the worthy; "and now for the recipe."

"Wait a moment, my dear Major," said the Captain; "in business matters I always like to proceed regularly. Let me draw up something in the shape of a little contract—it will prevent mistakes."

And going to a table, he requested the fair widow to supply him with pen, ink, and paper. This was soon done by the smiling lady, and the worthy Borderer spread a sheet before him, and dipped the pen in the ink. After a moment's reflection, during which he assisted the operations of his intellect by tugging violently at the black fringe upon his lip, he traced upon the page, in a large, sprawling hand, decorated with a myriad of ornamental spatters, the following lines:

"It is hereby agreed between Captain Julius Wagner, otherwise called Captain Bloody Longknife, and Major Gideon Hastyluck, a justice of Frederick, in the parish of Shenandoah, which is a fine country, or I'm a dandy, that in consideration of Captain Julius Wagner, sometimes called Julius Cæsar Wagner, giving up to the said Hastyluck the recipe for making rum punch, which recipe the said Wagner got from his aged and much deplored grandmother, who resided in Stafford County, and on account of never sending for doctors, a sort of people that she never could bear, succeeded in living to almost the truly surprising and wonderful age of a hundred years—that as aforesaid, in consideration of Captain Wagner's giving to the said Major Hastyluck the said recipe, the said Hastyluck shall vote for Winchester, when the next court comes to fix the county-seat, as they are bound to do, at the town of Winchester, which will prove in the opinion of us, the undesigned, the future seat of empire of the Valley.

"And to the faithful discharge of the conditions in this paper, binding on us, we the underwriters, pledge our respective words, and fix our seals—Captain Julius Wagner intending immediately to brew a flagon of the drink above mentioned, wherewith both parties shall wet the bargain."

Captain Wagner executed a masterly flourish beneath this document, which he evidently regarded with much pride and satisfaction—and then affixed his name in letters nearly an inch long. Major Hastyluck, with a business-like air did the same, and the Borderer put the agreement in his pocket.

"And now for the punch, Captain—the recipe and the 'flagon' which I think you speak of brewing in the latter portion of that document."

"It shall be forthcoming at once, my dear Major—at once."

And first carefully writing down the desired formula, the worthy soldier applied himself to mingling the new supply in silence. Ere long it was rapidly descending the insatiate throat of Major Hastyluck; as to the Captain, he was chuckling to himself and muttering:

"I've the majority now, or may the—hum! your health, my dear Major, your very good health!"

In this way was the town of Stephensburg sold for a flagon of rum punch and the recipe to make it. Kercheval, in his *History of the Valley*, says: "Tradition relates that Fairfax was much more partial to Stephensburg than he was to Winchester," but an opponent "out-generalled his lordship, and by treating one of the justices to a bowl of toddy, secured his vote in favor of Winchester, which settled the question." This is Mr. Kercheval's account—the reader is left to judge of the relative credibility of the opposing historians—that gentleman and ourselves.

XXVI.

THE DAGGER IN THE HEART.

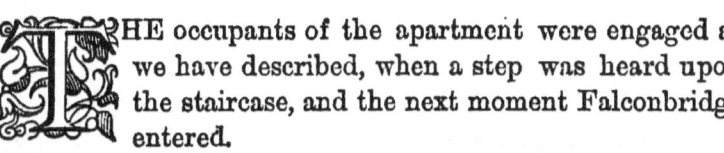THE occupants of the apartment were engaged as we have described, when a step was heard upon the staircase, and the next moment Falconbridge entered.

Since that night on which Captain Wagner had warned him in his gloomy and satiric tones against "panthers," and their wiles—since those mocking and mysterious words had resounded in his ears, Falconbridge had lived like one in a dream. His quick instinct told him that the soldier meant Miss Argal. There could be no doubt upon that point. His studied coldness toward the young lady, his grim expression when he encountered her, the shadow on his brow when her name even was mentioned—all this left no room for doubt.

Falconbridge had shut himself up in his room, and the storm began to mutter in his heart. His thoughts, like hounds unleashed, darted forward and backward, circling over the whole of his life, past and future. Then they returned with furious mouths to tear their master. Could this be anything but the merest dream, as wild and unreal as the sickliest chimeras, haunting the fancy of the invalid turning and tossing on the couch of fever? Suspect those brilliant, limpid eyes of dissimulation!—suspect that open and beautiful brow of concealment!—those tender lips of falsehood, of treachery! Treachery? Were women *treacherous?* Could eyes and lips and sighs and bashful glances lie? It was incredible, monstrous! If this were so, then everything was unreal—the world a mere phantasmagoria—and life a cheat, a lie, a miserable, horrible delusion!

Such thoughts do not pass through the heart for the first time without making it bleed. The brow which is racked and furrowed by them, never afterwards can be smooth. The sincere and noble honesty of this man's nature made the blow one of inexpressible agony. Suspicion was no customary guest with him—it pierced him mortally. Like a rusty and jagged blade directed by an unskillful hand, and turned from mere wanton cruelty in the wound, it stretched him on the bed of torture.

He pondered thus throughout the long hours of the dreary night, and for all those hours succeeding. He sent away the food brought to his room, untasted. More than once he mounted Sir John, and galloped toward Mr. Argal's—but it was only to return without going thither.

"Well, well," he said, on the morning when he re-encountered Captain Wagner as we have seen, "all this shall end. I will know; I will not labor under this terrible suspicion! Suspect her? I do not. I would as soon suspect an angel. Still that singular look of the soldier as he spoke!—those words full of sneering coldness! Yes, this shall end—I swear it!"

And passing his hand across his forehead, which was clouded and pale from suffering and want of rest, he descended.

"Give you good day, Captain," he said in his clear, noble voice; "I thought I heard your cheerful accents."

"Why, welcome, welcome, comrade," returned the soldier warmly, and grasping the young man's hand as he spoke; "I swear the sight of you is good for sore eyes, or I'm a dandy!"

The Captain seemed to feel what he said. His martial countenance always softened as he gazed at Falconbridge—his penetrating eyes grew wistful; this man who had fought against the hard, rough world so long, and encountered so much selfishness, falsehood and deception, appeared to experience a real delight in the company of his younger companion, and to regard him with a strange affection.

"I'm dooms glad to see you after having so long a slang whang with Fairfax," added the soldier, "but you are looking badly, Falconbridge; you are as white as a ghost. What's the matter?"

"Nothing, nothing, comrade."

"You want fresh air, or I'm mistaken."

"I really think you are right, Captain, and I'm going to take some. I see Sir John coming to the door."

" Oh, you ride—you are going to see "——

"Miss Argal," interrupted Falconbridge, with his proud, open look, full of sincerity and truth; "it is three or four days since I saw her."

And going to the door, he threw a critical glance at Sir John, who whinnied with pleasure at the sight of his master. The young man, with his delicate hand half covered with lace which filled his great barrel sleeves, caressed gently the white neck of the thoroughbred: and as he gazed at the beautiful animal, full of spirit and fire, his weary brow cleared up slightly.

All at once a hand was laid upon his shoulder. He turned round. Captain Wagner was beside him; and his face wore the same cold and gloomy expression which had characterized it on the night ride.

"Falconbridge," he said in a low, earnest tone, "have you any confidence in me—do you regard me as a true man —as an honest soldier—as a friend?"

"Yes," said Falconbridge, passing his hand slowly over the neck of the animal, and speaking in a very low voice.

" Well, you do me no more than justice. I swear to you that I love you as I would love a son, though you're no chicken, but a stout-hearted and stout-armed cavalier, or the devil take it! Well, I act as your friend when I say, take care what you do! Beware!"

And turning away, the soldier, who had lost all his cheerfulness, and gay spirit, slowly re-entered the house.

Falconbridge followed him with his eyes until he disappeared—turned even paler than before—and a sort of lurid light broke from his eyes. He evidently hesitated for a moment whether to follow and extract from the soldier a complete explanation of his meaning, or seek it from the person accused. His hesitation did not last long. He set his teeth together like a vice, leaped into the saddle, and driving the spur into the side of his horse, set forward like lightning on the road to Mr. Argal's.

He drew up at the door so suddenly that his horse was thrown upon his haunches. In a moment he had entered the house, and was in the presence of Miss Argal, who greeted him with the warmest favor.

"You have been away so long!" she said, in her caressing voice, and with a look from her black, lustrous eyes, full of such electric fascination that it turned the young man's head almost; "so very long—for nearly four days!"

XXVII.

FALCONBRIDGE PARTS WITH HIS MOTHER'S RING.

THE breast of Falconbridge thrilled with a vague excitement, and in the presence of the beautiful young woman, so innocent and pure-looking, his racking suspicions began to disappear, and his confidence to return. Were not those suspicions mere folly—a baseness and disloyalty even? Could any one look into that fair face, and believe for an instant that it masked a heart full of guile? For the instant his possessing thought disappeared—he no longer doubted—he yielded to the enchantment of eye and lip and voice.

But this change could not be permanent; Falconbridge was no weak and vacillating boy, whose moods at the moment govern his opinions, and actions. Those acrid and bitter meditations during the long hours which he had passed in loneliness and silence had impressed him too deeply. Thus his face became overclouded, and his head drooped. To the soft and caressing reproach contained in the words, "You have been away so long!" he therefore replied with sorrowful calmness :

" Are you sure you cared to see me?"

The young lady turned her head aside, and a slight color, like the first blush of morning, stole over her cheek. Then from the red lips came in a whisper almost, the words :

" *Very* sure."

"Falconbridge gazed at her for a moment with an expression of ardent love, mingled with bitter anguish, and said, in suppressed tones :

"You are so beautiful!—so very beautiful! Are you true?"

She turned her head quickly, and fixed upon him a glance which seemed intended to read his very soul. Then an expression of coldness and hauteur rose to the beautiful face, and she said with frigid ceremony :

"Are you aware of what you are saying, Mr. Falconbridge ?"

" Yes, yes—unhappily I am," was the young man's reply; "and I can understand your resentment. You find my accent harsh, my words insulting, even. You see that this question is not an idle jest, Miss Argal. You start at my address, at my coldness, the solemnity of my demand. But the question is not asked by chance. I most solemnly propound it! Not my lips, not my words, no! my heart, my soul cry out to you. Answer me, for pity's sake, for the sake of all that is pure and truthful!"

The cold expression in the eyes of the young lady grew ice. With a frigid erection of her superb head, she said :

"Are you unwell, Mr. Falconbridge, or is your mind affected?"

"No, no! I am well, if a man whose heart dies in his breast is well! I am sane, if a mind stretched on the rack may be called sane! I mean what I say—I have heard what makes me ask—do not demand what it is, I cannot reply. I suffer so poignantly that I must put an end to my distress, or it will put an end to me! For worlds—for the universe I would not pain you—I would die a thousand deaths rather—but "——

He was interrupted by the voice of the young lady. That voice had suddenly changed. It was no longer cold; her manner had passed from hauteur to anguish. Turning aside and covering her face with her handkerchief, she sobbed repeatedly, and at last uttered the broken words :

" If you—would not—pain me—why do you speak—so—cruelly to me—so unfeelingly—so "——

There the voice died away.

The accents went to the young man's heart. The sobs

smote down all his coldness. The sight of the lovely form bent down, and shaken with agitation, dissipated all his resolution, and drove away every suspicion, as the winds of March drive away the clouds from the clear blue sky.

All the profound loyalty and truth of his nature was aroused—all his abhorrence of injustice and unkindness. He took the young lady's hand in his own—pressed it ardently, and begged her forgiveness for his cruel and unfounded suspicion.

"Pardon me," he said, in his sincere, noble voice, casting upon his companion, as he spoke, a glance of unspeakable love, "pardon your poor friend for the harsh and insulting words he has uttered. I know not why I spoke so—I know not how these thoughts ever entered my unfortunate brain. Enough ; in pity let us speak of this no more. So we are friends again—are we not?"

And he bent forward to look into her face. That face was raised, and the black eyes were riveted upon his own with a sorrowful forgiveness, a tender melancholy which were inexpressibly beautiful. They swam in tears—but through the tears broke a sad smile which made the heart of the young man bound in his bosom with wild delight. Carried away by a rush of emotion, he pressed the hand which he held to his lips, and said, passionately :

"Do not weep—your tears make me wretched! Never shall I forgive myself for the cruel and unmanly conduct which I have to-day been guilty of. I came here with my heart on fire, my brain in a tumult—I have been unjust, insulting, mad, almost—I could not help it. I spoke thus, because my mind was whirling, my nerves trembling—because—because I love you!—yes, presumptuous as you may think the words in a mere stranger—I love you—with honest, faithful love!"

Enough—we forbear from pursuing further the details of the scene between the young lady and Falconbridge. We have little skill in reporting such dialogues, and must draw the veil over the rest.

He remained until late in the evening, and then returned at full gallop toward the Ordinary, his face the very impersonation of joy. At times he gazed wistfully upon his left hand, from which a ring was missing—a plain gold ring which had belonged to his mother. He had placed it upon the finger of the young girl, for she had plighted to him her troth.

Here we would gladly leave the young cavalier—with his face smiling, his cheeks glowing—his pulse beating joyfully as he galloped on through the prairie and forest. But the fatal current of our narrative keeps us beside him. Those smiles are brief ones—the bloom of the happy cheek evanescent as the frail spring blossom—the blow awaits him.

He dismounts at the door of the Ordinary and enters. The fat landlord presents him with a letter which he opens, smilingly.

Ten minutes afterward he is seated in his chamber, his brow leaning upon his crossed arms, resting upon a table —his cheeks as pale as a ghost's—his forehead moist with icy perspiration. The shudders which pass through his frame rattle the paper still clenched in his nervous grasp— but no groan issues from his lips.

XXVIII.

THE LETTER.

THIS is the letter accompanying another paper which is stained with blood.

"MR. FALCONBRIDGE :—After much doubt I address you, to warn you, as a friend, against allowing your affections to be ensnared by Miss B. Argal. I have no right, sir, to pry into your matters, and maybe I will get no thanks, but your courtesy to me makes it impossible for me to see you duped. Captain Wagner will not speak out—he says that he has already said more than he had a right to—and I will, therefore, do so myself. The paper which I put in this letter will tell you all. The poor young man was a distant relative of mine, and died at my house. He wrote the paper just before his death. I will add no more, except that I have no private grudge against Miss Argal, and so remain, Your real friend,

SARAH BUTTERTON."

The paper was written in a firm hand, obscured in several places by stains of blood, and ran as follows :

"STAFFORD, VA., *May*, 1747.

"I am about to commit suicide. Before putting an end to my miserable life, I will relate the circumstances which impel me to the act. My mind is perfectly sane, my memory good—I will speak calmly. This is my history :

"I was left an orphan at twenty, with no brothers or sisters around me—my only brother, who was older than myself, having perished on a sea-voyage. I was rich—the entire property of my parents having reverted to myself. I enjoyed country life on my property, and was fond of the society of young ladies, but never loved any one until I met with Bertha Argal. Her father rented a small farm near my own considerable estate, and I met with her frequently, and conceived a passion for her. She was, and is the most beautiful woman that my eyes ever beheld. Unfortunately she is destitute of all those noble qualities which should accompany beauty. She is false, and as cold as ice—heartless. But I will not say more—let the event show.

"I loved her passionately, and very soon commenced paying her my addresses. She received them with manifest favor. It was not long before I confessed my affection, and she told me with tears and blushes, that she loved me as ardently as I said I loved her. I will never forget her words or her looks; they are engraven on my memory. Well, to be brief, we were contracted in marriage; it was fixed for a day not more than three months off, when my elder brother, who had been given up as lost at sea, five years before, suddenly made his appearance. He had been taken prisoner by a Spanish vessel, carried to Cadiz, and thrown into a dungeon there, as a suspected character; his identity being mistaken. He had finally been liberated however, and so came back. I need not tell anybody who knows me, that I did not regret this, or grudge my brother the estate, which as eldest son he deprived me of; reducing me from an independent gentleman of large possessions, to a dependent on his bounty. I loved him, and he loved me. I looked up to him; he was my superior in mind as in strength and stature; and I was content to occupy my rightful position of younger brother and inferior.

"Not long after his return, Harley saw Bertha Argal, and in spite of his knowledge of my engagement, loved her. In this there was no disloyalty—no intention to become my rival. He would have scorned the imputation, but he loved her. He could not help it. The dazzling beauty of the girl, her fascinating, bewildering witchery, were too much for his resolution. I saw that he loved her, but at first gave myself no sort of uneasiness about it. I knew that Harley was the soul of honor; would as soon cut off his right hand as commit a base action; and as to Bertha Argal, I was quite at rest. At that time I laughed at the idea of treachery in a creature so pure and beautiful. Well, the sequel will show. Six months after my brother's arrival, the young lady began to grow cold toward me, and warm toward my brother. I told her of it; she laughed in my face. She grew fonder and fonder of my brother. I became angry. She sneered at my anger. If I was displeased, she said, at my brother's attentions, why not bring it to the decision of arms? we both wore swords! These satirical words impressed me horribly; the young lady was coming out in her real colors. I said nothing, and terminated my visit; but I went again the next day, for I had no will to resist; I was mad about her. Thus things continued until a month ago. Then I found that she had been poisoning my brother's mind against me. He became cold to me, and ere long my presence in the house, our father's house, became an evident constraint on him. One morning, however, he returned from Mr. Argal's, whither he had been on business with a strange glow in his cheek, and greeted me with long disused affection. He seemed to look at me compassionately. Something told me that this foreboded evil, and I galloped over to see Bertha. I had guessed correctly, She embraced that occasion, she said, to inform me that I might give up all thoughts of marrying her; she had no reason to give; it was her decision! She looked like a queen as she spoke, and I remained for a moment looking at her, pale and silent. Then I said, 'Was this what made Harley so kind to me, so compassionate? Did you inform him of your intention?' 'Well, sir,' was her reply, 'suppose I did? I beg you will in future confine yourself to your own affairs, and not subject me to the inquisition.' She was furious, but as beautiful as an aroused leopardess. I was white with rage, but I loved her passionately still. I glared at her for an instant, and then replied, 'This will end badly, Miss Argal—no young lady can trifle with a gentleman with impunity.' Her lip curled, and she said, coolly, 'Oh, you mean you are going to fight Harley? Well, why don't you try it, sir? Are you afraid that he is a better swordsman, and will finish you? I have no doubt this is your objection, and I don't believe you would dare to face him!' I solemnly declare that these were her exact words. I leave the readers of this paper to decide if in many cases they would not have produced that awful tragedy, a mortal contest between brothers. I said nothing, however; I looked at her with pale and trembling lips only, and went away. Three days afterwards, Harley was called to Mr. Argal's again, and on his return looked serious and troubled. 'Miss Argal is a singular person,' he said to me after dinner, with great gloom; 'can she wish to place you and me, Charles, opposite each other with swords in our hands? I should so imagine from her conversation to-day; a strange person!' I did not reply, except by some commonplace. I loved the young woman still with too passionate a love. I could not speak against her. For more than two weeks thereafter, I was her slave, her dog. I crawled back when she lashed me away, and tried to kiss the hand which struck me. I say this, because all the truth shall be known. I have no resolution—I never had any; I am the powerless victim of this infatuation; and if this moment Bertha Argal were to enter the room, and smile on me—even after all—I would obey her in anything she commanded

"But my narrative must come to an end. Four days ago I went to see her for the last time. She met me with scorn and satirical smiles, which soon became sneers. So I had determined not to be whipped away, had I?' she asked: 'I had come sneaking back to moan out that she no longer loved me; that she loved my brother, which she now begged leave to inform me was a fact, and that I was wretched.' 'Yes,' I said, 'all you say is true.' 'Then you are a fool for your pains, sir,'

THE MASTER OF GREENWAY COURT. 141

she said, 'and your presence makes me sick. *You*, a brother of Harley Austin! *you*, with your feeble snivelling complaints, and begging, the brother of that strong, resolute man! Yes, sir! I love him, and he shall love me; and if you don't like that, you may put an end to yourself; it will be a matter of very small interest to me!' I looked at her as she spoke, and shuddered. She was super-humanly beautiful; I would have given all the countless worlds of the sky, had I possessed them, to have clasped her for a single moment in my arms. She saw her influence over me, and her lip curled. 'You haven't resolution, however, for the act,' she said; 'if I were a man, and fortune went against me, I'd do as the ancients did, get rid of life. And now, sir, you will please leave me, I am tired of you. Ah! here comes Harley!' And turning her back on me, she hastened to the window, and smiled at the visitor.

"I set my teeth close, put on my hat, and went out. Harley and I passed each other with some constraint on his part; I was quite calm, for I had made up my mind. I returned to the hall and wrote on a piece of paper which I knew would meet my brother's eye, the words: 'Think well, before you marry Bertha Argal, brother. She has broken my heart—attempted to drive me to a bloody combat with you, knowing who would be victor, and now advises me to end my despair by my own hand. I obey, for life has no longer any charm for me. Farewell.' I signed this, and have come hither to Mrs. Butterton's to write and leave this paper.

"In five minutes I shall be dead.   CHARLES AUSTIN."

These were the words which Falconbridge read—then his glance fell upon these others in addition, in Mrs. Butterton's hand-writing:

"The poor young man was found dead when we ran at the explosion of his pistol. This paper was lying on the table. Mr. Harley Austin returned it to me, not wishing to keep it; he has since left the country."

Falconbridge remained motionless throughout the entire night. As the sun streamed in, he raised his face, which was covered with a deadly pallor, and groaned.

XXIX.

THE THREADS OF THE WOOF.

HOURS, days and weeks have fled away since the scenes and events which we have endeavored to place before the reader's eyes. The year wanes fast. The brilliant sunlight of October has yielded to the hazy influences of November. The sky is no longer blue: the trees are dismantled of their splendid trappings. Under the chill heaven of a leaden color, the broad face of nature resembles some great hall, from which the gorgeous hangings have been torn, the trophies of banners removed—in which the lights are slowly going out, as after a great revel, when the guests have all departed.

The plover cries and the partridge whistles on the wind-swept hills—the wild geese wing their way toward the south—the crane stalks with a sombre and weird air among the shallows of the water-courses, dreaming, you would say, of other lands—and from the northwest wander cutting blasts, preluding the approach of winter.

But the human hearts beneath the chilly sky beat as before. The personages of our drama follow still, the bent of their diverse passions, humors, and desires. The hot-blood in their veins pulsates, and hastens to and fro, as strongly.

Lord Fairfax and Captain Wagner hold interminable discussions on the state of the border, and the best means of defence, now that the Indian inroad may be soon expected. The worthy soldier is content to pass his time thus—alternately debating with his lordship, and pursuing his own special campaign against the enemy at Van Doring's Ordinary: he sleeps, and eats, and drinks, and philosophizes, not without many camp expletives, uttered in a jovial and sonorous voice, the sound of which seems encouraging to the Earl, for he greets these outbreaks on the part of the Captain, with his uniform grim smile.

Meanwhile George is occupied by his own affairs also. He surveys the surrounding lands assiduously for the Earl; sleeps often in the woods, his head resting on his knapsack; and it happens that the direction of his toils is often toward the south.

There the great Fort Mountain raises its double wall, blue against the dun heaven, and within the embraces of the shaggy arms—perched like an eagle's nest in the declivity of the mountain—he sees the cottage in which Cannie lives. He loves the little maiden now with the fondest devotion. She has become all the world to him, and dwells in his thoughts wherever his footsteps turn—in the prairie, and the forest, by night and by day; it is always Cannie of whom the youth is dreaming; around her he weaves that tissue of romance and fancy which the bounding heart of youth adorns with such resplendent gems. George goes often to the mountain dwelling, and there all the outer world disappears. He is alone in the great universe with one whose grave, sweet smile lights up his life—whose frank, open brow is the mirror of truth and goodness—in whose eyes he finds the charm which only exists for the youthful lover. And Cannie now no longer looks upon him as a stranger. He has become day by day, more an influence upon her life—her innocent heart beats fast when his tall and erect figure enters the doorway—when his sunny smile, lighting up the firm lips, and frank, true face, beams on her. She does not disguise her affection now, for she knows it is returned—but her fondness for her youthful companion never betrays itself in a manner repugnant to the most delicate maiden modesty. It is Cannie's nature to be honest and true—but she is ripening into a "young lady" now; and so George can only guess from the serious smile, and kindly eyes, her secret.

Their lives glide on thus, and no incident breaks the spell which is woven day by day more closely around the young hearts of the maiden and the youth. The old grandfather alone with his books, his chemical machines, or with whatever occupies his attention; they are by themselves in the world of reverie and fancy. It is true, that from time to time, as they wander like happy children along the mountain side, or to the lofty brow of the sleeping giant, that a shadowy figure follows and marks the way they take—but this figure is unseen by them. It is the young Indian whom the reader has once looked upon, on that beautiful day of October—hidden among the leafy branches of the great oak, and descending to follow, then, as now, the footsteps of the pair. He still preserves his air of grave and lofty dignity—his eyes have the same expression of mild truth and honesty—his lips move as before, and utter the sad murmur which seems to indicate a possessing thought. His eyes never wander from the form of Cannie when she is in the circle of his vision—he seldom betrays any other emotion than a jealous, watchful guardianship over her; if his features contract slightly, and his broad bosom heaves, when she bestows upon her companion some little mark of her affection, this exhibition of feeling is soon suppressed; the old gravity returns; and the young chief glides into the deep woods, and disappears, as lightly and silently as a shadow.

And Falconbridge—what of him? Has the darkness which enveloped all his life upon that awful evening, when he read the letter of the suicide, been dissipated?

Wholly.

A few days afterwards he encountered Captain Wagner at the Ordinary; the soldier, who had been informed by Mrs. Butterton of the step which she had taken, almost feared to meet the young man, or witness his agony. He expected to find Falconbridge bowed to the earth with anguish—to hear only groans and stifled sighs—to see, in the pale cheek, the lack-lustre eye, the drooping form, those evidences of suffering which betray the victim of despair. Instead of such a figure, he saw Falconbridge happy, smiling, buoyant. His head rose proudly erect; his eyes shone with a joyous light; his lips were wreathed with smiles; he was the picture of one across whose brow a cloud has never passed. The worthy Captain started, and looked with unfeigned astonishment upon his companion. The quick eye of Falconbridge discerned at once the meaning of this expression. He laughed gaily, and then said, with earnest simplicity:

"I know why you start so, comrade—why you are astounded at seeing me thus happy-looking. That well-meaning lady, your friend, has doubtless told you of her warning to me. It was honest and kind in her—but it made me very miserable."

"And then," said Captain Wagner gloomily, "what happened afterwards?"

"What happened? Why what could happen, comrade? I went to the person charged with this awful duplicity and heartlessness. I asked her to say what was the real truth—and I heard it. She raged at the accusation; vainly attempted to extort from me the author—and then giving way to her feelings, burst into tears, and told me all, explained everything."

"Oh! she explained everything, did she?" said Captain Wagner, with gloomy irony; "no doubt she made all quite clear."

"Oh, perfectly! How could your friend have seriously thought that paper written by the poor unfortunate youth who killed himself, an actual narrative of facts?"

"It was all a romance then?" said the Captain, with the same sardonic contortion of his lip, "it was only a little imaginary story which he amused himself in writing, to wile away the time before he blew his brains out!"

"Captain, Captain!" said Falconbridge earnestly, "your voice has a terrible sneer in it; your curling lip betrays scorn and incredulity!"

"Well, it betrays what I feel," returned the soldier, looking at the young man with wistful and gloomy eyes; "it talks plainly, does this curling lip you speak of, or I'm a dandy! But I'll uncurl it; I'll sneer no more; I'll not wound you Falconbridge—and have only to say that 'twas truly unfortunate that this mad youth made up such a horrible story."

"*Mad!*" said Falconbridge, with a quick glance at his companion, "then you heard of his madness!"

"No," said Captain Wagner, "but I have no doubt that is the fair young lady's explanation."

"Yes, assuredly! who could have doubted it? The truth is that the unhappy lover's tale was only the sick fancy of a diseased mind. He did pay his addresses to Miss Argal—he did love her passionately—but she told him frankly a hundred times that she could not respond to his affection. She tried to do this as kindly and tenderly as possible, but her reply only enraged him. There was a tendency to madness in his family, and this made her peculiarly anxious to soothe him. He would not be soothed however; in their last interview he yielded to a crazy fit of wrath—he rushed furiously away with his hand upon his forehead, and three days afterwards Miss Argal heard with inexpressible astonishment and horror that he had put an end to his life. The statements of the paper were the mere fabrications of his rage and madness—the creations of a diseased intellect, aiming at revenge. That is all. Is not the explanation perfect?"

"Yes," said Captain Wagner, as calm and cold as ice, "perfect. I have rarely heard anything so simple. And what did you do with the dead man's letter?"

"I begged it of Mrs. Butterton, she yielded—it is ashes."

Captain Wagner moved his head up and down with the same icy expression; set his teeth firmly together; and, after a moment's silence, said in a low voice:

"Falconbridge, are you a fatalist?"

"A fatalist?" said the young man, looking curiously at his companion, "surely not, comrade. God rules us and directs our lives—all issues rest in his merciful hands, and we are told that not even a sparrow falls without the knowlege of the kind Father of the Universe. I trust in all to him—as I pray to him night and morning as my mother taught me at her knee. No, I am not a fatalist."

"Well, from this moment I *am*," said the soldier, with a sombre glance; "I don't deny your religious views—but I am none the less, from this day, a fatalist!"

With these words the Captain entered the Ordinary, and Falconbridge, with a serious expression, mounted his horse to go to Mr. Argal's.

This was the state of things, in connection with the main personages of our narrative, at the moment when we again take up the thread of events. From this time forth, each day and hour, everything ripened and advanced toward the catastrophe of the drama.

XXX.

THE ARREST.

ACROSS the prairie, sobbing mournfully now in the chill, autumn wind—under the bare boughs of the forest, studded here and there with evergreens, which only looked more cheerless from the surrounding desolation—through the sparkling waves of the Shenandoah, and into the rugged defile of the Fort Mountain, George passed at a rapid gallop, his eyes full of gloom, and his brow contracted.

Lord Fairfax had informed him that on this day "Old Powell," as he was called, would be arrested on the charges made against him by a justice named Hastyluck, and the officials would probably go early.

George had received this information on the night before, with utter horror and astonishment, and had besought Lord Fairfax, if the charge were witchcraft, to dismiss it as absurd and ridiculous. His lordship had replied coolly that this was quite out of his power, even if consistent with his convictions; all he could promise was, that no act of oppression should be performed; and with this George was compelled to be content.

He scarcely slept, and at daybreak was on his way to the mountain.

Never moderating the speed of his horse, whose mouth was filled with foam, he rapidly ascended the steep bridle-path and reached the door of the little mansion.

The scene which greeted him made his cheek flush and his eyes flash fire.

The officers of the law had already arrived, and placed the old man under arrest. One of them was curiously examining the strange coin which George had seen on a former occasion, and which the man had picked up from among some books on a table—the other was about to place upon the wrists of old Powell a pair of iron hand-cuffs, in spite of the tearful and trembling prayers of little Cannie, who had clasped the arm of his shaggy overcoat, and begged him, crying, not to use them.

George advanced quickly into the apartment, and confronting the officer, said sternly :

" That is quite unnecessary, sir ! Mr. Powell cannot escape from you !"

The officer turned hastily, and said with an insolent scowl:

" Who are you, pray ?"

" My name is of no importance," George returned, with a hauteur in strong contrast to his democratic opinions; "it is enough, sir, that I command you in the name of Lord Fairfax to conduct the prisoner unfettered to Van Doring's Ordinary."

And putting his hand into his breast he extended toward the person whom he addressed a slip of paper, upon which was written:

"I desire, and if necessary require that the prisoner Powell may be treated with all respect, and especially brought to Court without hand-cuffs.

" FAIRFAX.

"GREENWAY COURT, 5th Nov. 1748."

George's foresight had led him to ask this favor of the Earl, which had been readily granted—and the vulgar official had no courage to resist. He scowled at the young man, whose cold, fixed look cowed him in spite of himself, and putting the hand-cuffs in his pocket, growled :

" Well it's nothing to me ; and you, old fellow, just come

along with you? You'll have a hard time of it, cuffs or no cuffs."

"It'll be harder'n he thinks," here put in the other worthy with a sneer. "If I ain't mistaken, this is a counterfeit—he's a coiner, as I've heard hinted."

A flash darted from beneath the shaggy white brows of the old man, and he reached forth to take the coin from the hands of the speaker. But the hand fell at his side. An expression of scorn which might have become a royal prince, passed over his features, and he turned away.

"Mr. George," he said, bowing with courtly gravity to the young man, "I need not say that I thank you from my heart for this kind and thoughtful action. Of the result of this foolish business I have no manner of fear. I commit my child to you, in my absence—it is enough, to so honest a gentleman."

Then adding calmly to the officials, who were evidently impressed in spite of themselves, by the dignity and coolness of his bearing,—"I will be ready in a few moments to attend you,"—the old man entered the inner apartment. He soon returned wrapped in a comfortable overcoat, which reached beneath the knee, and issuing forth, mounted the spare horse which had been brought for him. How those intelligent gentlemen, the constables, had expected him to hold the bridle with his hands secured remains a mystery to this day—but the obstacle no longer existed—and with a tender kiss upon Cannie's tremulous lips, and another bow to George, the prisoner set forward, between the two officers.

We shall pass over the scene between George and Cannie —such distressing pictures are not to our taste. He consoled her with every possible assurance calculated to calm her emotion—but all was in vain. The girl begged him, with tears in her eyes, and nervous sobs, to take her to her grandfather, and it was one of the hardest tasks which George had ever undertaken, to resist these moving entreaties. He did resist, however, by an immense exertion of will, for he knew that to yield would be to add to the child's unhappiness by showing her the old man, formally arraigned for trial—and all Cannie could procure from him was a promise that he would go at once and see that her grandfather was not treated cruelly.

"That should never be!" George said, with that flash of the eye which betrayed the depth of his character, and the strength of will lying beneath the calm exterior—"he would go at once! there was nothing to fear!"

And leaping on his horse, he put spur to the animal, and galloped at full speed down the mountain.

Cannie followed him with her eyes, which the tears almost blinded, and prayed inaudibly for strength and protection from One in whom she was accustomed to place all her trust. She saw George disappear, in the forest—than reappear in the open space, galloping violently as before: and finally, on the banks of the river, saw him join the officers and their prisoner.

Then the whole cavalcade disappeared, and Cannie fell upon the bench of the little porch, covering her face with her hands, and uttering sobs so passionate that her bosom, and the long, fair hair, which had fallen, and now rested upon her shoulders, were shaken, as by a convulsion.

XXXI.

LIGHTFOOT.

SHE preserved this attitude still, when a footstep was heard upon the path near at hand, and raising her head she saw the young Indian, whom we have twice alluded to in our chronicle.

He was clad as before, in fringed leggins, joined by a pliable garment of soft doeskin, reaching to his waist, which was encircled by a leathern belt, upon one side of which were secured a bundle of arrows:—his feet were protected by ornamented moccasins, fitting tightly to the high instep and nervous ankle:—above his brow drooped, as before, the variegated plume, his badge of chieftainship. As he leaned upon his long cedar bow and looked upon the child, his bare breast slightly heaving, and his noble features full of tender pity and affection, he presented a subject for a great painter.

Cannie rose quickly to her feet, and hastening to his side said hurriedly:

"Oh, Lightfoot! I thought you were far away! I know you will help me! Can you take me over the river? Grandpa is to be tried, and I must not, cannot stay here!—Lightfoot, you are a good, true friend."

She stopped, overcome with agitation:—one hand resting on his arm, her eyes turned up to his face beseechingly. The young Indian looked into the sweet countenance with a sudden color on his swarthy cheek, which betrayed the extent of the interest he felt in the speaker. But when he spoke, his words were calm and measured; long training had made self-control a second nature with him. We shall not record his reply in the broken English which was all he possessed—though the sad, musical tones made that defective dialect not destitute of a singular charm.

"Is not Lightfoot the true friend of the Mountain Dove?" he said. "He has known her very well, and loved her for many moons—and her father has been kind to the poor Indian who left his tribe to wander here among the places of his childhood."

"And you have been kind, very kind to us, Lightfoot. You have more than once kept the Indians from attacking us—and I would have died that day when the moccasin bit me, if you had not brought the herb to cure me. And now, Lightfoot, you must be my friend. You must take me over the river to Mr. Yeardley's—I know he will let me go in his wagon to the court. Will you, Lightfoot?—do not refuse me, dear Lightfoot!"

The swarthy cheek again colored slightly, but the voice was calm when he said:

"Lightfoot loves the little dove of the mountain—he will do her bidding now and always—he would willingly die for her."

And with these grave words, which were accompanied by a sudden flash of the eye, in which might have been read an expression of deep tenderness, the young chief assumed the attitude of one who waits patiently.

Cannie hastened into the house, threw a cloak upon her shoulders, tied her chip hat under her chin, and came forth again quickly. The two then rapidly descended the mountain—the Indian often taking the little hand to assist his companion over some obstacle in the path—and thus they finally reached the river. From a sheltered nook, overshadowed by a great drooping pine tree, Lightfoot silently produced a gum-log canoe, and placed the girl in it. A sweep of the long paddle sent it ten yards into the current, and they were soon on the opposite side of the river. As carefully concealing the skiff as before, the Indian and his companion then hastened on, and before very long, came in sight of Mr. Yeardley's. Lightfoot allowed the girl to go on alone—and from his hiding-place saw her enter the rude mansion of the settler, before which a light wagon, drawn by a pony, was standing. In ten minutes she came out again, with the rough, but good-humored borderer, who placed her in the vehicle, got in himself, and drove off.

Lightfoot leaned upon his cedar bow, and followed the wagon until it was out of sight, with his sad smile and look of wistful affection. He was thinking of Cannie's parting words, as she pressed his hand in both of hers and said :

"Come to our house to-morrow, Lightfoot!—you are my dear, kind friend!"

The words had made his breast thrill, and a joyful light illumined his features. Then the sadness came, and he murmured :

"She loves the pale-faced youth. I am naught to her. But Manitou will speak. It is well."

With these words he turned and disappeared in the forest.

XXXII.

HOW CAPTAIN WAGNER OVERTHREW HIS ADVERSARY.

IN the main apartment of Van Doring's Ordinary, the worshipful justices of the County of Frederick were assembled, to take into consideration all questions touching the order, defence, government, and general condition of the region under their supervision.

The Ordinary had been selected for the place of meeting at the request of Lord Fairfax. As one of the pieces of business which would come before the worshipful justices, was the selection of a permanent locality for the court, and as Winchester and Stephensburg contended for the honor, and emolument in question—said his lordship—it would be fair to meet on the present occasion at neither of those places. Thus they would enter the arena of friendly competition impartially, and without undue advantage.

These views had received the approbation of the enlightened justices, and they had accordingly assembled from every direction at the Ordinary of Mr. Van Doring—riding every description of animal of the horse species, and clad in the most extraordinary diversity of apparel. Some of them were gentlemen of the first class, and these were well dressed, with some pretensions to grace and elegance. But the majority were like Major Hastyluck, rather unfavorable specimens of their species—low-browed, sharp-faced, wiry, keen-looking individuals, who evidently had an eye to the main chance under all possible circumstances, and, like a celebrated gentleman of more modern times, thought it well to be "shifty in a new country."

A large crowd of a nondescript character had assembled on

the occasion—hunters, trappers, settlers—many of them portly Germans, others trim, active Scotchmen:—and this crowd moved about in front of the Ordinary, drank systematically of Mynheer Van Doring's Jamaica, and during the first hours of the day, entered with enthusiasm into the business of trading horses—the animals being, for the most part, plain to the inspection of all, at the long rack in front of the tavern door.

About twelve o'clock a decided sensation was created in the crowd by the appearance of a large English chariot, drawn by four glossy horses, from which vehicle, when it paused before the door, descended his lordship, the Earl of Fairfax, Lieutenant of the County of Frederick, and President of the body of justices. Lord Fairfax, who carried into the wilds of the New World something of the English idea of the propriety of full dress, on occasions of ceremony, was very richly clad. His coat was of brown cloth, decorated with embroidery; his waistcoat of yellow silk, ornamented with flowers in silver thread; from his bosom protruded a mass of snowy ruffles, and his peruke was carefully powdered. Around him, as he issued from the chariot, he drew the folds of a rich red velvet cloak —and then inclining his head slightly to the admiring crowd, he entered the Ordinary.*

A quarter of an hour after the appearance of his lordship, the sheriff was heard uttering his loud brazen "Oyez! oyez! oyez! Silence is commanded—humhum—humhum—hum! —God save the King!"—and the justices took their seats at a long table, at the further end of the apartment, the Earl occupying a large arm-chair in the centre. A little gentleman, with an irresistible business air, sat at one corner of the board with a huge volume bound in leather, lying before him—and near the door, at a respectful distance from the

---

* The chief details of this description are faithful to accurately preserved tradition. The tradition was communicated to the present writer by the son of a gentleman who visited the Earl at Greenway Court—saw his handsome chariot, and red velvet cloak— and dined in state at the broad board,

members of the court, the crowd—among whom might be seen Falconbridge, George, and Captain Wagner, conversing—looked on with interest.

The clerk read some previous proceedings in a monotonous voice—the justices consulted in a low tone with Lord Fairfax;—and then the Earl leaned forward and said, turning his head first to the right, then to the left:

"Is the court prepared to vote upon the selection of a county-seat? I need not inform you, gentlemen, that the question will chiefly lie between Stephensburg and Winchester. I shall, therefore, request each justice, as I address him, to pronounce one or the other name, which I will note down as it is uttered."

A considerable sensation among the crowd greeted these words, and a hubbub of voices for a moment deafened every one.

"Silence in the court!" cried the sheriff, with fierce indignation; "silence, or the court-room will be cleared!"

"No, sir! Winchester, or the devil take it!" resounded clear and sonorous in the sudden silence, and the sheriff started up with ferocious abruptness.

"Silence! Captain Wagner, you are disturbing the court! Silence!"

"My dear friend," said the voice of Captain Wagner, as that worthy advanced from the mass, with clanking spurs and sabre, "I have the utmost possible respect for this most honorable court, and the little remark which fell from me was spoken confidentially to a friend, who is an advocate of Stephensburg. Now, I'm only a poor soldier, and nothing of a lawyer, but I will maintain that Winchester, and no other place, ought to be selected for the county-seat. I have my reasons," added the Captain, mysteriously, "and if this most honorable and respectable body would listen to the said reasons, I could satisfy their minds, or may the "——

What followed, or nearly followed, was lost in the Captain's huge beard.

The ghost of a smile flitted over the countenance of Lord Fairfax :—it was his favorite music, the sound of that martial and sonorous voice—and he recalled all at once the "declaration of war" by the soldier, on his arrival in the Valley. As to the Captain, he pushed up his great black moustache with his finger—ran his eyes along the line of justices, among whom were Mr. Argal, and Major Hastyluck—and finally concentrated his gaze upon the face of the Earl, with an expression which said, plainly, "Honor bright, my lord!"

The lurking smile came again to the Earl's face, and turning to the court, he said:

"Gentlemen, if it is your pleasure, we will listen to Captain Wagner's reasons for selecting Winchester. He is well acquainted with the country, and its interests, and if you permit him, may throw light upon the question."

A glance of much admiration from the soldier rewarded his generous enemy; and when the court acquiesced in the Earl's recommendation, the countenance of the worthy, which before had been filled with the elements of fear, was now fringed with the radiance of hope, and expanded with the delight of a great orator who feels that the moment has arrived for his triumph. The Captain bowed his head, then raised his martial brow erect—and extending one arm persuasively, plunged with eloquence into the middle of the subject.

It is again, as on a former occasion, matter of deep regret to the faithful historian of Captain Wagner's exploits, that the absence of professional reporters, at that remote period, renders it impossible to accurately record the vivid eloquence of his speeches. As in the case of Patrick Henry, and other celebrated men, the legend of his power alone remains. We may safely say, however, that the eulogium pronounced upon the town of Winchester, by the military orator, was one of transcendent beauty and stirring impressiveness—while Stephensburg dwindled away into a tenth-rate cross-road assemblage of huts, unworthy of the attention of any one for an instant. The Captain concluded by a pathetic and affecting appeal to the honorable justices to be guided in their decision by no considerations of self-interest, by no preference for persons—to remember that unborn millions would be affected by their determination, and form their opinion of the members of the court by the manner in which they discharged, on this great occasion, their solemn and responsible obligations.

With this eloquent appeal the Captain ended his oration, and retired modestly into the crowd.

The smile on the Earl's face had come back in full force—and turning to his associates, he said:

"Gentlemen, you have heard the reasons given by Captain Wagner, but I imagine you have discovered in them nothing to largely modify any opinions which you may have before made up. If the members of the court are ready to vote, I will submit the question."

As no objection was made, the Earl called in turn the name of each—making a mark as they responded, either under "Winchester," or "Stephensburg," which were written upon a sheet of paper. The result was that the first had five marks, the latter but four—and Winchester was selected as the county-seat of Frederick by a majority of one.

As he inscribed the last vote—that of the worthy Major Hastyluck—a slight flush invaded the swarthy cheek of the Earl, and he leaned back haughtily in his arm-chair. The result seemed to cause him no less surprise than dissatistion; and for a moment he remained silent, looking coldly at the court. Then with an irritated flirt of the hand he tossed down the paper, saying, simply:

"Winchester is chosen."

The Earl's displeasure did not last, however. It plainly

subsided after the transaction of some additional business of a common-place nature; and when a short period for rest was taken by the court, who went to supply themselves with cups of Jamaica, Lord Fairfax approached Captain Wagner, and said, calmly :

"Well, you are victor, sir—I congratulate you upon your triumph!"

"My lord," said Captain Wagner, making the military salute, "there is something finer than to get the better of an adversary—it is to act toward that adversary with the chivalry and fairness that your lordship has displayed on this occasion."

It was the Captain's honest opinion, and the ill-humor of the gratified Earl completely disappeared.

XXXIII.

THE WIZARD OF THE MASSINUTTON.

IT was not until late in the evening that the case of the singular inhabitant of the Fort Mountain came up for examination.

He was brought from the private apartment in which he had been confined, into the main room in which the array of justices were seated behind the long table, and directed to sit down until he was called—"when," added the individual who had arrested him, "you'll have a chance, my proud-looking old fellow, to say if you are guilty, or not guilty, and I've got my opinion as to how it'll turn out."

With these comforting words the vulgar officer retired, and left his prisoner to himself. That personage seemed to pay no manner of attention to him who thus addressed him. Had no one been beside him—no voice sounded in his ears—he could not have exhibited a more perfect unconsciousness of being spoken to. He was looking with a gloomy and fixed glance at Lord Fairfax, who occupied his former position in the middle of the line of justices: and thus, motionless, stern, wrapped from head to foot in his old gray over-coat, shaggy and soiled with long use, he presented a singular spectacle. His long gray hair half covered his face, which inclined forward, and the keen eyes, burning beneath the bushy white eyebrows, were never removed for a moment from the face of the Earl.

The rude crowd swaying to and fro at the door, regarded the prisoner with superstitious interest; and as the shades of evening began to descend, and his figure grew gradually less distinct in its outlines, they watched him with as much intensity as if they had expected him ere long to melt into thin air, and disappear, with a disagreeable smell of sulphur only left behind.

The remote and retired life of the old man, his systematic non-attendance upon any occasions of public assemblage in the small towns, or at social gatherings—the mysterious manner in which he had arrived a year or two before, no one knew whence—and above all, the dense smoke which was frequently seen, even in the hottest days of summer, curling above the summit just beneath which his cottage was situated—all these things had strangely impressed the rude and credulous inhabitants of the frontier, and led them to bestow upon him the name by which he was known throughout the region—"The Wizard of the Massinutton."

What had induced the drunken justice, Hastyluck, to set on foot a prosecution against him for diabolical proceedings, it was difficult to say. It may have been some private spite —or the attempt of a sottish hanger-on to bolster up a damaged reputation by an affectation of zeal in his office of justice—or lastly, the mere enmity of a small, ill-natured mind against one apparently without friends.

However this may be, it is certain that Hastyluck set the matter on foot; and in his vagabond wanderings among the rude and ignorant settlers—especially those from the witch-haunted land of Germany—he had experienced little difficulty in impressing upon their minds the idea that every misfortune which had ever happened to them had been caused by the " Wizard of the Massinutton." More than one of these superstitious people were now present, prepared to testify with the utmost distinctness against the prisoner— and Major Hastyluck, who had spent a considerable portion of the day in swilling Jamaica in Mynheer Van Doring's inner room, now rubbed his hands and regarded the *two* wizards seated before him with maudlin triumph.

"The prisoner, Powell," said Major Hastyluck, in a thick and stammering voice, "will now be arraigned."—

Lord Fairfax, whose place had thus been unceremoniously assumed by the drunken Major, turned with a frown to that gentleman, and said with some hauteur:

"I pray you, sir, permit the business of the court to proceed regularly."

To which cold words Major Hastyluck, who was quite beyond the influence of hauteur, responded with the remarkable words, uttered with shocking indistinctness:

"Hans Doppelkraut 'll tell you!"

After which the Major assumed an expression of much dignity, and attempted to pare his nails with a goosequill.

The Earl bestowed a withering glance upon his associate, which, however, fell powerless, and making a sign to the sheriff, that excitable gentleman summoned the prisoner to stand and say whether or not he was guilty of witchcraft. The prisoner, thereupon, rose and said, "I am not guilty," in a calm and indifferent voice. Then taking his seat, he fixed his eyes as before upon Lord Fairfax.

Carl Zellycreffer being called, testified in broad German, that his child had been afflicted with internal dropsy and rickets, which he believed to have been caused by the wizard. Being interrogated as to the foundation for this opinion, his reply was unsatisfactory.

Hans Doppelkraut succeeded this worthy. Hans testified that he believed his cattle to have been destroyed by the wizard's shooting them with hair balls, as no marks of disease, or violence were discovered upon them :—his neighbor, Flangel, who was too sick to attend, was certain that his illness was caused by the wizard's changing him into a horse, bridling and saddling him, and riding him at full speed over the very top of the Fort Mountain, to a meeting of witches and wizards in the "Hog Back." He, the witness, did not know how this was—but he could say, that in his opinion his own cows had been made dry by the prisoner, by fixing a pin in a towel for each cow—hanging the towel over a door, and drawing the milk from the fringes. The officer had told him they had seen a towel at the prisoner's house : —and that the "Hog Back" was the most probable place for a meeting, such as neighbor Flangel had declared he was ridden to, saddled and bridled, with heavy spurs dug every instant into his sides—which marks, by some witchcraft of the prisoner, were, however, not visible when he returned to his human shape.

Having given this perspicuous testimony, Hans Doppelkraut stood aside, and Joe Gunn, hunter and trapper, was called.

Joe Gunn, for his part, didn't know whether there was any sech thing as witchcraft or not, and only hearn about it. He had been acquainted with hunters who said their guns were bewitched and wouldn't shoot straight—and when Black, one of his hounds, couldn't be got to hunt of late, he had burnt him in the forehead with a hot iron—after which he didn't know whether he hunted or not, for, like an ongrateful varmaint, he run away. Major Hastyluck there had told him, Joe Gunn, "strange things was in the wind nowabouts"—and asked him if he was well; when he, Joe Gunn, told the Major that he did have a little tetch of the rhumatiz from sleeping out o'-nights on the ground, the Major had asked him solemnly if he was sure that this was not caused by Powell. He, Joe Gunn, replying that in this miserable world there was nothing whatsoever that was nat'rally sartin but unsartinty, the Major had advised him to draw a picture of the wizard on a plank, and shoot at it with a bullet containing a bit of silver. His old woman wouldn't hear of any such waste of precious metals, and he fired away at the picture, drawn on the fence in charcoal, with an ordinary bullet. The Major told him the bullet would hit the old wizard all the same as if he was really there—and so, not wanting to kill anybody, and knowing Long July Ann, his rifle, sent the ball right where he put the bead, he aimed at the right shoulder, and put it there. If the talk about wizards was true, the prisoner ought to have an ounce of lead in his right shoulder—which he, Joe Gunn, wouldn't like to have in his own—and that was all he knew about it.*

A singular expression of surprise passed over the face of the prisoner, who nevertheless did not move.

"Search him, search him, according to the law of witchcraft!" came with maudlin energy from the drunken Major on the bench:—and many of the justices evidently acquiesced in the propriety of this proceeding. But before the officious worthies of the law could approach, the prisoner rose slowly to his feet, and opened his lips to address the court.

---

* "The belief in witchcraft was prevalent among the early settlers of the Western country. To the witch was ascribed the tremendous power of inflicting strange and incurable diseases, particularly on children—of destroying cattle by shooting them with hair balls, and a great variety of other means of destruction—of inflicting spells and curses on guns and other things—and lastly, of changing men into horses, and after bridling and saddling them, riding them at full speed over hill and dale to their frolicks and other rendezvous. . . . Wizards were men supposed to possess the same mischievous power as the witches. . . . . The diseases of children, supposed to be inflicted by witchcraft, were those of the internal dropsy and the rickets. The symptoms and cure of these destructive diseases were utterly unknown in former times in the country. Diseases which could neither be accounted for nor cured, were usually ascribed to some supernatural agency of a malignant kind. For the cure of the diseases inflicted by witchcraft, the picture of the supposed witch was drawn on a stump, or piece of board, and shot at with a bullet containing a little bit of silver. This bullet transferred a painful and sometimes a mortal spell on that part of the witch corresponding with the part of the portrait struck by the bullet. . . . . The witch had but one way of relieving herself from any spell inflicted upon her in any way which was that of borrowing something, no matter what, of the family to which the subject of the exercise of her witchcraft belonged! I have known several poor old women much surprised at being refused requests which had usually been granted without hesitation, and almost heart-broken when informed of the cause of the refusal. When cattle or dogs were supposed to be under the influence of witchcraft, they were burnt in the forehead by a branding-iron, or when dead, burned wholly to ashes. This inflicted a spell upon the witch, which could only by removed by borrowing as above stated. Witches were often said to milk the cows of their neighbors. This they did by fixing a new pin in a new towel for each cow intended to be milked. This towel was hung over her own door, and by means of certain incantations, the milk was extracted from the fringes of the towel after the manner of milking a cow. This happened," adds the reverend historian with dry humor, "when the cows were too poor to give much milk."—*Doddridge's Notes :* pp. 376-7, *in Kercheval's History of the Valley of Virginia.*

At the same moment a stir was heard at the door, some pitying exclamations were uttered by the crowd, and through an opening which was speedily made for her, Cannie advanced into the court room. The wagon of good Mr. Yeardly had broken down, and she had just arrived at the Ordinary—trembling, pale, shaking with an indefinable fear.

The sight of the old man, however, seemed to give her strength. The power of a resolute will, and a devotion which spurned all fear, came to her assistance—without shedding a tear, or hesitating a moment, the young girl, with the air of a little queen, went to the side of the prisoner, and throwing one arm around him, nestled close to his bosom.

But the trial was too much for her—the agitation she had undergone too excessive—the proud and defiant look which she directed at Lord Fairfax and the justices, was succeeded by a nervous tremor, and burying her face in the old man's breast, she clung to him, and sobbed wildly:

"Grand papa! grand papa! they shall not take you from me! They shall not!—no they shall not, while I am alive!"

A flood of tears followed these words, and for an instant a dead silence reigned throughout the apartment. All eyes were fixed upon the tall gray-haired man, clasped in the embrace of the beautiful and devoted child—and as they stood thus, bathed in the red light of the declining sun, there was something so proud and noble in the forms of both, that the crowd was hushed and awed.

The silence was broken by the prisoner.

"My Lord," he said, calmly, in his cold, austere voice, "my Lord and Gentlemen of the Court, I beg you to take notice that this presence of my child was against my wishes—I would scorn to make use of any such vulgar trick to excite your sympathies. This absurd accusation of witchcraft has been heard—the witnesses have testified—I might go to my house again, cleared of the foolish imputation—but there is still another charge to be brought against me, I believe. Before that charge is made, I crave a few moments' private conversation with the presiding justice of the court—my lord Fairfax. In making this request, I am not impelled by any fear of the result, or any wish to conciliate your lordship's favor. My child is agitated—I would be home again—I have other reasons, my Lord Thomas of Denton —Fairfax, I should say. I pray that I may speak with your lordship."

At the words "Lord Thomas of Denton," the Earl gave a visible start and leaned forward in his chair, vainly endeavouring to read some secret in the countenance of the prisoner. But that countenance defied all his penetration—it was cold and impenetrable—a mask might have conveyed more expression.

Lord Fairfax drew back with a deep sigh and a bewildered look, which was extremely unusual with him—but said nothing. Then seeming suddenly to recollect the request of the prisoner, he rose to his feet and said hurriedly:

"I pray the court to suspend its business for a brief period. I am willing to grant the private interview which the prisoner craves. I know not the character of the communication which he is about to make to me, if it be a communication—but trust I may rely upon the good opinion of my honorable associates, that nothing will be taken into consideration by me without their privity and advice."

Major Hastyluck, who had been for at least an hour without a fresh potation, cheerfully replied for his brethren, that they had perfect confidence in his lordship—and then the Major showed the example by staggering pompously from his seat toward the inner room.

Lord Fairfax, still absent and looking with vague curiosity toward the prisoner, made a sign to that personage, and passed up the staircase to his private room.

The old man, with soothing words and a smiling caress, entrusted Cannie into the hands of George, who hastened forward to offer her his arm, and then wrapping his shaggy over-coat more closely around him, stalked through the group of insolent and astounded bailiffs after the Earl.

In a few moments the door was locked behind them, and they were alone together.

XXXIV.

THE PRISONER AND THE JUDGE.

THE two men looked at each other for some moments in silence. There was something striking and impressive in this silent examination by each of his adversary; and points of great similarity were not wanting, at least in the carriage of their persons.

Neither of them had anything in common with the humbler class of human beings. Both men, in their attitudes, bearing, and poise of head and feet, were plainly of that rank accustomed to command and not to be commanded,—to question but not to be questioned. An indifferent spectator would have said, however, that the mysterious "wizard" was the superior, and the stronger of the two. There was something superb and haughty in the figure no longer bent, but as straight as an arrow, in the eye flashing clearly beneath the shaggy white eye-brow, in the proudly compressed lip, the forehead raised calmly aloft. Lord Fairfax had the air of a nobleman, but the stranger that of a monarch.

"Well, sir," said the Earl, betraying unmistakable astonishment, for no man had a quicker eye for the indefinable evidences of superior character. "Well, sir, now for your private communication. You have made a somewhat singular request, and used a mode of address which indicates former acquaintance. Where and how did you learn that 'Lord Thomas of Denton' was my name upon my patrimonial estate, and there alone? Speak, sir!—let us end this mystery. I listen!"

And sitting down, his lordship motioned with cold courtesy toward a chair opposite to his own.

His companion did not take the offered seat, but said coolly:

"Then you do not recognize me, my lord?"

"No, sir; I find, it is true, something strangely familiar in your features, but"——

"Possibly I may assist your recollection," interrupted the other; and throwing off his long overcoat, he stood before Lord Fairfax metamorphosed from a rude backwoodsman into an English gentleman clad in the most courtly and imposing costume. His coat was richly embroidered in scarlet—his frill snow-white,—his waistcoat of blue silk, loaded with decorations, and falling over knee-breeches of the finest material.

"Have you forgotten me?" he said coldly, as he saw the Earl give a great start and suddenly turn pale.

Lord Fairfax almost recoiled, as the stranger advanced toward him, but by a powerful effort summoned his strength again, and replied:

"I have not, sir. You are Sir William Powys!"

"Yes, my lord," returned the wizard with a frown, "I am Sir William Powys! Sir William Powys whom your lordship's father stripped of nearly all his possessions in Yorkshire—who swore enmity thirty years ago against your family—whose body bears the scar of a pistol ball lodged therein by your lordship, in the right shoulder here, as that hunter by a strange coincidence, declared—who has left the Old World, as your lordship has left it, to come to the New, and who here, as there, finds one of the house of Fairfax eternally in his path, set in judgment over him, to oppose him, and strive to direct him, in all his acts; to endeavor—vainly! vainly my lord!—to thwart and to crush him! Not content with alienating from me the heart of my daughter, and marrying her against my wishes!—not content with shipwrecking my happiness and hope in the Old World, your lordship has followed me hither!—you assemble a body of low yeomen to try an English gentleman for *witchcraft!* Had I not requested this interview, the vulgar fellow who arrested me yonder would have preferred in addition a charge of counterfeiting coin!—against me. *me*, my lord! *me!*"

And the old man, with flushed cheeks and forehead, looked down upon the Earl with a fiery wrath which made his countenance almost terrible in its indignation.

Lord Fairfax did not immediately reply. He seemed endeavoring to control a sentiment as violent as that of his companion. His compressed lips and heaving bosom indicated the struggle which was passing in his mind, and he was silent for some moments. The effort at self-control was successful. His features slowly grew calm. The flush disappeared from his face, and returning the other's gaze with cold solemnity he said:

"Sir William Powys, what you have just uttered is an injustice unworthy of your character, and unlike your blood, which, in all its representatives with whom I am acquainted, has been violent and implacable, but neither unfair nor ungenerous. You know well that I have had no part in originating this silly prosecution of you for witchcraft. You know that I am simply *among* these people, not of them,—as the Lieutenant of the county, as an official bound to act officially. So much for that. And touching the subject of counterfeiting, it was mentioned in my hearing but an hour ago. These are the wrongs which I have inflicted upon you, as you declare, in the New World!"

The Earl paused a moment, then continued gloomily:

"Of events in England I would rather not speak: except to say that you have here done me equal injustice. I do not believe that my father was harsh toward you—but let that pass. In a single accusation, you are just. I did force a quarrel with you and wound you,—I regretted it. I still regret it; it was unnecessary. But touching the last charge,— here, Sir William Powys, I have nothing to blame myself with. I honestly loved your daughter—she honestly loved me; in spite of your hatred for my family, she became my Countess—if against your wish, as you say, still not without your legal consent. But enough, sir. These memories move me bitterly. Let the past sleep. I do not speak angrily as you see, Sir William; I address you as your rank and position demand. I have done, sir."

There was so much nobility and sincerity in the tone of the Earl, that his words evidently affected the listener strangely. The menacing expression disappeared, and a gloomy calm succeeded.

"My lord," he said, "I so far acquit you of this present annoyance as to fully believe that you had no part in it. The pain it has occasioned both me and my child, no less remain. There is, besides, no certainty that in future it will not be repeated—and thus I have reason when I say that the name of Fairfax is my evil genius, for you are the real master and controlling influence in the country. But I pass that by. You have said that my family is implacable. That is only partly true of myself; but I shall not discuss the question. I shall simply say that toward yourself personally I have no ill feeling; indeed I am conscious of having more than repaired all your injuries, as some day you will know."

Lord Fairfax made a motion with his hand and said with noble simplicity:

"I would rather have it so than otherwise, sir."

The words seemed to dissipate still further the enmity of his companion. He sat down, and when he spoke again, his voice was greatly changed. It was almost sad.

"My lord," he said, "this is a strange and sorrowful world—have you not found it so?"

"Eminently," replied the Earl, sadly.

"I am more than seventy years old; you must be nearly or quite fifty. Well, at our respective ages, men should strive to forget the passions of their youth—the enmities and hatreds which sear the soul. You have wronged me—I have wronged you. There let it rest. I am willing to forget all, and to go upon my way without cherishing any thoughts of vengeance in my heart. I will do more: I will right the wrong I have done you;"—here the brows of the speaker contracted painfully—"but not now. Let us come to the business which made me request this interview."

The Earl inclined his head with great courtesy, and listened.

"Nearly two years ago," said his companion, "I bought of your agent here—I never expected to see you in Virginia —the tract of land upon which I live with my granddaughter. I removed from my small estate on the seaboard, because the chills and fevers of that region, for a portion of the year, render it dangerous to her constitution; and again because she derives singular benefit from a mineral spring in the 'fort' yonder. I brought with me only a man and a maid, intending to return in the cold season, but have remained. One of the reasons for this decision, in addition to the health of my granddaughter, was the discovery of a mine of gold and silver, upon the tract, which I have worked with the utmost success."

The Earl bowed with the same calm courtesy, and the speaker continued:

"I know that by the charter granted to Lord Culpeper, from whom you derive your property in this province, you are entitled to one-fourth of the proceeds of all mines of gold and silver discovered upon all lands within Lord Culpeper's grant, and I have accordingly laid aside carefully one ingot from every four, in a box marked "Lord Fairfax." In relation to the coin discovered by the bailiff, in one sense it is counterfeit. I cast it from pure gold in a mould of clay, as the amusement of an idle moment; and inasmuch as its value, from the absence of all alloy, is one-fourth more than that of real coin, I imagine my moral innocence of the charge of coining may be established. I have made this explanation," continued the speaker, "in order to propound to you an interrogatory. I do so that there may be no misunderstanding, no ambiguity. Shall I be permitted to remain in this region undisturbed by legal annoyances, or must I go with my child to another? The heart beats chill at seventy, my lord, and a man is disposed to quiet. I would ask no favor; I would have you reply as a mere matter of business; I address myself to you as Lord Proprietor of the Northern Neck in which I live, and chief executive officer of the country."

"As such I reply, Sir William," said the Earl, calmly, "that your further sojourn in the region shall be, as far as lies in my power, wholly freed from all annoyance. If I were not disposed to make you this assurance, with reference to yourself, I should do so for your granddaughter's sake. I cannot forget that she would have been the cousin of my children. No more of that. In regard to the fourth part of all gold mines, I do not claim that right in my charter—or, if you insist, I reply that I wish the child to receive the sum which you have laid aside—as a present from her uncle by marriage. I pray you, sir, not to refuse me this trifle. I shall not stop here, with your permission, in my privilege of displaying my affection for my little niece. I am truly proud to think of her as such; a more perfect young princess I have never seen than the child, as she came to you in the court-room. But enough, sir. I shall not let you offer me this gold again, as I think you intend; let us return and terminate this business. All shall end at once."

And opening the door, the Earl made a courteous gesture to the old man, who had again donned his long coat, to precede him, which resulted in their issuing forth together. In the two hearts thus close to each other, there was no longer any enmity; but in the elder's there was pain, and a cruel hesitation.

They entered the room where the members of the court

were seated, and in ten minutes Lord Fairfax had impressed upon his associates, in private conference, the entire absurdity of all charges brought against the prisoner. Indeed the honorable justices were rather ashamed of themselves; and many looks of disgust were directed toward the person of Major Hastyluck, chief instigator and persecutor, who was slumbering serenely with his face on the table. The toils of his arduous position had overcome this watch-dog of justice; after all his labors and his Jamaica, he "slept well."

The Wizard of the Massinutton was thus promptly discharged, and in a moment two soft arms were around his neck, and a face wet with tears was pressed to his thin cheek.

Cannie was crying on the old man's bosom.*

---

* The following extract from "A visit to the Fort Mountain," in the *Southern Literary Messenger* for February, 1841, will indicate the origin of the character of "Old Powell;" the first lines describe the Massinutton:

"On the left bank of the creek, the mountain crowds against the narrow road—on the right, a granite escarpment of a thousand feet frowns down upon you—and the ravine itself, clothed with a luxuriant growth of pines, cypresses, and laurels, deepens the gloom of the overshadowing rocks. . . . On a sultry day, dispersed along the comb of the precipice, groups of these vultures (turkey buzzards) may be seen, with their broad, rusty wings, half expanded to the breeze—resembling so many spirits of darkness, brooding over the gulf of perdition. The view from the bank is splendid. Passage Creek is diminished to a rivulet, whose murmurs are faint as the dying wind in the pines around us. The highway along its bank, seems but a winding footpath, over which the millboy's horse – didst think it was a small brindled dog with a white spot on its back?–steals without any apparent effort or motion of its own. What a majestic mountain is this across the defile! It looks like Atlas, strong enough to sustain the world upon its shoulders. Within this fort a comparative abundance of wild game is still to be found, particularly wild hogs descended from the domestic breeds, but fierce as the monsters of the Pyrenees. It is called "Powell's Fort," after one of the first settlers of the country, the valley of the creek is also known as "the Fort." There is a curious and popular tradition cherished in the neighborhood regarding "Old Powell." It is said that he was an advocate of a specie currency, and to assist the Government in the promotion of a specie circulation, (established a hard money factory on his own responsibility, and coined thousands of the genuine "*Carolus* III.—*Dei gratia*"—procuring his metal from mines in the vicinity only known to him. Suspected, and fearing detection, he barreled up his immense treasure, and buried it at various places in the mountains. Without disclosing the secret he died, and the barrels of silver still remain undisturbed because undiscovered."

XXXV.

THE RESEMBLANCE.

THE old man gently caressed the soft hair of the child, and gazed into her face, which was all April smiles and tears, with a depth of tender affection which made the countenance, ordinarily so proud and cold, almost beautiful and winning.

Then raising his head, Sir William Powys, or the Wizard, if we may be allowed to still employ the name by which he was most generally known, looked around upon the crowd, who regarded him with strange and superstitious interest. There were many persons in the assembly whose heads had moved significantly from side to side when the strange personage demanded a private interview with Lord Fairfax. No good would result for his lordship, these wiseacres declared, from yielding to this demand. Once alone with him, the wizard would be sure to "bewitch" him—he would cast a spell on him, and then vanish in a cloud of brimstone. Some of these philosophers were by no means certain that if this were not the case, the mysterious wizard would not be seen issuing from the window of the tavern, mounted upon a handsome flying horse, once Lord Fairfax; now destined to bear the prisoner away in triumph to some diabolical revel of witches in the depths of the "Hog-Back."

It resulted from this condition of public feeling, that when the wizard, who had fulfilled the expectations of the more moderate among the wiseacres, by procuring a prompt acquittal through his interview with the Earl, looked round upon the crowd, they recoiled with an unmistakable expression of dread, and left him standing, almost alone, with his child, in the middle of the apartment.

A slight curl of the firm lip greeted this movement, and the wizard was about to turn away indifferently, when suddenly his eyes were riveted upon a richly-clad figure, framed, as it were, in the doorway, and gazing upon him with deep interest and sympathy.

That figure was that of Falconbridge, who, having watched the absurd trial, and witnessed the scene between the prisoner and his daughter, now rejoiced at the result, and regarded them, as they stood wrapped in each other's embrace, with kindly smiles and pleasure.

The wizard fixed upon the young man, as he stood thus framed in the doorway, like a picture, one of those glances which seem to penetrate into the soul of the person upon whom they are riveted. There was much in the gallant and graceful form of Falconbridge—in his proud, laughing face, and elegant costume—to attract attention; but the look now bent upon him was not one of simple admiration or curiosity. It expressed surprise, deep feeling, and a species of wondering doubt.

The young man perceived the glance directed toward him, and without understanding it, approached, and said, kindly:

"I am rejoiced at your acquittal, sir; as much for your own sake, as you seem very old, as for your little daughter. My father taught me to respect and bow to purity and devotion wherever I met with them, and I think I cannot be mistaken in saying that your child is both innocent and courageous—faithful and noble-hearted."

With these words, which were uttered in that tone of simplicity and sincerity, which characterized his voice, the young man held out his hand to Cannie, extending the other toward the old man.

The girl's soft, little fingers glided into those of Falconbridge, and a grave, sweet glance, shining through the tears in her eyes, rewarded the speaker.

"Thank you, sir," she said, in her low, musical voice, "for speaking so kindly to us—to grandpapa. You are not like those people who have gone—your face is kind."

And Cannie pressed the hand frankly, and looked "thanks!" with her whole heart.

The old man had, however, drawn back unconsciously when Falconbridge greeted him. He had not taken the hand. Still, looking at him with that strange air which we have described, he said:

"What is your name, sir?"

The words were almost rude, but the tone in which they were pronounced did not so impress the hearer. The wizard plainly intended no slight—it was some mysterious sentiment of wonder which spoke in his voice, in his abrupt question: and the young man comprehended this instinctively.

"My name is Falconbridge, sir," he replied, wth a courteous inclination; "I have but recently come to this region."

"Falconbridge! I thought so! I was sure of it!" murmured the wizard. "Strange! Strange! who would ever have believed!"——

There he suddenly stopped. By a sudden and powerful effort he controlled his emotion; his countenance subsided again into its customary calmness, and he bowed in return, taking the hand which was still half extended.

"I thank you, Mr. Falconbridge," he said, coolly, "and beg you will not attribute my singular question to any disposition to affront you. You bear a very remarkable resemblance to a person whom I once knew; this must be my excuse for the very rude reception I have given to your kind speech and sympathy."

"It is nothing,—I scarcely noted it," returned the young man, smiling, "and as to any kindness, I am sure, sir, that I deserve no praise. My heart leaped when your child came so bravely to your side—and I bow to, and honor her. I have never seen a princess or a queen—but I think she is worthy to be either!"

"Oh, sir," exclaimed Cannie, blushing, "you make me feel ashamed! It was nothing for me to come to grandpapa's side. He is all I have in world, and I love him dearly, with my whole heart. And you, grandpapa," added Cannie, turning and whispering to the old man with a smile, "you know you love *me* just as dearly."

"That is very certain," was the low reply, accompanied by the look which always came to the face when it was turned toward the girl; "and now, my child, let us go to our private room. We must remain here all night—but we will return home early in the morning."

"Come with me, sir," said the voice of Lord Fairfax, at the speaker's elbow, "I have ample room for you and your daughter at Greenway Court—it will be far more comfortable."

"I thank you, my lord," returned the other, with a ceremonious inclination, "but the nights grow chill, and my daughter is delicate."

"The blinds of the chariot may be easily closed, sir," said the Earl, looking wistfully at Cannie.

"Your lordship will not consider me ill-bred—that is to say ungrateful—if I still decline your goodness. If my child should wish at another time to visit Greenway Court," added the old man, exchanging a look with the Earl, "it will give me true pleasure to bring her thither—or to entrust her to our good friend here, Mr. George. May I take that liberty, Mr. George?"

That liberty! thought George, as his heart gave a bound at the idea of a long gallop through the prairie, with Cannie's arm around his waist; but he suppressed his delight, and replied with extreme gravity and politeness, that it would give him very great pleasure.

"And now, my lord," said the wizard, "let me, before I

leave you, say how much I am indebted to your lordship, for my release from this prosecution—a prosecution which I dreaded far more for the grief it caused my child than on my own account. I am old, and care little what comes to me—whether of weal or woe—but she is young and tender-hearted. Thanks! thanks, again for our freedom!"

The speaker was standing as before, with his arm around Cannie, and by them stood Falconbridge, smiling. Not only the Earl, but George, and Captain Wagner, who were near at hand, were struck with the singular resemblance between the three, and afterwards spoke of it. One was seventy, and gray-headed; the second twenty-three or four, and in the bloom of manhood; the child, a girl of fifteen, with innocent, sweet eyes, and tender lips. But the resemblance was as perfect in all three as if they were the offspring of the same parents.

For a moment they remained thus motionless, then bowing again, the wizard retired with Cannie to a private room, having arranged with Mynheer Van Doring on the way, for a vehicle in the morning.

Lord Fairfax turned to Falconbridge, and said;

"I think you have not yet consulted me upon your affairs, Mr. Falconbridge. If it suits your convenience at the present moment, you might accept a seat in my chariot, and sleep at Greenway. What say you, sir?"

"I accept your lordship's offer with many thanks," was the reply.

And very soon the young man and the Earl were rolling toward Greenway, beneath the new risen moon, which mingled its light with that of the setting sun, and communicated to the dreary stretch of prairie land a wild and mysterious charm.

As to George, and Captain Wagner, they remained at the Ordinary for reasons best known to themselves, but easily comprehensible by the reader. George staid because Cannie would spend the night there; the Captain because his eloquence had triumphed in favor of Winchester; and the fair Mrs. Butterton was, no doubt, ready to thank, perhaps to reward him.

Meanwhile the chariot containing the Earl and Falconbridge rolled on in silence. The few common-place words had died away. Lord Fairfax seemed deeply preoccupied.

At last, as they approached the clump of trees, indicating Greenway, the Earl raised his drooping shoulders, uttered a long, deep sigh, and muttered:

"I wonder if a single heart beats still for me, in dear old England. No, I think not one!—not one!"

XXXVI.

CAMPAIGN OF GENERAL LONGKNIFE.

THE Captain twirled his moustache. We would call the attention of the reader to the fact, which we have hitherto omitted to mention, that Captain Wagner was always engaged in twirling his moustache. Or, if the statement seems extreme and improbable, let us simply say that he was often thus laboriously occupied, and seemed to derive much innocent satisfaction from the ceremony.

On the present occasion he gave to the martial appendage a jaunty and gallant curl toward the eyes; then he looked at Mrs. Butterton, who was busily knitting opposite the Captain, and the table by the Captain, upon which was deposited the Captain's warm glass of punch and unfilled pipe.

Monsieur Jambot, for the moment in deep disgrace, was forlornly carrying on a sleepy conversation with Mynheer Van Doring in one corner—a ceremony which resulted between the two in an awful mutilation of King George the Second's English. In another corner George and Cannie were talking in a low tone, and assisting what they uttered with smiles and confidential glances.

"My dear Mrs. Butterton," said the Captain, "have you any commands in Belhaven—or, as these new-fangled folks will call it, *Alexandria?* It's a shame to be re-christening so promising a child—or I'm a dandy!"

"Any commands in Belhaven?" asked the lady with a little simper and flutter; "why do you ask, Captain?"

"Because I think it likely that I'll go back soon to amuse myself. You remain here, I believe."

These cold and cruel words made the lady's heart throb. Then Captain Wagner cared nothing for her!

"Yes," she said, faintly, "perhaps till the spring."

"I would like to do as much myself," continued the worthy, "but the rascally Injuns, whose scalps I was to have, won't come, and it is repugnant to the feelings of a soldier to be living on that honest fellow, Fairfax, without doing him any service in return."

"Why, Captain," said Mrs. Butterton, with evident admiration in her eyes, for one who spoke in this free and easy way of so great a nobleman, "why, Captain, his lordship is delighted at your visit, and I heard him with my own ears say, no longer ago than this morning, that you were worth a thousand pounds a year to him in good spirits!"

"All flattery!" returned the soldier, "or I'm a dandy! I have remonstrated with Fairfax about that bad habit he has of trying to ingratiate himself with people by flattering them. He knew you were my friend—that you would repeat it—and he is trying to get around me."

"Oh, Captain! How can you talk so of his lordship!"

The worthy laughed.

"He's only a man like anybody else, my dear Mrs. Butterton; it's not his fault that he is called Earl and Baron. I'm free to say he'd be a dooms good fellow under any circumstances. I like Fairfax. He's no pretender. And I repeat that I don't like to be eating and drinking, as *I* eat and drink, at his expense, when the Injun devils decline coming along and getting themselves done for! I was sent for to eat Injuns, not beef! to drink blood, not Jamaica! And these Injuns—where are they? Nowhere, or may the —hum!"

The soldier terminated this sentence by swallowing a mouthful of punch, which seemed to refresh him greatly.

"Why, Captain," said Mrs. Butterton, "you are certainly

mistaken about the chance of an inroad. They say there's no certainty of peace from day to day."

"My dear madam," returned the Borderer, "it has been my habit for a number of years to hunt up Mr. 'They Say,' and when I have heard his views to go and lay my plans precisely to the contrary. I have no respect for 'They Say.' I know the rascal—he is as completely ignorant of what is really going on as a mole! Even if the Injun rascals do come along, let Fairfax send down for me! I can't be neglecting my most important affairs dangling hereabouts, and chopping arguments with his earlship!"

"Your affairs?" persisted the lady, smiling, "why, Captain, you have no *business* in Belhaven, have you?"

The conversation was taking the direction which the cunning Captain desired. He smiled.

"Well, really," he said, "I hardly know how to reply to you, my dear madam—to reply without touching upon a most delicate subject—you comprehend?"

The lady blushed, but said nothing.

"It is true," continued Captain Wagner, "that many people would say I had no *business* whatsoever to attend to in Belhaven, like merchants, and shopkeepers, lawyers, and all that small fry, who are thinking all the time of money and nothing else—not like us soldiers, of honor and glory, and—hem!—love."

"Of—love?" asked Mrs. Butterton, faintly. What *could* the Captain mean?

"I would not refer to these matters with any one else, my dear madam," said the worthy, edging his chair across to Mrs. Butterton's side, and speaking in low, confidential tones; "but you are my good friend, and are well acquainted with—the lady."

"The lady"—— And Mrs. Butterton's voice died away in her throat.

"The fair Emmelina, your friend," whispered the Captain, bending over. But his companion's agitation made her turn away her head—she could not reply.

"Miss Emmelina," continued the subtle campaigner, in the same confidential tone, "is, it is true, past the bloom of youth. She is nearly my own age, indeed, I fancy, and this might seem to many persons an objection. But is it really such? I am tired, my dear madam, of your school-girls and young misses—your sweet young creatures, full of sentiment and romance—who clasp their hands when they look at the moon, and read poetry verses and say, 'Oh, how beautiful!' I don't say I never admired 'em, but I'm past all that, or may—ahem! I now admire the ripe flower, not the bud—I confess I want a wife, and it has seemed to me that Miss Emmelina, your friend, whom you have so often praised, would make a noble spouse—and likes me well enough to give me a fair start—don't you think so—Emmelina?"

And the Captain scratched his nose, and regarded the ceiling, after this tender exclamation, with an absent and pre-occupied air, which was very striking.

As to Mrs. Butterton, that fair lady remained for some time silent and blushing—then, on being again pressed by the Captain, replied that she thought—she had hoped—she —No! Emmelina was *not* calculated to adorn the married state. No doubt Captain Wagner would think—and here Mrs. Butterton assumed a tone meant for hauteur—that she was unjust and unfriendly. Yet candor compelled her to say that she knew Emmelina well, but in spite of a most tender friendship for that lady, must say she was in the sphere she was best calculated to fill—that of an old maid. In that sphere, said Mrs. Butterton with animated feeling, Emmelina was worthy of all praise. She had her little faults, such as a propensity to gossip, a disposition to pry into her neighbors' matters, and a talent for adding to and coloring all that she repeated, which no doubt arose from her smartness. She had certainly been the cause of that terrible fight at the corner of King Street, where the two lovers of her corner neighbor bruised each other so awfully, and created such a horrible scandal; but she, Mrs. Butterton, was quite sure that Emmelina had never expected any such misfortune to take place in consequence of her communicating the trifle which she did to one of the young men—it had given her great pain, and she had deeply regretted it. With these, and a few other little drawbacks—such as an undue love of money, a disposition to spend nothing more than she was absolutely compelled to—a strong dislike and suspicion of every one who did not belong to her particular church, she was very well in her way, as an old maid. Out of that condition, she, Mrs. Butterton, very greatly feared that Emmelina would not be a very perfect character. She was little suited for a wife, still, if Captain Wagner thought differently, it was no affair of *hers*. She hoped he would not find out too late the failings in Emmelina's character.

Having made this lengthy speech, which the Captain listened to with silent attention and a subtle smile, Mrs. Butterton applied herself to her knitting in a more hurried manner than before, and assumed an air of studied indifference.

"My dear madam," replied the Captain, with earnest and solemn feeling, "I thank you for this interest in me, but are you not misled somewhat in your estimate of the sweet Emmelina, by the opinions of those persons who dislike her? Are the fair sex at all given to gossip? I do not, I cannot believe it, my dear madam! I will never credit the assertion! True, I have heard it said that when they get to be old women—even after the tender and still blooming age of twenty-five, they experience the extremest pleasure in the circulation of intelligence about their friends. The irreverent and low-minded individual who made this statement in my hearing, added, that *the truth* was so dear to these angelic newscarriers, that much of their existence was heroically and fondly dedicated to the task of decking it in bright apparel, and presenting it in such a manner as to forcibly impress it on the minds of those who made its acquaintance. 'The poor, plain maiden Truth,' this wretched person added, 'scarcely knew herself when she was thus pranked out; and none of her old friends could recognize her.' Now, all these base insinuations I abhor and utterly reject and despise! Attribute to the fair sex any such poor, narrow conduct? regard them as laboring under this '*disease*,' as the low fellow worded it—as the victims of a sickly craving? Never! never! I don't respect the man who allows his mind to be filled with such base prejudices! What, madam! Acknowledge that the beautiful and superior sex—the better half of human beings—fritter away their time and intellect on little smirking gossip and tittle-tattle! Believe that they go round and smile and whisper, and stab people in secret behind their backs—and when they meet them afterwards, squeeze their hands and look into their eyes with tender friendship! Believe that when the female mind should grow in dignity and sweetness, that it only waxes smaller and more narrow—festering away into nods and smirks, and 'guggle—guggle—guggle—whish—sh—sh—sh!' beneath the breath! Credit this statement, madam! think thus of the ladies!—never! never! The cynical and sneering may believe it, but Captain Julius Wagner? Never!"

The worthy uttered these indignant words with such solemnity and emphasis that Mrs. Butterton experienced a sentiment of admiration for the speaker and his lofty views, amounting almost to enthusiasm.

What he said of women was quite worthy of his generous and liberal heart, she replied, and did him honor. It was rare to find a gentleman so magnanimous toward the fair sex, and she would not have him think that she intended to speak harshly of her friend Emmelina. She had alluded to those little foibles in her character, without the least intention or desire of doing her injustice—and perhaps she was mistaken in her. It was more than human nature could accomplish, to become free from every failing—and Emmelina was, perhaps, no worse than many others.

"Again I thank you, my dear madam," said the Captain; "you are a friend indeed! But let me ask if there is not a chance of all these little foibles disappearing after matrimony—I mean in case I were to become the happy—hum!—possessor of the beauteous Emmelina? I have frequently observed this singular change. There was my friend, Dick Thonderguste—he married a perfect vixen, and I assure you, on the word of Wagner, that in six months you wouldn't have known her—she was so meek and mild! There, again, was my old playmate, Charley Ryan, who always smiled when people got angry. He married his cousin, a quiet, sunny little thing, who seemed as good-natured and soft as a May morning. And what was the consequence? In a year, madam, Mrs. Ryan was a tartar—yes, a terror to her household, including Charley! I never dared to go and see him—she looked so black at me. I would sometimes call on Charley when I knew she was out; but when her footstep was heard on the porch, I would take my hat unconsciously, wring Charley's hand with deep commiseration, and got off, if possible, without meeting the lady. You see I was afraid of her—of that timid little thing!—I, Captain Longknife!—and all this has induced me to suppose that marriage frequently changes the fair sex. Don't you think so, my dear madam?—and might it not change Emmelina—Emmelina!"

And the worthy again gazed at the ceiling.

"It may," said Mrs. Butterton, curtly but sadly too.

"If I return to my home yonder," however added the Captain,"I shall take with me the satisfaction of reflecting, madam, that I have been of some service to you. It rejoices me to reflect that this day the town of Winchester has been selected as the county seat. I rejoice upon your account wholly, madam; for confidentially speaking, I regard the village of

Winchester as the poorest place on the habitable globe. It is a failure—it always will be!—there are no men of public spirit there—no natural advantages—and mark me! there is no future for Winchester! Stephensburg, on the contrary, is the pearl of towns, the diamond of villages. It bids fair to become a gigantic city. Fairfax is a man of intelligence, and he understood this, and preferred Stephensburg. But for you I should have gone for it—when, of course, madam, it would have been chosen. But I could not desert a friend, one for whom I had so great a—hum—regard; so real a—hum—attachment! I declared war against Fairfax on my own private account—I went about to see the justices—I made a little speech—it was nothing," said the Captain, modestly, "a mere series of remarks—and I beat his lordship, ha! ha! I say, my dear madam, that if I go, I shall take away with me this pleasing reflection—if I go."

"Why do you go?" said Mrs. Butterton, fixing upon Captain Wagner her most significant glance.

The Captain sighed, and looked deeply depressed.

"Because—I have not told you—" he said in almost a whisper, "because there is another reason, stronger than any I have given."

"Another reason?"

The Captain accidentally secured one of the lady's hands, which hung at her side.

"Because I have been defeated once, madam, and am afraid to remain near the enemy—like a coward! afraid! Because I am subjected to the pain of seeing what I wish to possess, ever before me, yet beyond my reach! Because I am humiliated, mortified, lowered in my own opinion, by finding myself distanced by a professor of the frivolous art of dancing and music playing"—here the Captain darted a terrific scowl, full of gloomy rage, at the unconscious Monsieur Jambot—"and because it does not become a soldier to get on his knees and beg, or crouch like a hound to be cut! These, madam," said Captain Wagner, with an air of touching sorrow, "are the reasons which impel me to leave this neighborhood—which drive me away from your side! If I thought this fair hand, which I hold, cared to rest in my clasp—if I thought it would not drop mine like a hot—hum—indifferently:—if I thought it would retain me, when I was going away forever—then I would stay, for it is my most coveted treasure. But this is folly—farewell! farewell!"

Having uttered these whispered words in a tone of dignified misery and unfaltering resolve, the Captain made a motion to withdraw his hand and go. But strange!—unexpected!—astounding event!—event wholly unanticipated or thought of by the Captain!—the hand which he would have released would not suffer that ceremony to be performed. With a gentle pressure it retained the soldier's, and the owner of the hand turned away her blushing countenance, but not before she had bestowed upon her companion a glance which said plainly as glance could say: "If another defeat is all that you fear, you need fear no longer—for the enemy whom you are afraid of is ready to capitulate—the hand which you think cold, is ready to rest here, in your own for life!"

The fair Mrs. Butterton may not have made use of this elegant and graceful speech, which we have skillfully attributed, therefore, to the "glance of her eye," but before the interview terminated, the overjoyed Captain received from the lady's lips the assurance that she was willing to become Mrs. Captain Wagner.

The rest of the company could not tell what made the Captain's countenance shine so resplendently as he finished his punch at a single gulp, or why Mrs. Butterton was so gay and so sorrowful by turns.

We know the meaning of the first of these emotions; the second is as simply explained. The dame was looking with pity at her disappointed suitor, Monsieur Jambot.

XXXVII.

THE EARL AND FALCONBRIDGE.

IN the large apartment at Greenway Court, whose picturesque decorations—stags' horns, guns, old swords, and long tapering rods—were lit up by the cheerful fire-light, and the more steady radiance of two candles in the tall, silver candlesticks, the Earl and Falconbridge talked long, and on many subjects.

The young man speedily found that nothing need now detain him in the region. There was no longer any occasion to proceed to the far South Branch of the Potomac, whither he had promised himself a trip with George, who had completely won his heart. The lands which he came to look after, were all laid down upon the rudely-traced maps which Lord Fairfax spread before him: his title was secured beyond all question; and the slight quit-rent only, a mere nothing, guaranteed the right of property conclusively.

It was then that, passing away from business, the host and his guest conversed on other things for hours—those long hours of the autumn night, which glide by rapidly like joyful dreams, for the happy and light-hearted, but which lag so drearily for those whose spirits are oppressed.

Falconbridge listened with a strange interest to the melancholy tones of this singular man. Everything about the Earl excited his imagination. Here, beyond the Blue Ridge Mountains, in the Virginia wilderness, he conversed with one who had once shone among the most splendid noblemen of the English Court; who had lived in the brilliant circle of which Bolingbroke, and Somerset, and Shaftesbury, and Joseph Addison were the ornaments; who had written for the "Spectator"—and been equally distinguished in fashion and in letters: this exile was his host, in the lonely mansion, and in his melancholy monologue, there was an irresistible attraction, a strange spell which the young man could not throw off. He leaned forward in his chair, and gathered every word which fell from the grim lips; every word was a new thought, a new emotion.

The gallant face of Falconbridge had in its turn strongly impressed the Earl, though he exhibited little evidence of the fact. We have said that his long commerce with the great world had made him wonderfully penetrating in his views and judgment of character. He thus comprehended quickly the man with whom he was conversing. In Falconbridge he recognized an organization of singular nobility and sincerity. The spirit breathed by the Almighty into this clay, was plainly of extraordinary delicacy. He understood the silent indications of eye, and lip, and smile, and gesture; he saw in the nature of this youth, the scorn of falsehood; the love of truth; the pride of which made him bow only before honesty and what was noble and sincere; all the traits which go to form that lofty character, the true gentleman.

The Earl saw all this at a single glance, and watched with a grim and wistful interest, the emotions chasing each other rapidly across the eloquent face. He saw that he was appreciated; and this is always an agreeable conviction with men of proud, strong natures, and original minds. The colloquy thus came at last to embrace a great variety of subjects; the different worlds in which the two men had been dwellers; England over the sea, and Virginia here, with all that made them what they were; the aims of noble manhood, the philosoply of life; the past, the future, and what lay beyond the future of this world, in the undiscovered realm of silence. These mortals who represented from a different point of view a single class—the class who take the pole-star Honor for their guide, and sail toward the course it points, through gloom and tempest, whether that sail be in a crazy skiff or a mighty ship—these men, both eminent for lofty traits, for cultivated intellects, and noble instincts, recognized in each other something strangely similar, and gave their confidence unasked.

Falconbridge spoke without reserve of his life, his surroundings in the Lowland, his amusements—of everything: and the Earl gave a picture in his turn of life in England, without, however, touching upon his private history. It was only in certain moods, and in presence of such old acquaintances as Captain Wagner, that the stern and melancholy nobleman threw off his mask of cold reserve. His manner to Falconbridge was perfectly polite, but perfectly ceremonious too; the young man was plainly nothing more to him than a very agreeable stranger.

"Virginia, Mr. Falconbridge," he said, "is England simply under a different form. It is true that our white retainers, essentially parts of the soil, are replaced by negroes who are legally serfs for life; but I question which is the happier of these classes."

"I know our servants are happy," replied Falconbridge, "and we love them as they love us. I have an old nurse who is quite as dear to me, as many of my relations. She nursed me in my childhood; has loved me in my manhood; and I am less her master than she is my mistress! for she scolds, and reprimands, and makes me do just what she pleases. I would rage at one half she says from any *man* in the world, however much above me, but I can't rage at her. I love her because I know she loves me, and I think I would defend her at the peril of my life."

"I really think you would," returned Lord Fairfax, looking at the speaker with grim interest; "you have a cordial nature, Mr. Falconbridge."

"I don't regard my feeling as at all meritorious, my lord. I should be more than a heathen were I not to love the old nurse who has loved me so faithfully. I would see to her comfort before that of the greatest lady in the province, and would rather she would smile on me than have his Excellency, the governor, take off his hat to me. That would seem very simple to you if you knew how she has loved and cherished me."

"I can understand," said the Earl, with the same melancholy smile. "You are a perfect democrat, and would rather talk with some old 'Colonel' on Tide-water, than with the greatest Duke of England."

"You are laughing at me, my lord," said Falconbridge. "What would a Duke take the trouble to talk with me for?"

"There might be no inequality," returned the Earl. "I mean, Mr. Falconbridge, that in England, there is a very absurd mode of viewing the people of the American provinces. They are regarded as persons of an inferior race, which is simply nonsense. A very great number of persons in the Colonies here, are either descended from our nobility—the sons and grandsons, it may be, of "younger sons," but of course no less inheriting the family blood—or they are the offshoots of that "untitled nobility," as they have been called, the country gentlemen of England. This class, sir, is after all the real strength of the British Empire: our peerage is the flower, simply, of the vigorous plant. What matter if a coronet, or noble order, does not decorate these men? They are the life-blood of the Anglo-Saxon body; the foremost men of all this world, as Shakspeare writes it; and the time may come when our exhausted stem will look with pride upon its flourishing offshoots, growing in the soil of the west. Thus, sir," added the Earl, gravely, "I may now have the honor of conversing with a young nobleman above my own poor rank; one who is such by right of blood, if not by title."

Falconbridge laughed as he listened to this grave statement.

"I am afraid you flatter me, my lord," he replied, "we are only gentlemen."

"Gentlemen!" returned the Earl, "*only* gentlemen? My dear Mr. Falconbridge, you will find, as you go on in life, that this is an unphilosophical phrase. It is no slight task to be "only" this. It is better to be a gentleman than a lord—and the greatest lord can be no more. I pray that the historian of my life, if I shall have one, may give me that noble title only. 'Tis my sole ambition, sir, I crave no more. My career has been troubled and unhappy; my fortune adverse. I am growing old in a foreign land—alone in this wilderness after living at the finest Courts in Europe —but this does not afflict me very greatly, 'tis a matter of small importance. If my 'scutcheon is untarnished, my name free from all stain, I shall think myself fortunate and happy."

There was something so noble and moving in the melancholy earnestness of the speaker, that Falconbridge unconsciously stretched out his hand. The Earl pressed it gravely, and said:

"I take your hand as 'tis offered, sir—as the hand of an honest gentleman—and now, sir, I will no longer detain you with my talk. You are young and must require rest, and I too am weary after this annoying day, in which I have filled a position which is far from agreeable to me."

With these words the Earl rang his little bell, which was promptly answered by the appearance of the old body-servant, and with grave inclinations the two men separated.

The Earl sat down in his carved chair, as the door closed, and leaning his pale face upon his hand, mused long and moodily. At last he rose with a deep sigh, and muttered:

"The eyes and lips of this youth have a singular effect upon me; they are wonderfully similar—wonderfully. Well, well, I have arranged an idle trap for him yonder. He must see it, and I will question him. Folly! folly! but what is life, but a tissue of folly?"

And Lord Fairfax slowly left the apartment.

XXXVIII.

THE PORTRAIT.

FALCONBRIDGE found a cheerful fire burning in the wide fire-place of his sleeping apartment, for the November nights were growing cold, and rendered it necessary.

Old John saw that all was disposed agreeably for his master's guest, and then respectfully edging toward the door, quietly disappeared. Falconbridge was left alone, seated in front of the fire, into which he gazed long, with thoughtful eyes. His mind had been filled with new emotions lately; his life subjected to many novel influences. The beautiful woman, the melancholy nobleman, the jovial Borderer, the wild region, into which he had been so grimly welcomed by the Indian assault; all these personages and objects had flooded his life with new thoughts and feelings, and were now the subject of his vague reverie.

From time to time a smile would flit over the handsome features of the young man; and then a frown and an expression of pity would succeed. Miss Argal was the origin of the happy smile, the strange letter of the mad lover who had killed himself, caused the frown, and the commiserating shadow.

Falconbridge mused thus for more than an hour, taking no notice of the pattering drops which fell down from the wax candle on the silver candlestick, without observing that the fire was dying out, and that the dimly-lit apartment began to grow chill, as well as to assume a weird, ghost-like appearance in the flickering light of the single candle. As the light wavered to and fro, immense shadows chased each other across the walls and the ceiling; a melancholy "death-watch" tapped in the wainscoting; and a bough of one of the trees creaked nervously against the pane of the window. A fanciful imagination might have seen shadowy faces, peering in through the dim panes, or fancied that goblin fingers were tugging at the grating bells in the old belfries.

Falconbridge heard all these weird, low sounds, but did not heed them; he pursued his reverie. But finally his meditations came to an end; he banished them from his mind, and drawing a long breath, rose erect, and looked around him. As his eyes fell upon a picture hanging above the mantelpiece, he almost recoiled.

It represented a gentleman of about twenty-five, clad in an elegant costume, covered with embroidery. The white hand, half covered with lace, was thrust into the scarlet waistcoat, and the figure was erect and proud. The strange circumstance, however, which impressed the young man so strongly, was the startling resemblance which the portrait—for such it plainly was—bore to himself. It was not so much a resemblance, as a perfect copy of his own features. No trait was different, no detail wanting. The clear eyes, large, frank, filled with smiling pride; the clearly defined lips, expressing equal resolution and good humor; the raised head, the smooth forehead, the brown curling hair, all was identical with the traits of the real man. Had the picture descended from the canvas into the apartment, and any one been asked which was Falconbridge, which the other, he would have found it impossible to decide.

The young man's astonishment was so great that he remained for a long time gazing with deep wonder, and in silence upon the picture. Then taking the candle from the table he held it above his head, so that the light fell in a clear stream upon the portrait, and muttered:

"Why, that's no picture! 'Tis my other self!"

He sat down again, but could not remove his eyes from the strange portrait. Could it possibly have hung there, when he occupied the room before, without attracting his attention? He could not believe it. Why, then, had it been hung up since? Had Lord Fairfax placed it there? Was it intended to attract *his* notice? Whose could it be? what original sat for it? It was plainly no recent picture; whence did it come, and why was it here in his chamber, with its eyes fixed on him with that motionless stare?

The young man's mind was filled with conflicting thoughts. He could arrive at no conclusion; the strange picture was as absolute a mystery to him at the end of an hour, as when his eyes first fell upon it.

It was not until the old clock on the stairway struck *twelve*, slowly and solemnly, that Falconbridge, finding the apartment grow cold, retired to sleep. The strange copy of himself followed him in his dreams; the eyes shone on him in slumber, as when awake.

He slept uneasily, and started more than once; but finally toward daybreak fell into a sweet and soothing slumber, which was undisturbed by the haunting eyes. From his murmured words and smiles, it was plain that the young man was dreaming of his home in the Lowlands. His strange past, the stranger picture, the life around him, had all disappeared: he was far away from the valley and the mountains, in his own land again.

When he woke, and saw the bright sun streaming in, he smiled and welcomed it. Then a sudden movement proved that he recalled the night before. He turned his head quickly.

There was the picture.

XXXIX.

THE OLYMPIAN IRE OF CAPTAIN LONGKNIFE.

CAPTAIN WAGNER had just mounted Injunhater, and happy, triumphant, his chin in the air, was about to set out from the Ordinary for Greenway Court, when all at once, Falconbridge emerged from the forest, and galloped toward him.

He rode one of Fairfax's horses, whose speed he had well tested, according to the recommendation of the Earl, and in the bright morning sun presented a very attractive appearance.

"Whither bound, comrade?" said the Captain, reining in the active Injunhater, "you come on like a thunderbolt!"

"I am a very harmless one, Captain," returned Falconbridge, "and the Ordinary is my mark."

"You are from Greenway?"

"Yes."

"Any news?"

"None at all; his lordship, whom I left a short time ago, is quite well."

"He always is that, or the devil take it! He rides over the mountains enough to make anybody well and strong. You had a pleasant time?"

"Very pleasant."

"And a sound night's rest, doubtless?"

"Well, yes—I slept well enough; but a strange thing happened."

"Strange? What was that? Did you have any more visions?"

"No, Captain, but I saw myself."

"Saw yourself? Oh, you mean you were guilty of the vanity of looking into a mirror, of which there are not so many in this region. Well, companion, when one's as good looking a fellow as you are, that's not unnatural, or may the devil take it!"

"I did not say that I saw myself in a mirror—I was on canvas."

"On canvas!"

"Yes, my actual self, Captain!"

And Falconbridge described the portrait, the manner in which he had seen it, and the effect which it had produced upon him.

"Strange enough," said the soldier; "and did you mention it to his lordship?"

"He alluded to it himself at breakfast, and asked me if I had slept well with this *second* nocturnal visitor—you remember the first?"

"Yes, companion, and what was the explanation?"

"A very simple one. His lordship had placed the picture there as an agreeable surprise to me. It was the portrait of a friend of his who had been long dead—and my resemblance, he said, to this friend, had impressed him, upon our very first meeting."

"Well," said the soldier, "all that's very interesting and striking. I never saw the picture, but mean, as soon as I arrive, to go up stairs and look at it. Did you arrange your business?"

"In half an hour. I need not have come from the Low country hither."

"And you return?"

"Well, yes, I imagine so, Captain," said Falconbridge with some hesitation, "before very long."

"I'm glad to hear it," was Captain Wagner's apparently unfriendly reply. "I think of going down to see Gooch who, I'm told, sails for England in the spring, and we might jog along together."

"Then you have business with Governor Gooch?"

"Yes—about my lands."

And Captain Wagner gave a twist to his moustache, which made that decoration stand out prominently from his martial countenance.

"I own, or shall very soon own, my dear comrade, some of the prettiest pieces of ground in the Virginia valley. I will be mysterious, I will shirk the subject for the present, but I have said what I have said," added the soldier in a determined voice, as though some opponent disputed his statement. "My property lies in and around the town of Winchester—a noble place, Falconbridge, the pearl of the entire universe. It is my intention to make Gooch build a fort there, appoint me commandant, and commission me generalissimo of the frontier."

"Oh! really? But he could do worse."

"Thank you, comrade—and to be frank, I agree with you. Once commandant of an armed post, let me hear of the rascally Injuns daring to set foot on my ground! Let me hear that any of the copper-nosed scoundrels think of coming to the place or the neighborhood! I'll march on 'em, and exterminate 'em off the face of the earth! I will make the Opequon and Lost River run with their blood! I will choke those streams with their miserable carcasses, as I'm told Julius Cæsar did at the battle of Marathon in Africa! I'll cut 'em into slices, and fry, and eat 'em! If I don't I'm a dandy, Falconbridge!"

With which words, the Captain assumed a terrific frown, made a farewell sign to his companion, and setting spur to Injunhater, went on toward Greenway.

Falconbridge laughed, and dismounting, gave his horse into the hands of an ostler, directing him to lead the animal back in the afternoon to Greenway. Then he ordered his

9*

own horse, Sir John, to be saddled, and was ere long curbing that intelligent quadruped, with a joyous hand.

To his inquiries regarding the wizard, his daughter, and George, Mrs. Butterton replied that all three persons had set out some hours before on their return to the Fort Mountain—George riding his sorrel, the old man and his daughter occupying the landlord's sole vehicle. It was very plain, added the dame, that Mr. George was a friend of theirs.

Replying to this significant observation with a smile only, and saluting the lady with a low inclination, Falconbridge set forward at a round pace, for Mr. Argal's.

He had not seen Miss Argal for almost a whole—day.

XL.

THE BEGINNING OF THE END.

IT was only a few days after these scenes, when as Falconbridge arrived one morning in sight of Mr. Argal's he saw, affixed to the drooping boughs of an elm, in the midst of many hounds, the large chestnut, which was the favorite-riding horse of Lord Fairfax.

As the young man entered he saw the Earl, who wore his hunting costume, seated near Miss Argal, and engaged in earnest conversation with her. Mr. Argal was not visible.

The young lady did not seem overjoyed at Falconbridge's appearance—indeed her greeting was rather cool than warm. It was no more than she could have bestowed upon a common acquaintance—and although the nice sense of delicacy possessed by Falconbridge led him to approve of this reserve in the abstract, he could not divest himself of the idea that something more than the presence of a third person actuated the young lady in her demeanor toward him.

He had caught, indeed, as he entered, one of those strangely fascinating glances fixed upon Lord Fairfax, and the circumstance, trifling as it was, made his heart sink unconsciously. It was folly, he reflected, to expect a young lady, because she had plighted her word to one gentleman, to assume toward all others an air of coldness and indifference; but none the less did the electric smile which Miss Argal had directed toward the Earl make the pulse of Falconbridge throb with disquiet, and his brow contract.

Lord Fairfax rose courteously and greeted the young man with grave politeness.

"Give you good day, Mr. Falconbridge," he said; "I am glad to meet you again."

"Many thanks, my lord,—I trust you are well."

"Perfectly, sir. I am always well when I move about, as I have been doing now since daybreak."

"You have been hunting, I imagine, from your dress."

"Yes, all the morning. I had a chase after a deer, but made nothing of it. It led me some miles to the west, and I stopped here to see Mr. Argal and his family. I believe they are friends of yours, are they not, sir?"

"Oh yes—is not that true, Miss Bertha?" said Falconbridge, smiling.

"Certainly, sir, we are friends," was the young lady's reply. But the expression of the face seemed to say, "that is all"—in her voice there was something strange and indescribable; but its tones were plainly altered.

The quick ear of Falconbridge, sharpened and rendered nervously acute by the depth of his infatuation, did not fail to mark the change. The furrow in his brow became deeper, and he fixed upon the young lady one of those clear and searching glances which aim at reading the thoughts of those who are the objects of them.

The tone in which Miss Argal had spoken was either accidental, or she thought that she had gone too far. The indifferent, almost cold expression disappeared from her eyes —the beautiful face broke into smiles, and holding out her hand, she said:

"Friends should treat each other more kindly than you do us, Mr. Falconbridge—I have not seen you for a very long while!"

And with this ambiguous speech, which conveyed the idea to Lord Fairfax that the young man had not called for a month—but to him, the meaning that *twenty-four hours* was a "very long while" for him to be away from her,—the young lady bestowed upon Falconbridge a new edition of the glance at the Earl which he had intercepted on his entrance.

"At your age, Mr. Falconbridge," said the Earl, with his weary smile, "I would have made many visits to Mr. Argal's here, especially if I were detained, as I believe you are, sir, at that dull old Ordinary yonder. Pray leave it, and come and stay at Greenway Court as long as your affairs engage you in the region. It is really inhospitable in me to permit a gentleman like yourself to thus tarry at a roadside tavern, so near my house."

Falconbridge inclined his head courteously and replied:

"Many thanks to your lordship. But I shall soon return now—I have been away too long already from home."

"Ah, that need not draw you, I fancy," said the Earl, smiling; "when a young seigneur goes on his travels in Europe, we are accustomed to give him the length of his tether."

The young man smiled in return, and shaking his head replied:

"That may be true of young seigneurs, as you say, my lord, but I am not such a person. My father is in straitened circumstances, although we live well—requires my assistance, and I must go back soon.

The Earl gravely inclined his head, and then turning to the young lady, said:

"Do you expect your father to return this morning, Miss Argal? I now remember that he desires to consult me upon some land business, and my visit may save him trouble."

"Yes, he will soon return, my lord," was the reply; "I am sure he will not stay long."

"I will wait then, madam."

And the Earl resumed the chair from which he had half risen. He did not look at Falconbridge. The expression of the young man's countenance would have surprised him. He was gazing at Miss Argal with unaffected astonishment

—and he had abundant reason for doing so. Mr. Argal had announced in his presence, on the evening before, that business of importance made it necessary for him to go into Maryland, and had begged the young man to be as much with his daughter as he found it convenient—it would relieve his mind. He had gone on the journey, which would occupy two or three days, at least—and now Falconbridge heard the assurance given to Lord Fairfax by his hostess, that her father would "soon return," that he "would not stay long"—as though he had ridden out for an hour simply.

We shall do Miss Argal the justice to say, that no sooner had she uttered the words, than she blushed and seemed to regret them. She darted a rapid glance at Falconbridge, played with the ribbon at her belt, turned carelessly a handsome bracelet on her snowy arm—and ended by winding around her finger with graceful indifference one of the profuse curls of her raven hair.

She hesitated for a moment; looked out of the window, and said:

"Perhaps I have unintentionally misled you, my lord. I now remember that my father has ridden to some distance, and may not return so soon. If your lordship, however, will remain until the evening, I shall esteem it a favor. The neighborhood is very lonely."

"I regret that 'tis impossible, Miss Argal. I promised to leave a deed which I have in my pocket, for a new settler in the region, who will call for it. If my body-servant were with me, as is sometimes the case when I hunt, I might comply with your most obliging request."

The young lady turned the bracelet round again on the white arm,. beat the floor with her foot, and then said:

"Our servants are all away; but Mr. Falconbridge might take it for you, my lord. He might then return"——

The mark was overshot. Lord Fairfax greeted the proposition with an unmistakable stare of astonishment. As to Falconbridge, his face turned crimson, and from his eyes darted one of those flashes which at times indicated how dangerous he was when aroused.

"That is—I mean"—said Miss Argal, with some agitation, "I meant that your lordship might be worn out with fatigue—you might be greatly in need of rest—and as all our servants are in the woods, I thought I might treat Mr. Falconbridge, as a friend,—without ceremony. If I have offended you, pray pardon me," added the young lady, fixing upon the young man her saddest and most beseeching glance. "I am very young and inexperienced—I did not think—if I have shocked you"——

And turning away her head, Miss Argal seemed overcome with emotion.

The young man no longer betrayed any anger. There was nothing but sadness now in his eyes. He did not reply for an instant; when he did speak, it was only to say:

"I freely pardon any apparent slight, Miss Argal—I am sure you did not mean any—as I am sure that his lordship feels that I would willingly spare him fatigue were he greatly exhausted."

"No, no, sir," said the Earl with a low inclination, "by no means. I am quite rested, and feel as fresh as possible."

"But you think my conduct unbecoming, my lord," murmured the young lady, "to treat Mr. Falconbridge with such rudeness and want of ceremony—I fear you regard me as thoughtless and ill-bred—I pray Mr. Falconbridge will pardon me!"

The cloud disappeared from the brow of the Earl. That voice of subtle and wonderful melody dissipated all the displeasure which he had felt. Indeed he seemed fully under the spell of her beauty, and had more than once displayed during the progress of their interview that admiration which he had conceived for her on the first day of their meeting,— and which lingering unknown to him, in the depths of his nature, had come at last to be something more than a vague sentiment of pleasure in her society.

As she spoke now, or rather murmured in her low sweet voice those words, "I pray Mr. Falconbridge will pardon me!" all traces of displeasure disappeared, as we have said, from his countenance, and the cold swarthy face almost glowed:—that dark eye shone strangely.

"My dear Miss Argal," he said with something approaching feeling, "I pray you do not think so very seriously of a trifle—I am sure Mr. Falconbridge so regards it. 'Twas nothing,—mere thoughtlessness I am sure. And now I am constrained to leave you. Pray present my regards to your father on his return, and beg him to call on me at my house. I need not say that I shall feel honored should you choose to accompany him—at any time."

With these words, Lord Fairfax bowed low, and left the apartment. Falconbridge followed him to the door, declaring his intention to remain. No sooner had the two men disappeared than the sad and submissive expression vanished from Miss Argal's face, her head rose erect, her brows contracted furiously, and she imprisoned her red underlip between the white teeth,—so unmistakable was the fire of anger in her eyes.

When Falconbridge returned, in five minutes after bidding the Earl farewell, he found the young lady in the position in which he had left her—leaning sadly on the arm of her chair, and presenting the image of a statue of sad sweetness and regret.

He had never loved her more than at that moment.

XLI.

PROGRESS.

TWO days after Mr. Argal's return, he set out for Greenway Court, accompanied by his daughter, who had delivered the Earl's message, and expressed a desire to "breathe a little fresh air."
Her father had readily acquiesced in this proposal, and mounting their horses—Mr. Argal his stout cab, and his daughter her slender-legged filly—they were soon upon the road. There were two routes to Greenway Court. One led by the Ordinary; another branching to the right, and following a mere bridle path, wound over the prairie, and approached the house on a different side.

In compliance with the request of the young lady, who said she was heartily tired of the common road, they pursued this latter, and very soon arrived at the Earl's.

He met them at the door, and exhibited a satisfaction upon seeing Miss Argal, very unusual with one who seemed hard to arouse or interest. He assisted the young lady from her animal, gave her his arm, and led her into the mansion with grave courtesy. Mr. Argal followed, and they were, all three, seated ere long before the crackling fire of light sticks, which was far from unpleasant.

Whilst her father and the Earl were engaged in discussing the business matters which were the occasion of the visit, Miss Argal amused herself looking over the bookshelves; and finally bore away a volume of the "Spectator," in which she very soon seemed to become absorbed. She presented a fascinating picture as she sat by the window, poring over the book. One of her plump, white arms, from which the wide sleeve had fallen back, sustained her bent head, the elbow resting on the window-sill, the rounded wrist, adorned with its fine bracelet, half buried in the profuse curls of her ebon hair. Her full, but graceful figure, was inclined forward, and her black eyes were nearly concealed by the long, dark lashes, almost resting on the rosy cheek.

She was still poring over the volume, when a grave and courteous voice said behind her :

"Pray what have you there, Miss Argal—a romance from my collection?"

"Oh no, my lord, I never could read romances," was the smiling reply; "it is a volume of Mr. Addison's 'Spectator,' which I admire very much."

"And I also, madam," replied the Earl. "He is a writer of rare wit and humor."

"Oh, he certainly is!"

"Pray what paper did you open at—his attack on the ladies, and their fashions? It created a great talk, I remember, at the time."

"So I suppose, my lord; but I was not reading that. I was interested very much in this paper."

And she held up the book with her fascinating smile. The Earl looked at it. The paper was one which he had contributed to the "Spectator" in his youth.

"I have heard that Mr. Addison and Mr. Steele wrote together," said Miss Argal; "can your lordship tell me which of them wrote this? It is so elegantly composed—so delightful!"

The Earl smiled. He had prided himself much on his literary reputation, and the old leaven of a former vanity had not spent its strength.

"I am almost ashamed to reply after such high commendation, madam," he said; "but truth renders it necessary for me to say that I am myself the author of that number."

"You, my lord! Have you ever written for the printers?"

The Earl smiled again: there was something singularly delightful to him in the young lady's admiration and surprise.

"I am obliged to say yes," he answered. "I knew Mr. Addison, and esteemed him highly; and rather received, than conferred a favor by having a place in the "Spectator." Indeed, the man himself was of such conspicuous gifts, that the greatest noblemen, much more my poor self, were honored by his friendship and conversation. He lived but simply when I knew him first, and dressed very meanly: but you forgot what he wore, and the poor apartment he occupied, when his calm, clear voice began. He would smoke his pipe and converse for hours, and I still recall his smile, with its extraordinary sweetness and serenity, as though his thoughts were fixed upon some delightful recollection, or unseen spirits were whispering to him. All who knew him admired and loved him; I was honored by his friendship. He was a very great man; I am not—that explains all, madam."

"And *you* wrote this beautiful paper?" said Miss Argal, with a contemplative air, "this paper I was reading with so much interest?"

"I believe so. And I think you will find my name affixed at the end."

The young lady turned the leaf, and said, innocently:

"Why here it is, sure enough! 'Thomas, Lord Fairfax.' I ought to have looked."

Had she looked? Yes. The connection of the Earl with the "Spectator" had been known to her, and she had sought for and found, and commenced reading the number marked with his name.

After some more conversation on literature, the book was replaced on the shelf, and at the same moment a savory odor invaded the apartment. The dinner hour had arrived, and with a little urging Mr. Argal remained.

Dinner was served after the English fashion, in courses, and the three persons remained at table until the sun began to stream through the western window. Miss Argal had summoned all her wonderful powers to attract the admiring attention of the Earl, and she had succeeded. She had commenced by flattering his vanity; she ended by impressing upon him the fact that she regarded him with a mixture of respect and affection, which she struggled against, but could not overcome. The conversation had turned upon marriage and the philosophy of that relation; and the young lady, in the most casual and unintentional way, had declared that for her part, she never could understand the taste of women for "mere boys." Young men were no favorites of hers. They were so terribly vain, and prided themselves so much upon their youth and beauty; they seemed to bestow their affection as a sort of favor on the ladies, and, indeed, she never could bear them, the vain creatures! If she ever thought of marrying, she would select some one else. It should be a serious person;. no matter if he had reached or even passed middle age. She would be sure at least of his love, and could rely upon his judgment and his protection. She would rather a thousand times trust her happiness to such a one, than to a giddy-pated youth, however handsome he might be.

All this was uttered by Miss Argal in the most innocent and careless way: the mere outpouring, it appeared, of her confiding disposition. And it thrilled the cold heart of the weary exile with a new and delightful emotion. His vanity was soothed and flattered—his admiration was excited by the lovely speaker—his ears drank in the music of her voice, and his eyes dwelt with unaccustomed intensity upon her countenance, so instinct with beauty and fascination.

When, very soon after dinner, Mr. Argal declared the necessity of his departure, the Earl pressed him warmly to remain. The young lady, as before, discovered that she was laboring under a cough, but this only hurried her departure. Mr. Argal thanked his lordship, but said that it was absolutely necessary for him to return that evening. And so the horses were brought up, and the Earl assisted the young lady to her seat in the saddle.

Did her ungloved hand retain his own, as it had retained Falconbridge's on that evening of their first meeting? Was the slight but clearly perceptible pressure intentional?

The Earl stood on the porch and watched them until they were out of sight; the languishing smile of Miss Argal as she departed, still before him. As he turned finally, and re-entered the house, he muttered:

"I have never seen a beauty as superb, or a more brilliant mind! Let me beware! Love a woman again? It would be monstrous!"

But all the evening he was thinking of her.

XLII.

IN THE MOUNTAIN.

HALF an hour after the departure of Mr. Argal and his daughter for Greenway Court, Falconbridge drew up before the house, and leaping from his horse, entered the mansion, smiling and joyful.

His love for the young lady had reached that point now, that out of her presence he scarcely lived. His life was concentrated into those hours of each day when he sat by her, and looked into her eyes. All the rest was a dull, cold blank to him, with no pleasure in it all. He *existed*, simply, there at the Ordinary, and passed all his moments in musing upon the interview which had passed by, or on the one which was to occur again on the morrow. As he mounted his horse to go away, his form would droop, his eyes become gloomy—when he put spur to Sir John, to go and see her, he was the picture of buoyant joy and light-heartedness.

These words will explain the emotion of the young man, when one of the servants informed him that Miss Argal had departed, and above all, departed for "Lord Fairfax's."

As the words were uttered, he felt a dizziness, a sudden sinking of the heart. Lord Fairfax's! She had gone to Greenway Court! All the scene, when that morning she had insulted him so carelessly, rushed back; he remembered the whole interview; he saw her glances, her wiles, her witcheries to attract his lordship. For a moment, then, he stood still and gazed at the servant with an expression which almost frightened her.

It was for a moment only. His presence of mind returned, and simply requesting her to inform Miss Argal of his visit, on her return, he issued forth and mounted his horse again.

Should he go thither? Yes! He would go and be a witness of what he felt was the scene at Greenway—a witness of her smiles and cajoleries, and fascinations, aimed at the Earl—he would go and sup full upon his jealousy and resentment!

And digging the spur into the side of Sir John, he set forward like lightning upon the road to Greenway.

A mile from Mr. Argal's he suddenly drew rein, so suddenly that Sir John reared and almost fell upon his haunches. Was it advisable to go there? Would she relish this persistent pursuit of her—this jealous supervision, as though he suspected her fidelity to him? Was it worth while to go and suffer, and get no thanks, rather coldness for it? No! He would return to his lonely chamber and see no one.

And he turned his horse's head in the direction of the Ordinary, going along now very slowly, his head drooping, his brow overshadowed.

"No, no," he murmured, "no, I cannot go back there. Mrs. Butterton would annoy me with her wearying conversation—I need movement, fresh air."

With these words he stopped and looked round. The Fort Mountain raised its great ramparts and seemed to beckon him; the prairie, swept by the wind, whispered to him. He had met George in the morning, at the Ordinary, on his way to the "Fort," and now remembering the fact, directed his course straight toward it.

He at last reached the river; pushed his horse through the current, and skirting the noisy Passage Creek, ascended the winding bridle-path toward the cottage of the wizard.

As he went onward many wild sights and sounds greeted him, and dissipated, in a measure, his possessing thoughts.

A great eagle rose, with slow, flapping wings, from a crag near at hand, and swept away into the opposite mountain: a stag flitted across a distant opening, and disappeared; more than once he heard in the tangled thicket near at hand, the stealthy tread of a panther or a bear, crackling over the dry twigs, and rustling the dead leaves of the forest. He went on without heeding these things, however, and soon reached the steep knoll upon which the wizard's cottage was situated. As he arrived at this point, he all at once saw, in the porch of the house, a pleasant little rustic picture.

On one of the benches a young girl was seated, graceful and smiling; and her smiles seemed to be occasioned by the attempt which a young man, occupying a lower seat at her feet, was making to place a wreath of pale primroses on her forehead.

Beside them was stretched, indolently sleeping, a huge black bear, to whose presence no attention at all seemed to be paid.

Cannie and George were so much interested in their occupation that they did not hear the foot-falls of the horse, and it was not until Falconbridge had tied Sir John to a bough, and ascended the declivity on foot, that they became aware of his presence.

The bear rose with a growl, and exhibited a ferocious mouth filled with white, sharp teeth, but at a word from the young girl, accompanied by a warning tap on his head from her little hand, lay down quietly again, and dozed serenely.

The boy and the girl welcomed Falconbridge with the warmest cordiality, and Cannie, with a smile, informed him that he need fear nothing from "Bruin," who was a long tried friend and pet, and quite harmless. With these words she pushed the animal with her small foot, and bade him move. Bruin acquiesced with perfect good humor, and rising lazily, waddled off to a sunny knoll, and lying down, speedily went to sleep again.

Cannie, meanwhile, had entered the house, and announced the visit of Falconbridge to her grandfather, who soon came forth and welcomed him. They were still exchanging courteous expressions, and the young man was looking with great interest at Cannie, when another incident occurred. A sudden fluttering in the air attracted their attention—a suppressed croak was heard—and an immense hawk, with an arrow through his wing, fell almost at the young man's feet.

"Why, Lightfoot is here!" said Cannie; "he has shot the hawk that was after my pigeons!"

"Who is Lightfoot?" asked Falconbridge, whose gloom began to yield before the innocent smiles of the girl; "another friend, like the bear?"

"Oh, no sir! he is an Indian. He is a true friend, however. He once saved my life, and we love him, even George. There he comes—he has been to see us twice lately—he lives in the mountain."

As Cannie spoke, the young Indian was seen approaching down the abrupt, almost precipitous path which led upward to the summit. From the tall mass of rock above, he had seen and transfixed the hawk, and now came to pick it up. He was welcomed with great affection by Cannie, and when she pointed to Falconbridge, and said: "This is another good friend, Lightfoot," the Indian stretched out his arm, and shook hands, as he had learned to do, with a grave dignity and courtesy which might have graced an emperor.

10

XLIII.

HOW AN ANIMAL CHANGED THE DESTINIES OF THREE HUMAN BE-
INGS.

THE day was spent happily by all. That confidence which soon springs up between persons of sincere and truthful natures, made the hours glide away without constraint or ceremony.

The Indian and Falconbridge were not regarded in the light of strangers by the old man or his daughter; and as to George, we already know that he was on a footing of the most perfect familiarity and friendship. As they sat on the little porch, and looked forth on the beautiful scene of the forest and mountain, dancing streamlet and moss-clad rocks, a cheerful and inspiring influence seemed to fill every bosom, and Falconbridge was no exception. The shadows which had lain upon his brow slowly passed away. His equanimity returned. From the little mountain cottage, nestling in a gash of the great lofty range, he looked down as it were upon the events of the morning, there in the Lowland, and regarded them in a different and more hopeful light.

Had he not suffered himself to be carried away by a mere rush of jealous and irrational suspicion—by a fit of angry disappointment at not meeting the young lady? What reason was there to find fault with her for accompanying her father on a ride across the prairie, when he doubtless had some business matters to transact with Lord Fairfax? Could he blame her—was there any, the least, ground for complaint or dissatisfaction? Indeed, ought he not to feel some shame at having charged her with unworthy motives even in his imagination?

. When his reflections brought him to this point, the whole matter was ended. A noble nature always suffers deeply from the consciousness that it has committed an injustice ; with such the recoil is always powerful; the longing to make amends is irresistible. Falconbridge determined to be, in future, more kind and unsuspicious than he had ever been before !—and thus having banished his absorbing thought, he became cheerful and even joyous again.

Every object around him increased this sentiment. The fresh bracing air caressed his cheeks and forehead, and filled his pulses with buoyant life. He inhaled it with delight, and felt the last traces of his gloomy thought disappear. His companions were not unsuited to the scenes, nor to his change of mood—Cannie looked up into his face with her bright smile, her tender eyes, and air of confiding affection. She had not forgotten how he came to the side of her grandfather on the day of the trial, and greeted him in his sincere voice, full of sympathy and kindness—how he had held his hand out to herself, and said she was a little countess, and a good daughter. She had recalled his tones and looks and words, on her return, with strange pleasure; and now met him as a friend whom she had known and loved. And Falconbridge derived no less pleasure from the countenance of Cannie. He thought many times during the day that there was something in the clear eyes and innocent lips strangely familiar —he seemed to have met with the girl far away in some other land, of which he retained only a shadowy recollection. Unable to define or explain this emotion, he at last yielded himself up to the charm, and was happy at her side.

If he turned from Cannie or the old man, or George, who was a favorite with him, it was to gaze with much interest on the graceful young Indian. Lightfoot evidently excited his curiosity and admiration. There was something simple and majestic about the Indian—the evidence of the possession of those traits which Falconbridge had been taught to love and reverence all his life; true native dignity, simplicity and goodness. A close observer would have said, indeed, that these two youths of different race and training had come of the same blood. Both bore themselves with an unconscious pride,—both had the native truth and honesty of the forest, in eye and lip and tone of voice.

"You are from the Lowland, I believe, sir?" said the old man in his calm, collected voice, "the Tide-water region?"

"Yes, sir," returned Falconbridge; "from the banks of Chesapeake—and I seem to have met with you, or some one nearly resembling you, somewhere"——

And the young man seemed to reflect.

"Yes," he added suddenly, "it was in Williamsburg one day! You were conversing with his Excellency the Governor, on Gloucester Street—were you not, sir?"

The old man smiled, but replied guardedly.

"I have visited Williamsburg, sir, and I am acquainted with his Excellency."

"I was sure of it, Mr. Powell—I was there at College, and was walking out that evening with a friend, when I saw you. Did you live near the town?"

"No, sir," returned the other, "higher up the country. You see I have come up still further into the mountains, and perhaps I shall spend all my days here. There is something strangely noble to my eye in these bristling ranges, and I should like to sleep my last sleep on the summit of one of those peaks."

"And I, too," said Falconbridge musing: "true, it is a matter of small importance where the poor body rests when the spirit has left it—in the depths of the ocean, in the desert, in the air as the Indian race prefer—in the lowland or the mountains. But something of the old preferences govern us even in this. For my part I would like my grave to be on the summit of this very mountain—on the forehead itself of the sleeping giant, if I may call it such—yonder, where that great eagle is swooping toward the immense pine against the sky, full in the sinking sun. And that reminds me, George," added the speaker, turning to his companion, "that we should set out for home unless we wish to be benighted. I have had a happy day, sir, and thank you all for it."

With these words Falconbridge rose.

"I have something to give you for Lord Fairfax, sir," said the old man, "as you no doubt will see him. I will procure it, and request you to take charge of it."

He retired as he spoke, and soon returned with a small package, secured with a heavy wax seal, which he handed to Falconbridge. The young man thought it somewhat singular that it had not been entrusted to George, who was going straight to Greenway, but said nothing, and bade all farewell.

George, however, was not ready: a circumstance which he explained by saying that he wished to discover if the stories about carrier-pigeons were true—and especially if Cannie's favorite one " would carry a message " from Greenway to the mountain. He accordingly proceeded to coax the pigeon to descend by scattering some crumbs, and gradually approach it, as it tipped about, picking them up. Cannie had meanwhile called Falconbridge's attention to her prince's feathers, cardinal flowers, and primroses in a bed near the fence, and the young man bent down and examined them with a pleasure and interest which was rather on account of their mistress than their own, but no less delighted the smiling girl.

As he did so, he did not observe that in turning round he had dropped from the breast pocket of his doublet the package which the old man had entrusted to him.

George soon secured the pigeon, and imprisoning it carefully in his bosom, announced his readiness to depart. With many cordial pressures of the hand, and kind words, the two young men then mounted their horses, and were rapidly proceeding on the way to their respective abodes.

They parted at a point where they encountered the road leading from Greenway to the Ordinary—George turning to the right, Falconbridge to the left—with friendly smiles, and a promise on George's part to come soon and see his friend, at Mynheer Van Doring's.

Falconbridge rode on, busy with his own thoughts, and had nearly reached the Ordinary, when suddenly he remembered the package entrusted to him by the old man, which he had intended to deliver to George for the hands of the Earl. He put his hand into his doublet—it was gone! Greatly annoyed at the circumstance, and wondering how he had lost it, he thought at first of retracing his steps, but gave up the intention, as the setting sun preluded night, and he would not be able to find it.

Promising himself to search for it on the succeeding morning, he continued his way.

The search on the next day proved useless.

Ten minutes after the departure of the young men from the mountain cottage, and soon after Cannie and her grandfather had entered the house, the bear Bruin descried the glittering object, and either attracted by the color, or liking the flavor of the wax, bore it off to a spot in the forest, and amused himself in mouthing and tearing it. Unimportant as it seemed, the circumstance had an influence almost fatal upon the destinies of three persons.

XLV.

IN WHICH CAPTAIN WAGNER REQUESTS MONSIEUR JAMBOT TO PULL HIS NOSE.

THE spectacle which greeted Falconbridge as he entered the doorway of the Ordinary, was one of those tableaux which are only presented upon extraordinary occasions, and under peculiar circumstances.

In the middle of the apartment, Captain Wagner and Monsieur Jambot were locked in a tender, and fraternal embrace, upon which Mrs. Butterton looked with tears of joyous agitation and hysterical delight.

What had caused this fine picture? Let us explain.

Since the evening when Mrs. Butterton yielded to the onset of the valiant Borderer, the bosom of Monsieur Jambot had been consumed by a gloomy internal fire. He had speedily discovered the result of that low-toned conversation between the Captain and the widow—and the discovery was gall and wormwood to him. He had flattered himself, with that talent for hope which characterizes his nation, that all obstacles to an union with himself would disappear from the mind of Mrs. Butterton—that she regarded Captain Wagner with nothing more than ordinary friendship—and that he himself had only to wait, and the prize would be his own.

When he now found his rival successful, his own hopes all crushed, the demon of revenge invaded his breast; and he set about obeying its dictates.

On the evening of the day to which we have now arrived, he clad himself carefully from top to toe, and paid minute attention to every detail of his costume and appearance. His silk stockings were irreproachable; his coat almost as good as new; his frill immense and snow-white; his cocked hat resting gallantly on his powdered peruke, the model chapeau of a noble chevalier. Indeed Jambot was truly a chevalier of Touraine, of no means; but vastly ancient race,—and had much of the *bel air* in his carriage when he chose to adopt it —he was a noble still.

In this guise he presented himself before Mrs. Butterton, and declared with deep sadness that in the distant land to which he was soon about to proceed, he would always remember her, and speak of her to his friends with admiration and respect.

The fair lady looked surprised at this announcement, and said:

"Why, where are you going, Monsieur Jambot?"

"I go to my native Touraine, madame," returned Monsieur Jambot with a touching air, "I am desolated to announce this to madame, but 'tis necessary. I go to the home of my race, to my native land. My worthy aunt has had the politeness to die—I have some *rentes*—my cousin, the Vicomte de Louvais, will give the poor exile home—or in the most hospitable mansion of my uncle, Monsieur le Chevalier de Sautry, I shall linger out, it may be, these few sad years, which, alas! will pass themselves so far from madame!"

With these words Monsieur Jambot assumed an expression of mingled love and sorrow, which really became him, and had no little effect upon the widow. She had liked Monsieur Jambot—had indeed thought seriously of bestowing her hand upon him—a possession which he evidently coveted. He was poor and homeless, but then he was gallant and chivalric; he might be romantic and unfit for business, but then he was devoted and kind-hearted—he would love her and wait upon her; she might do worse than become Madame Jambot. These reflections, we say, had more than once passed through the mind of Mrs. Butterton, and now when the *triste exilé* as he often called himself, spoke of departing—when he addressed her in a strain of such touching regret and affection—the heart of the lady felt all its old impressions revive, and the graces of Captain Wagner for the moment quite disappeared from her memory. She therefore responded to the touching address of her admirer by looking sadly at him, and saying :

"Are you really obliged to go, Monsieur Jambot?"

"'Tis better," replied her sorrowful companion; "'tis best for the peace of mind of madame's poor friend. That friend will not make himself too free with those events, he will say those tragic events, which have come to desolate his life, to crush his hopes, to make the life of him but a mocking dream, a chimera, which disappears! May the friend of the poor chevalier be happy in one who goes to love her much, though not so greatly as another! May he feel in his native home, at the board of De Sautry, or on the battlements of the Chateau de Louvais which makes itself admired by all upon the green banks of the Loire, that he has still a friend —a fair and beautiful friend in the distant land from which he now goes to depart—may he know that one whom he has loved, with a love so profound, so devoted, so ineffable, has not forgotten him, but thinks still of him, and perhaps in the bright days will murmur, 'Finally he loved me very much, this poor sad chevalier—this exile!'"

The head of the fair widow sank. The mournful words impressed her deeply, and revived all her old affection. There was more than one emotion in her heart as she gazed at him now, sadly and kindly. There was pity, regard, that sympathy which the female bosom never fails to conceive for the man who loves with real devotion—there was more. Monsieur Jambot was thus, after all, a nobleman! His family were Chevaliers and Viscounts! He was going back to the battlements of castles and chateaus, the possessions of his uncles and cousins! As Madame Jambot, she would have sat at the right hand of the noble De Sautry, and De Louvais—been a member of that elevated and refined society—this was lost to her! Such reflections were passing through the mind of the lady, and they were not without their effect upon her. She had abundant reason to know that all that Monsieur Jambot said was true—and her head drooped as she gazed at him. It is no more than justice to add, however, that pity and grief at parting with an old friend were the chief causes of her sadness. The tone of her companion was hopeless and resigned—he was yielding like an honest chevalier to a more favored rival,—without complaint, with the air of a gentleman who is unfortunate and retires. Could she suffer him to depart without assuring him of her lasting affection?

These reflections had so much influence upon her, that the fair Mrs. Butterton begged Monsieur Jambot to come and sit beside her. He obeyed with a resigned and touching air, which deepened the impression produced by his words.

The lady then proceeded to reply to his sad address. Gracefully evading the allusion to "another," she professed for Monsieur Jambot a lasting and most affectionate regard. He had proved himself, she said, a true friend, on very many occasions—she had found from many circumstances, that he was as reliable and devoted in his regard, as he was kindly and sincere in his feelings, and she could not give him up—she could not bid him farewell—he must not—must not—go!

With these words, the last of which were uttered in a broken and agitated voice, the fair widow turned her head away, placed her handkerchief to her eyes, and uttered a sob.

The sound seemed to act like an electric shock upon Monsieur Jambot. He uttered a deep groan—cried, "Oh heaven! She weeps!"—and falling upon his knees, caught her other hand in his own, and pressed it ardently to his lips.

It was just at this moment that a heavy step resounded behind Monsieur Jambot, a tremendous growl was heard, and a sonorous voice, full of wrath and astonishment, cried :

"Ho there! On his knees, or the devil fly away with me!"

It was Captain Wagner:—Captain Wagner astounded; Captain Wagner furious; Captain Wagner boiling with fiery jealousy and indignation, and threatening with his drawn sword to let loose the bloody dogs of war upon his enemy.

Monsieur Jambot rose quickly to his feet, and returned the look of the Captain with one equally ferocious.

"Ah? ventrebleu! Monsieur le Capitaine goes to get angry!" he hissed in a mocking and satiric tone. "Monsieur is of the jealous!"

"No sir! I'm not jealous," returned the Captain, "but it is my intention to spit your carcass on this little trinket —to skin you, and eat you, hind legs and all, Monsieur Frog-eater! If I don't I'm a dandy and a kitten!"

With these awful words, the Captain advanced straight on Monsieur Jambot, who had whipped out his little dress-sword, and did not budge an inch; and in an instant the weapons clashed together.

A grim pleasure at his opponent's pluck came to the face of the Captain, and gravely saluting with his other hand, he made a lunge at his foe which would have carried out the terrible threat just uttered, had it not been for an unexpected circumstance. This circumstance was nothing less than the disappearance of the valiant Captain's head, shoulders, arm and sabre, beneath a huge horse-blanket, from the folds of which the weapon of the soldier made ineffectual slashes in the air.

The hysterical Mrs. Butterton had performed this feat. In her agitation she had seized and made use of the huge wrapping, and it had answered the purpose which she designed. Captain Wagner resembled, as he struggled and struck out wildly, one of those luckless individuals whom the Venetian "Ten" doomed to the stiletto, a mantle being thrown over their heads before the blow.

In an instant he extricated himself, breathing fire and slaughter; but it was only to find his sword arm drawn down by the entire weight of Mrs. Butterton's person.

"For shame, Captain! for shame!" cried the lady, with blushing agitation, and pouting; "how could you treat Monsieur Jambot so badly, so cruelly!"

"Badly, madam!" thundered the Captain, with Olympian indignation and astonishment. "Cruelly! Did I not see him with my own eyes kneeling there! Did I not see him kissing your hand, madam, and making love to you?"

"And if he did kiss my hand, what of that?" said the lady, with a more obvious pout still; "my hand is my own, and no one else's!"

"That may be, madam," returned the soldier, still irate, but growing cooler at these significant words, "but I'll none the less have Monsieur's blood!"

"You shall not fight with him, or he with you!" cried the widow, again, alarmed at the Captain's ferocity; "I tell you it was nothing; Monsieur Jambot *is going away!*"

And Mrs. Butterton rapidly related the particulars of the interview; forgetting, however, to mention the unimportant circumstance that she had urged the nephew of the Chevaier de Sautry not to depart. The history quite changed the feelings and intentions of the worthy Captain. He grew gradually cooler, and soon recovered all his equanimity, when he reflected that his rival was about to go. Had he not been guilty, indeed, of wanton insult and annoyance to that gentleman? Was his ferocious attack well calculated to advance him in the estimation of his lady love? Did he not owe Monsieur Jambot a full and frank explanation—an apology, and a disclaimer of all intent to outrage him?

These thoughts passed *seriatim* through the mind of the worthy, as he listened; and at the end of the relation, his mind was made up. Replacing his sword in its scabbard, he fixed upon Mrs. Butterton a look full of sorrowful but ardent adoration, and said;

"I am glad that you arrested me in my course, madam! I was wrong. But in certain states of mind, I have always observed that the most intelligent men act like fools, or *non compos mentis* people, as the Greeks say. You understand me, madam," said the Captain, with immense significance; "and I leave you to decide. As to Monsieur Jambot, I am willing and even desirous to assure that gentleman, for whom I have a very high esteem, of my regrets. I was wrong—I was a fool and ninny, or I'm a dandy! Monsieur Jambot, I have grown a pair of long ears, I'm a donkey, or the devil take it! If it will be any satisfaction, and productive of any pleasure to you, you are at liberty to pull my miserable nose, or cut off, with that handsome sword of yours, the lengthy ears of which I spoke—only I beg of you to pull with a gentle and tender hand, and to leave enough of the said ears to grow out again—or the future historian of my eventful life will write in the book which he makes about my adventures, the words, 'Captain Longknife was destitute of ears!' which would be shocking and mortifying to my descendants—to my very great grandchildren!"

With these solemn words, Captain Wagner bowed courteously to Monsieur Jambot, and added :

"I am ready to shake hands, my dear friend, and beg your pardon—I'll do it—if I don't, I'm a dandy!"

"Shake hands!" cried Monsieur Jambot, whose temper was excitable, but as generous as the day, "it shall not be that we shake hands, *Mon cher Capitaine* and friend—that we embrace!"

As he spoke the worthy Jambot extended his arms, and the two bloody foes were locked in a fraternal embrace. The chin of Captain Wagner reposed affectionately between the shoulders of his friend; the countenance of Monsieur Jambot appeared above the arm of the other; and to make the whole complete, the fair lady who had caused all the commotion, stood by crying—but laughing too, and rejoicing at the result.

It was then that Falconbridge entered, and stood silent with astonishment; but all was soon explained to him.

"The fact is, my dear Falconbridge, your friend Wagner is a fool," said the Captain; "but when a man grows jealous he sees things double, or I'm a dandy! I remember hearing about a black fellow who knocked up a courtship with some king's daughter or other, by his nigger-witchcraft, and ran off with her *—after which he got jealous without any reason, and choked her to death with a bolster. Falconbridge," said the Captain, with affecting solemnity of accent, "beware of jealousy!"

---

* This somewhat free description of the "noble Moor" of Shakespeare, and his means of influencing Desdemona, was uttered in the hearing of the writer, by a worthy, who added that the name of the lady, as well as he could recollect, was *Arabella.*

XLV.

THE LAMIA.

THE passion of Lord Fairfax for Miss Argal ripened rapidly, and soon attained its full strength. It was one of those fatal infatuations which paralyze the reason, and lead captive the wills of the strongest and most resolute men.

From that evening when George encountered him in the Massinutton, and when they met Miss Argal and Falconbridge on the prairie, the Earl had not ceased to think of her with a singular emotion. There was something in this young lady which no one could describe—an impalpable and wondrous fascination—which, when it had once been felt, was an influence on the life, an irresistible spell which could not be thrown off. Her beauty was but a small part of this magnetic power. Her face, it is true, with its rosy cheeks, crimson lips, and framework of black curls, was of rare loveliness: her figure, both full and undulating, both sweeping and redundant, was enough to attract admiration; but the secret of her influence lay deeper, and was difficult to define. It was chiefly, a keen observer might have said, in the eye, and its expression, or its thousand expressions, rather. It was a strange and wonderful pair of eyes. The *lamia* of the poets—that mythological creature, with the form of a woman, and the instincts of a serpent—might have afforded an illustration of Miss Argal at times. Indeed, this serpent-like glance, dark and glittering, but full of caressing sweetness and subtle fascination as well, almost always shone from beneath her long silken lashes. It was a sidelong and wary glance, as if the person were *watching*

—a cunning and yet confiding gaze, lying in wait, as it were, for its prey. It could coax and cajole, and beseech, and wheedle—it took all characters, and bewildered the mind, but ended by bringing the victim to her feet.

It was wonderful, miraculous, almost, what a magnetic power lay in those eyes—a power to fascinate, to persuade, to bend the reason, however strong-willed and imperial. It had been nothing to draw the ardent and impulsive young man to her side—Falconbridge was ripe for a passionate attachment—he was young, unsuspecting, an admirer of the beautiful; with a heart which the first beautiful woman might enslave from the very enthusiasm and warmth of his nature. But Lord Fairfax! To win that cold and collected man!—to turn the old dry nobleman, past middle life, into a bashful and embarrassed lover! To move a heart long unmoved—to bend a will so resolute and determined—to make that woman-hater, or woman-fearer, yield to her wiles, and follow her when she beckoned! That was truly an undertaking worthy of her ambition. She worked for it—and she achieved her end.

It is not pleasant to analyze such a character. We touch upon those mysterious and shifting motives and impulses as the mariner in the frozen regions of the North, in the gloomy night, treads cautiously and with repugnance on the floating mass of ice which envelops his ship. There was little *love* in question, on her part. She was attracted toward Lord Fairfax by his wealth and position—by the ambition of becoming his Countess, and thus becoming mistress, in fact, of one fourth, very nearly, of the province.

Thread by thread the web was woven. The Earl of Fairfax soon came to feel a passionate attachment for the fascinating woman, and to visit her regularly—sometimes in the absence of Falconbridge, sometimes when he was present. But he did not exhibit any indications of his passion beyond this. His cold mask was never thrown off for a moment. His countenance, with its grim, sad smile, scarcely relaxed—he was the same calm, and cynical philosopher as before, the same courteous gentleman, but no more. One thing was apparent, however, in his demeanor. He avoided Falconbridge, and seemed ill at ease in his society; but let it not be supposed from this that the Earl was conscious of committing an injustice in visiting the young lady. Miss Argal had distinctly informed him one morning, that she was not bound in any way to Falconbridge—that he was merely a friendly visitor who was lonely at the Ordinary, and came over to chat with her and her father. The Earl had thus set his mind at rest on the subject, and regarded himself as wholly irreproachable in the undertaking which he had determined upon now, the attempt to make Miss Argal his Countess.

We have forborne to describe the feelings of Falconbridge. The task was more than we were willing to attempt. There is something awful and darkly tragic in the picture of a noble and great heart writhing under the dominion of a mad passion for a woman, and feeling that his passion is a vain one. For to this conclusion had the young man now very nearly arrived. He could scarcely mistake the indications of Miss Argal's manner. She was no longer what she had been to him. All her delightful smiles, and caressing accents, had disappeared. She met him when he came with ill-concealed disinclination, and opposed to his questions and prayers for an explanation, an obdurate and unconquerable reserve. If she replied at all, it was only to say, with cold politeness, that Mr. Falconbridge really placed too much stress upon trifles; young ladies, like *their superiors, young men*, were subject to changes of mood; she was not well to-day; the discussion made her head ache; was there any news of interest at the Ordinary?—she supposed he would soon return home now, as he had said his business in the region was finished. She would advise him to. The air of the mountains, after October, was very cold—he would catch a catarrh—and she really would advise him, as a friend to return. Ah! there was Lord Fairfax! Would Mr. Falconbridge excuse her for a moment? His lordship was always pleased when she met him at the door."

That was all. And Falconbridge would grind his lip with his teeth, bow coldly as the Earl entered, and discover that he had to meet George, or Captain Wagner, at the Ordinary. He would go away raging; and bury himself in his chamber, and grow old hour by hour, in presence of his misery.

To this point the history of the persons had advanced, when we again return to particular scenes in the narrative.

XLVI.

HOW FALCONBRIDGE KINDLED A FIRE TO SEE BY.

IT was nearly sunset, and a heavy bank of lurid cloud, fringed with crimson, was piled up in the western horizon. It was plain that a storm would burst before the sunlight shone again, and every eye which witnessed the magnificent spectacle, was entranced by its grandeur and wild beauty.

Falconbridge alone, of all at the Ordinary, did not heed it. Seated in his chamber, his shoulders bending forward, his face pale, his eyes blazing at times with a menacing fire, he did not move or utter a word. The events of the last few days had almost paralyzed him. He seemed to be growing old. His face had lost all its bloom and freshness; his bearing all its buoyant grace and pride; he stooped like an octogenarian, who approaches the end of human life, after much toil and suffering and grief.

The mood of the young man's mind was piteous. Rage and despair, love and hatred, a thousand warring and discordant passions, held riotous carnival in the heaving bosom, and tore him with their burning talons.

He knew all now. He had become aware of Miss Argal's intentions with regard to the Earl; and though the young lady had not distinctly broken with him, he foresaw that she had resolved to do so, and would dismiss him on the first favorable opportunity. Thus, then, would end his wild and delicious dream. The passionate love, which permeated his very life-blood, would be swallowed up in this gulf of despair. He would be thrown off like a useless garment, whose gloss has departed—which no longer excites any emotion but contempt. The *Countess of Fairfax*, if they ever met again, would smile or sneer at their past relations, and greet him with an air of condescension or indifference. The Earl would not insult him, perhaps—he would treat him with great politeness; a former friend of his Countess would be entitled to so much attention; and he would be bowed out grandly from their presence, he, the silly young adventurer, who had presumed to be the rival of his betters!

The thought flushed the pale cheek, and brought a threatening flash to the eyes. He rose from his seat, and looked around him with a fiery glance. Where was he? Why was he inactive? Was he to sit down and groan, and submit to his fate—or go and dare the worst, and place everything upon a comprehensible footing?

Yes, he would go! He would see her for the last time. He would know, beyond all doubt, what she intended, what he might expect. He would endure no longer this horrible state of doubt—all should be plain.

Falconbridge acted quickly. He went and ordered his horse—passed through the main apartment without speaking to any one,—and was soon in the saddle. The sky began to grow darker, the distant thunder to mutter; and one or two vivid flashes of lightning darted across the zenith, revealing the lurid depths more plainly. Falconbridge paid no attention to these evidences of the approaching storm. He struck the spur into his horse's sides; and set forward at a wild pace, towards Mr. Argal's.

He soon reached the place, and the fiery light in his eyes deepened and grew more menacing at the sight which greeted him at the door. Lord Fairfax's horse stood there—indeed the Earl had spent the entire afternoon with Miss Argal, her father being again unavoidably absent, and the former excuse of her loneliness having proved successful in retaining his lordship.

Falconbridge set his teeth together like a vice, dismounted, and went and knocked at the door. It was opened by a servant, who did not move aside for the young gentleman.

"Miss Argal?" he said, making a step in advance.

Mistress had told her to say, replied the servant, if Mr. Falconbridge came, that she was engaged and must be excused for not seeing him.

That was all. The words sounded like a death-knell in the young man's ears. He simply bowed his head and departed. He almost staggered as he walked.

His brain was turning round. He mounted his horse again, and set forth on his return. Then he would not even have an opportunity of arriving at a distinct understanding! What she had done once she would do again. He was to be simply dismissed contemptuously, as if unworthy of attention,—as a common individual, whose society was disagreeable. Meanwhile, Lord Fairfax was sitting by the side of the young lady, laughing, it might be, at the disappointment of his rival, and basking in the love-light of her fascinating eyes, and those smiles which now shone for him alone.

The thought maddened the young man almost. He looked over his shoulder at the illuminated window, through which he descried the shadows of the young lady and the Earl, close beside each other. With a muttered imprecation, and clenched hands, the young man struck his horse with the spur, and galloped forward. But he did not proceed far. Just as the house began to disappear in the trees, he reined in his animal and waited—his resolution was taken.

He did not wait long. Lord Fairfax, as we have said, had spent many hours with Miss Argal, and now desired to reach his home before the outburst of the storm. He accordingly bade the young lady farewell. Falconbridge saw the two forms in the brightly illuminated doorway, and mounting his horse, set forward rapidly toward Greenway.

The Earl passed within five paces of Falconbridge, but the darkness, which had descended quickly, completely hid the motionless horse and his rider. It was no part of the young man's design to force an explanation of the character which he intended from the Earl, within sight or hearing of Miss Argal. He accordingly permitted the tall horseman to pass him at full gallop; and then giving rein to Sir John, he followed.

The Earl heard the quick trampling behind him, and wondered at it. The hour and the place were not calculated to remove his suspicions of the pursuer—but he continued his way without noticing the circumstance.

The hoof-strokes rapidly approached—he heard the quick breathing of the animal behind him—then, before he could speak, a violent hand was laid on his bridle, and the horse, suddenly arrested, reared erect almost, quivering with terror.

At the same moment a vivid flash of lightning revealed Falconbridge.

"Sir! Mr. Falconbridge!" exclaimed the Earl, in a voice of utter astonishment and no less indignation, "pray, what is the meaning of this very extraordinary proceeding?"

"I will inform your lordship before our interview ends," returned Falconbridge, in a deep, hollow voice, which his suffering had rendered almost unrecognizable.

"Are you mad, sir?" said the Earl, from the darkness; "release my bridle!"

"Willingly," was the cold reply; "you are no coward, and will not escape me!"

"Escape! coward! You shall answer for those words, sir!"

"I am ready to do so."

"In the darkness, no doubt," returned the Earl, full of contempt and aroused anger, "'tis the favorite cloak of assassins and lunatics."

The words were scarcely uttered when Falconbridge was heard leaping from his horse. Then a quick sound followed—the sound of steel striking against flint—and almost immediately a pile of dry leaves and prairie grass was blazing aloft, illuminating the forest and the threatening figures with its brilliant flame.

"Now," said Falconbridge, in the same hollow voice, "if your lordship is not afraid, you may dismount and listen to my questions."

The word "afraid" acted like magic on Lord Fairfax. He threw himself from the saddle, and gazing at his companion with mingled astonishment and anger, confronted him in the full blaze of the fire.

There was something strange and tragic in the scene as the two men stood thus. The ruddy light streamed full upon them, and they already had their hands upon their swords.

"Speak, sir," said the Earl, controlling his anger; "speak, and explain this astonishing encounter."

"I will do so," said Falconbridge, "and first I will propound a question to you, my lord. Have you visited Miss Argal to-day?"

"Yes, sir."

"Were you not there when I came to the door and asked for the young lady?"

"Yes, sir."

"Are you aware that the young lady is plighted to me?"

"Plighted, sir! No! She is not!"

"Does your lordship design giving me the lie?"

And the young man advanced a step, half drawing his sword.

"Mr. Falconbridge," said the Earl, without moving, "are you a lunatic? I design nothing, sir,—I reply to your question. I say that Miss Argal is not plighted to you, because she assured me that she was not."

"She assured you!"

"Yes, sir."

"My lord, I do not believe you."

The Earl's face flushed crimson.

"That is a deliberate insult!"

"Yes!"

"As such I receive it, and will make you answer for it, sir, at the point of the sword!"

"Good! good!" said Falconbridge, with gloomy pleasure, "now your lordship is talking like a man. I thought, as you had tricked an honest gentleman—supplanted him by craft and cunning in the heart of the only woman he ever loved—taken advantage of your rank and wealth to wile away the affections of a lady plighted to another—I thought, as you had done all this, my lord, pretending all the time that you were the best friend I had,—that you would now discover some means of evading my vengeance—of refusing me reparation at the sword's point! I compliment your lordship—you are not frightened at the sight of cold steel at least—you are aroused by my rudeness and my insults! That is well, sir! Let us end, then, all our differences at once, and on this spot—with no witnesses, no preliminaries, without ceremony!"

And drawing his sword, Falconbridge advanced upon the Earl, whose weapon was also in his hand.

But it was not raised. The momentary madness of anger had disappeared from the mind of Lord Fairfax—he seriously asked himself if he was not dealing with a madman. The additional consideration immediately presented itself, that a combat at such a time and place, without witnesses, would be productive of the most serious results to the survivor. No evidence that the contest was fair and honorable would exist. The simple fact would be that a man was killed; and there were plenty of persons ready to utter the word *murder*. If he killed the young man in that lonely spot, could he produce any evidence of the provocation which had led to the act? Would not many of the miserable newsmongers of the region say that jealousy and rivalry had made him waylay his adversary? As these thoughts passed rapidly through the brain of the Earl, he drew back coldly, and sheathed his weapon.

"Mr. Falconbridge," he said, without moving, as the furious young man advanced straight on him, "if you wish to kill me, do so. I will not even trust my sword in my hand. You may not be aware of the fact, but I am, sir, that the survivor in this combat will be regarded as a murderer. But understand me, sir, I do not refuse your challenge—you have outraged and insulted me in a manner which no gentleman can bear, and by heavens! you shall answer it! Go home, and do all things decently and in order. Procure your second, and write me a formal communication. Do not fear, sir! You have made me as desirous of this encounter as yourself, and I am willing, nay, I insist upon it—my blood or your own must flow, sir!"

With which words the Earl deliberately mounted his horse, and gravely saluting his adversary, continued his road toward Greenway.

Falconbridge gazed after him for a few moments without moving. The excess of anger in his bosom had somewhat moderated, as he listened to the collected voice of the Earl —but it soon returned in full force again. He had thought of Miss Argal and the two shadows on the wall. With lips firmly compressed, and a more fatal determination in his eye than before, he leaped into the saddle, and just as the storm began to roar around him, and extinguish the fire, darted forward in the direction of the Ordinary.

"The net is broken!" he muttered, with a bitter sneer, through his close-set teeth, "but the prey has not escaped!"

XLVII.

PRELIMINARIES.

"DUEL!" said Captain Wagner, when upon the following morning Falconbridge related to him the events of the preceding night—"a duel! and about that woman! By the snout of the old he-dragon! Falconbridge, both you and Fairfax are a bigger pair of lunatics than I took you for."

"So let it be," said Falconbridge, pale and collected as before, "and I do not conceal from you—I cannot—that Miss Argal is connected with the matter."

"*Connected* with it! Falconbridge, don't treat me like an idiot," said the Captain, gloomily, "I am sane in mind, and see somewhat further than my nose."

The young man made no reply.

"I knew it was coming in some form or other—this misery, and wretchedness and blood!" continued the Captain in a sombre tone, "I smelt it in the air—this bloody odor—or the devil take it!"

"You were right in your warning," muttered the young man, with unutterable despair in his altered voice! "Would that I had taken your advice."

"About the nature of panthers, eh?" said Wagner, as grimly as before; "well, I wish you had."

"It would have been well for me."

"But you did not believe me," said the Captain, frowning painfully. "And now see, Falconbridge, how things have turned out. You doubted the miserable old bear who growled at the pretty, variegated animal, with her shining coat, her brilliant eyes, her caresses, and smiles, and bright glances! You were almost ready to strike your sword hilt into the mouth that discoursed on the subject. And now, what has happened? You have felt the sharp claws which I told you of! You have rolled into the mortal hug! The long, glittering teeth which mangled Charles Austin and left him in a pool of blood are gnawing you—you are her prey!"

A groan answered the words. It was irrepressible.

"Yes, yes," murmured the young man with cruel agony, "yes, yes, that's all true—I am lost!"

"Not that either! no, you're not, by the snout of the dragon!" returned the soldier; "things are not that bad at least. Don't cry for spilt milk—look the thing in the face. Let me speak like a doctor, comrade, and probe your wound, though you shudder and cry out. I mean well—do you love that woman still?"

"I know not," was the low reply.

"Then you do love her still. And now what do you design?"

"Nothing."

"That *means* nothing. Are you going to return to her, Falconbridge? Speak, and say if you are going back to crouch at her feet, to be whipped and spit on, and spurned like a dog! Are you going to cry and bewail, and beg her to love you, and make yourself her slave, her menial! Tell me this. Speak frankly, Falconbridge—are you going to return? If so, though I love you as I would love my own boy comrade, I'll wash my hands clear of the business."

"Rest easy," was the reply, in the same low voice, "I shall never see her again—except to get from her the ring which was my mother's."

A contraction of the pale brow and quivering lip betrayed the agony of the speaker, and he was silent. Then he added, in a voice which was almost inaudible,

"My mother gave me that ring on her death-bed, with

her blessing. She cried as she placed it on my finger, and I never removed it until the morning when—I was mad, companion! Don't mind me—you see—I am thinking—of my mother."

He was silent again. The words had forced their way by violence as it were, through the clenched teeth, and the pale lips. The eyes of the young man were dry and fixed—there were no tears in them.

"Falconbridge," said Captain Wagner, with frowning brows, "stop that talk; or you'll make me cry like a baby! To think of all this—of the way you have been tricked—of your honesty and true manliness—by the horns of the devil! it makes me flush—my nerves twitch! Would this woman were a man!"

Indeed a flash of something like fiery rage darted from the eyes of the soldier, and his hand stole down to the hilt of his weapon. Then, as he looked into the countenance of his companion, this flash disappeared; he bent down murmuring: and the old wistful, almost tender expression returned.

"Falconbridge," he said, "my miserable old heart is bleeding for you, as I think of what may happen in the next twenty-four hours. Whatever may be the result of that combat you announce as coming, it must be horrible."

"So let it be."

"There's misery and death in the matter—the blood of one or both of you."

"Doubtless," was the cold reply of the young man, who had completely mastered his emotion, and was calm again.

"Fairfax is an admirable swordsman; I have played with him; and you, do you use the short-sword?"

"Indifferent well."

"That is well—at least there will be a fair and aboveboard fight—no unequal combat. But I know not whether it is not unfortunate after all—if I do, may I be scalped!"

"What do you mean, Captain?" said Falconbridge.

- I mean plainly this—that in case you were ignorant of

the use of the small-sword, or completely out of practice, the affair could not take place—it might easily be arranged—as I hope it will be yet. Without a swordsman for his opponent, the Earl would retire—and you would necessarily do likewise."

"Never! There would remain the pistol!" was the quick reply, between the close-set teeth.

"A villainous weapon! No! If there's a combat it shall be with short-swords. That is fair and honorable—and now what are you going to do, Falconbridge?"

"I shall set out at once to find some gentleman of the neighborhood, who'll act as my second."

"Hum! then you know some?"

"One or two very slightly, but they cannot refuse me."

"Hum! hum!" repeated the Captain, still gloomy and thoughtful, but gazing at his companion from time to time with the strange, wistful glance which we have noticed, "and is there no possible way of accommodating this difference?"

"None on earth. If there is no regular duel, there will be a combat wherever we meet—the blood of myself or Lord Fairfax must flow!"

"Misery! misery!" muttered the soldier; "a wretched business in every way. And pray, why don't you ask me to second you, Falconbridge?"

"Because," said the young man, rewarding the speaker with one of his proud glances, full of thanks and feeling, "because you live with Lord Fairfax, and are naturally *his* second in the matter."

"Nothing of the sort," returned Wagner, coolly; "you're my friend as much as Fairfax, and by the dragon's snout, I'll not have you go looking for a friend, when his lordship can select one out of a hundred. Wait here, companion. I'll return in an hour. Do you promise?"

"You say 'an hour?'"

"Yes."

"I will wait so long, Captain—but sacrifice nothing for

me—have no jar with his lordship. I am not worthy of such friendship, or of such a sacrifice of feeling. I soon pass. See the sun there, comrade! He is mounting the sky—well, it is probable that I'll not see his setting. So be it. I am tired of my life, and death cannot come too quickly. In an hour!"

And with these gloomy words, which affected the rough Borderer strangely, the young man entered the building, and retired to his chamber.

XLVIII.

THE ARRANGEMENT.

THE Captain set out at a thundering gallop, and soon reached Greenway Court. Lord Fairfax met him at the door.

"Ah! welcome Captain Wagner," he said, speaking in his habitual tone of calmness, mingled with gloom; "I was just on the point of sending for you—to the Ordinary, where you have been, I think."

"Yes, my lord. I spent the night there."

"And you saw Mr. Falconbridge?"

"Yes, my lord. This morning."

"Did he speak of the events which occurred last evening?"

"As soon as I descended. I have come as quickly as possible to discuss in turn with your lordship, the arrangement of the whole affair."

The Earl inclined his head gravely, and pointed to a seat, which the Captain assumed.

"Speak, Captain Wagner," he said, calmly and courteously.

"I will do so, my lord," returned the Borderer, "and frankly. It is necessary, in this miserable business between yourself and Falconbridge, that I should act as the friend of your opponent. I like candor, and honesty—I prefer talking it out plainly. I am attached to you, my lord, I am your guest, and owe much to you—but I love this young man as if he was my own blood—my son; and he's a stranger here. Your lordship can find a friend who will be proud to act for you—any one of a dozen in the country near at hand—while Falconbridge is almost alone in this land. I announce this in advance, that no misunderstanding may take place—and now, my lord, I await your pleasure."

"Thanks, Captain Wagner," said the Earl, with a low bow; "it is pleasure indeed which I have experienced as you spoke. I thank you, sir, for this new proof of your confidence and esteem ; you rate me as I wish, sir, as a gentleman and an honest man. I not only acquiesce in your proposal to act for Mr. Falconbridge, and acquit you of all want of friendship in so doing toward myself—I was prepared to insist upon this very course. That we understand and treat each other with this confidence, is another proof of that esteem which I think we feel mutually, sir. Thanks, Captain Wagner."

And the Earl inclined again.

"Now to business," he continued; "I have already dispatched a request to Colonel Carter that he will wait on me here, and I think he will soon come. Do you bear any communication from Mr. Falconbridge?"

"No, my lord, I am not regularly in the position of his second yet, and have avoided becoming such, in order that I might act as the mutual friend of both—bound exclusively to neither."

"As the friend of both?"

"Yes, my lord—and you know that such is the real truth. As a friend then, in no wise connected with either, I ask, is no arrangement possible without bloodshed?"

"None, none at all," returned the Earl, with gloomy calmness; "I see no possibility of such a thing. You have doubtless heard the particulars of the encounter in the wood last night, and may easily understand that any explanation is impossible. Let me speak more plainly, and place the whole in a clear light. I have paid my addresses to Miss Argal in due form, and I think she is willing to become the Countess of Fairfax. Let us not speak further of this private matter, which I mention only to elucidate the rest.

Well, sir, I often saw Mr. Falconbridge at Mr. Argal's, and his attention to the young lady appeared somewhat particular. I accordingly demanded of her the exact character of these attentions, and she assured me that they were merely those of a friend. Was there any contract, definite or implied, between herself and Mr. Falconbridge? I asked. None whatever, was the reply. Why do you frown and sneer so Captain, with your lip?"

"I beg your lordship's pardon—'tis a deplorable habit I have acquired. Pray proceed."

"The rest may be related briefly. Once assured that Mr. Falconbridge had no claims on Miss Argal, and believing that he regarded her in the light of a familiar friend only, I paid her my addresses in a more marked manner. She received them in a manner which induced me to hope that my attentions were agreeable, and my visits became, accordingly, more frequent. Yesterday I spent the afternoon with the young lady. Mr. Falconbridge called, and, to my great surprise, was informed that Miss Argal was engaged, and could not see him. She explained the circumstance by saying that he had grown so moody and disagreeable of late that she must really endeavor to break off her intimacy with him—he made her melancholy. So the subject was forgotten, and I thought no more of the young gentleman until he waylaid me in the wood, and gave me the lie direct."

The Earl flushed as he spoke; but controlled his emotion and added:

"That is all, sir. I avoided a conflict then and there by promising to meet Mr. Falconbridge at another and more favorable time. You must see, Captain Wagner, that any overtures from myself are utterly impossible."

The soldier knit his brows and looked more gloomy than ever.

"It's a deadly looking mixture, or I'm a dandy!" he muttered, "and unless Falconbridge will move in the matter, all's over."

"What do you say, Captain?"

"Nothing much, my lord. I will go and see Falconbridge, and return as soon as possible, either bearing you the terms of an arrangement of the affair, or delivering his cartel."

"That is my duty," returned the Earl. "Mr. Falconbridge will thus have choice of weapons, time and place."

"There will be no trouble about that, my lord; now I'll go and see what I can do."

With these words the soldier mounted his horse, and returned rapidly to the Ordinary. All his attempts to move the young man were utterly in vain—the arguments of the Borderer fell back, so to speak, from his iron resolution, like waves from an ocean rock. At the end of an hour there was nothing remaining but the question of time, place and weapons. The Captain returned, and found Colonel Carter at Greenway, and with this gentleman he now discussed, formally, as the second of Falconbridge, the terms of the combat.

It was arranged that it should take place on the same evening at a spot within the Fort Mountain, which was secluded and favorable for the purpose, and then the Captain returned to the Ordinary.

He had never been more gloomy.

XLIX.

THE COMBAT.

AS the hour which had been fixed for the combat drew near, the four men entered the narrow defile of the Fort Mountain, and approached the secluded spot which had been selected.

They dismounted, tied their horses to the hanging boughs, and advanced slowly to the arena.

Captain Wagner and his principal returned the low salute of Lord Fairfax, and his friend, with one equally courteous, and then the seconds approached each other, and conversed for some moments in a low tone, which was inaudible to their companions.

The preliminaries were soon arranged, and the swords were produced and measured. They tallied exactly in length, and were of the same weight and temper. A nod from the Captain testified to his satisfaction.

At a sign from the seconds, the Earl and Falconbridge then removed their coats and waistcoats, and advanced to a spot indicated. They halted, saluted each other, and received the weapons from the hands of Captain Wagner and Colonel Carter.

"The terms of the combat are as follows, gentlemen," said the Captain. "You shall engage, and so proceed for as long a time as seems proper. But in no case shall any personal collision of bodies take place; there shall be no clutching, and no resort to other weapons than the shortsword. Should either weapon break, or the foot of either party slip, or stumble, the engagement shall terminate for the time. I will give the signal by raising my hand."

At the appointed signal, the two men advanced upon each other, and the weapons clashed together, the light of the sinking sun darting vividly from their burnished surfaces.

Both were excellent swordsmen, and soon felt that all their science would be necessary. The combat was thus guarded at first, and consisted of a series of fencing lunges, rather than rapid thrusts, as though each were feeling the wrist of his adversary. Falconbridge was the more active and supple of the two—the Earl stronger and heavier in his fence. Still, as the combat grew more excited, neither had gained any advantage—and the blood of both gradually grew heated. The Earl glared at his enemy, and a spot in each cheek began to glow; on his forehead the huge veins became black. Falconbridge was pale, but the fire in his eyes contradicted his apparent calmness: his lips were set together like iron.

Despite his most powerful exertions the Earl could not drive the young man back an inch; and his most deadly lunges were regularly parried. The old swordsman grew fiery and dangerous. His cheeks glowed as if from the light of a conflagration—he braced his gaunt frame until it resembled a bundle of steel springs, and advanced step by step upon Falconbridge. He did not yield or give ground—the points of the weapons played in the very faces of the combatants—the hilts were almost wrapped around each other.

Then, in spite of the exclamations and protests of the seconds, who hastened quickly toward them, a desperate, hand to hand, stabbing-match, rather than sword-play, commenced. Both the Earl and Falconbridge received slight wounds—but the sight of blood only enraged them more bitterly.

In another moment each would have mortally wounded his adversary, and so brought the combat to an end, when suddenly the two men were dragged violently asunder, and the Wizard of the Massinutton interposed his tall form, shuddering with strange emotion, between the adversaries. The respective seconds of the combatants had rushed forward, crying, "Gentlemen! gentlemen! this must cease! no poniard fight!"—but the towering resident of the Fort Mountain had forestalled them. He had seen the party when they entered the gorge of the valley, and divining their intention, hastened quickly toward them. He had arrived in time, and now stood between the hot swordsmen, his form towering high above even that of the Earl— his face, generally so pale, flushed with tragic emotion.

The Earl gazed at him angrily, and raised his head haughtily as their eyes encountered.

"Pray, what is the meaning of this interruption, sir?" he said. "Are you aware that you peril your life by this proceeding!"

"Yes, my lord," said the wizard, still agitated in every muscle of his tall, nervous frame by the singular tremor we have noticed. "Your weapon was within an ace of penetrating my breast; and Mr. Falconbridge also nearly struck me. But that is little!"

"Your meaning, sir! Stand back!"

"I will not! You may kill me, if the act will be productive of satisfaction to your lordship; but you shall not even do that until you hear what I came to say to you."

There was something so resolute and gloomy in the voice of the old man, and his eyes burned with such significance beneath his bushy white brows, that the Earl unconsciously dropped the point of his sword, and was silent.

"Your proceeding is extraordinary, very extraordinary, sir," he replied, coldly, "but I respect your age, and say no more. I only request that you will communicate to me speedily what you design to inform me of—I know not what it is—then we will proceed!"

"It is necessary," returned the wizard, "that your lordship should listen to it in private."

"Impossible, sir!" the Earl replied, impatiently shaking his head: "I cannot, and will not leave this spot until this matter is terminated!"

"You must!" was the resolute answer. "Yes, my lord, I tell you, and I know what I say—I tell you that you must hear me speak, and privately. This combat shall not continue, if it becomes necessary for me to interpose my own body between your swords."

"You speak in riddles, sir!" exclaimed the Earl; "stand back!"

"Strike, then, gentlemen," replied the wizard, calmly folding his arms, and not moving from the spot which he occupied between the combatants; "if you wish to shed blood, shed my own to commence with. I swear to you that nothing shall move me but the death-blow!"

And he confronted the Earl with a majesty and determination in eye, lip, and bearing, which produced an effect even on his angry opponent.

"Well, have your wish, sir!" said Lord Fairfax, frowning, "with the permission of Captain Wagner, I will retire for a moment, to the distance of ten paces—is it permitted, sir?"

"It is permitted, my lord," said the Captain.

"Well, let us make haste, sir," said the Earl: and sheathing his sword, he followed his companion, with quick steps. They had proceeded about ten paces, and the wizard had commenced speaking in a low, guarded tone, when the Earl was observed to start violently. As he did so, his head turned quickly, and he fixed upon Falconbridge one of those glances of lightning, which, on extraordinary occasions, made his eyes resemble flaming brands. His face was deadly pale, and the contracted lips revealed his white teeth set like a vice together. He no longer opposed the will of his companion, evidently—they walked a hundred yards, talking in a low, agitated manner, and finally disappeared behind a huge mass of rock, covered with moss and evergreens, which rose on the declivity of the mountain.

The three gentlemen who had been left by themselves in this unceremonious manner, waited patiently for a quarter of an hour. Then they began to look curiously toward the rocky screen. Another quarter of an hour passed slowly away, and Colonel Carter, at the request of Captain Wagner, had just gone to summon the Earl, when the two men were seen returning.

An extraordinary change had taken place in the bearing and appearance of Lord Fairfax. When he left the party, he had carried his head proudly erect, his eyes were flashing with anger, and the aroused thirst for blood—he had resembled a warhorse, snuffing the odor of battle, and champing at the bit which restrains him. Now, all this had disappeared. His shoulders were drooping—his cheeks were pale: his eyes, of late so fiery, were full of wistful light; and he gazed upon his companions with an expression of absent wonder which impressed them with the most vivid astonishment. Especially did they experience a sentiment amounting to stupefaction, almost, when they saw the Earl glance toward Falconbridge. In that glance there was no longer any enmity, any anger—all had vanished. It was a gaze almost tender in its character; and plainly an unconscious one to the Earl. The young man wondered at it, but replied only by a look haughtier than before, and calmly tested the metal of his weapon by pressing the point upon his boot.

Lord Fairfax soon recovered from his fit of absence, however, and by a great effort, summoned his habitual calmness.

He approached Captain Wagner, and Falconbridge, and bowing with grave courtesy, said :

"This affair cannot proceed, gentlemen, and the singular circumstances accompanying the fact, is the entire silence which I am compelled to observe at present upon the character of the considerations which render a further combat impossible."

Falconbridge flushed, and grasped his sword in a menacing manner.

"I am aware," continued the Earl, in the same calm voice, "that my words are enigmas, but I cannot prevent that. I will make any apology, or follow any course which Mr. Falconbridge may see fit to demand."

The seconds and Falconbridge greeted these words with incredulous wonder; but the Earl did not seem to observe it, and added :

"I propose, in all that relates to an affair in which Mr. Falconbridge and myself hold the position of rival claimants, to withdraw my pretensions, and retire from the field —his interests shall no longer suffer from my presence—and I am prepared to make him any apology which he requires, for anything in which he may have thought himself wronged, by any act of my own."

The words were uttered as calmly and coldly as before, in spite of a faint tinge which rose slowly to the cheek, and having finished them, the Earl bowed low and was silent. The seconds and Falconbridge had listened with an amazement greater than before; but this expression in the eyes of Wagner was succeeded by another of unmistakable pleasure. As the Earl ended his address, he bowed low and replied :

"As the friend of Mr. Falconbridge, I accept your lordship's proposal. We shall waive all further explanations or discussions, resting content with the general disclaimer, and offer which has been made. You will permit me, my lord, to say on the part of Mr. Falconbridge, whom I represent, that this proposition is no less characteristic of your lordship's magnanimity, than of your fearless disregard of appearances. And so, gentlemen, the matter's at an end—the fight's over—if it's not, I'm a crop-eared dandy!"

With this joyous outburst, the Captain twirled his moustache violently, and picking up the coats of the combatants, handed them to those gentlemen, with an air full of grace and politeness. With a clouded, and gloomy brow, Falconbridge yielded to his representative, and the whole party were soon again in the saddle, on their way back to the Lowland.

The wizard was slowly retracing his steps up the mountain.

L.

HOW FALCONBRIDGE RECÓVERED HIS MOTHER'S RING.

ON the day after the events which have just been narrated, Falconbridge set out from the Ordinary to visit Miss Argal for the last time.

We know the design of his visit. All was over—there was no longer any hope—the drama was played—he had fallen in the contest: but he must look upon her face once more for a moment; he must recover the plain gold ring which had belonged to his mother, and remained in the possession of the young lady.

As he thus drew near to the secluded dwelling in which he had spent so many happy hours, a painful and cruel shadow swept across the broad brow of the young man. His shoulders drooped; his lip quivered; and the heavy-looking eyes were half veiled by the long lashes which almost reposed upon the pallid cheeks. Falconbridge was passing through that baptism of silent agony which sprinkles the hair of youth with gray.

As if to mock him, the face of nature was serene and benignant. The chill winds had passed away—and that season which is called the "Indian Summer" had arrived. The landscape was still, and bathed in imperceptible floods of vapor—every outline was rounded, every angle had disappeared—the soft mellow haze rested like a veil of gauze on the distant mountains, the prairie and the forest. A dreamy and mild influence seemed to pervade the whole scene, and the genius of silence and repose was enthroned, where lately the fresh breezes of October careered onward, rustling the dry leaves.

But the young man scarcely observed the change. His own thoughts made the world in which he moved. An irresistible sadness invaded, and took possession of him; and he went along, unconscious of the landscape around him, dead to all but his own sombre meditations.

When Sir John stopped at the door, now so well known and familiar, his master looked up with a vague, absent wonder. Then slowly dismounting, he affixed his bridle to a bough, and approached.

He knocked at the door—no one answered. But hearing the sound of voices in the apartment to the right, which was used as a sitting-room, he turned the knob, and entered.

The sight which greeted him sent the blood violently to his heart, and an irresistible shudder ran through his frame. He leaned against the frame-work of the door for support, as though his limbs were about to fail him.

In the middle of the apartment Mr. Argal was holding, with a vigorous grasp, both wrists of his daughter, and endeavoring to soothe her. It was the appearance of the young lady, however, which made Falconbridge recoil, shuddering. She was scarcely recognizable. Her dress was in rude disorder—her black hair was hanging down on her naked shoulders in tangled masses, and the fiery dark eyes which burned beneath her knit brows, were filled with an expression of rage and wildness which was terrible. The small pearly teeth had bit the writhing lip until the blood flowed—and in every muscle of her body, as in her face, the visitor discerned an awful distortion.

It was evidently as much as Mr. Argal could do to hold her. The nervous force which she displayed was wonderful. The soft round arms seemed endowed with the strength of a giant—and in spite of his most powerful exertions, the writhing form almost escaped from her father's grasp.

"I tell you!" she cried hoarsely, and in a voice which the young man did not recognize as her own; "I tell you I saw him last night! He was lying in his blood! His eyes called to me—I will go to him!"

"There, daughter, you are unwell," muttered the heavy-hearted father, in a voice of deep anguish; "don't talk so, and sit down."

"I will not! I will go! There, the eyes again!"

"It is your fancy, my poor child."

"My fancy! It is false! I tell you there he is looking at me—there is blood on his bosom—blood for me to wipe away!"

"My poor child"——

"Let me go!"

The words were followed by a superhuman effort to disengage herself; but the iron grasp was not relaxed.

"I loved him! I never loved any one before! I loved him with my whole heart—and he is dead! That man killed him—he is gone!"

"No, my child," murmured the poor father, who had taken no notice of the young man's entrance, "he is not dead—there he stands."

"Yes, I see him—it is his spirit! He is coming like Charles Austin to call me; Edmund! Edmund! I am coming!"

And again the terrible struggle commenced. The sharp, white teeth caught the crimson lip and gnawed it cruelly—the round, supple form writhed violently in the grasp of Mr. Argal. The paroxysm was succeeded by an interval of comparative quiet, and the frame of the young lady exhibited evidences of exhaustion. A few more struggles ensued, and then they ceased. Her features relaxed; the burning eyes filled with leaden langour; the form drooped slowly, and murmuring, "I loved him only!" the girl fainted in the arms of her father.

Without speaking, he bore her to the sofa, and placed her unresisting figure on the cushioned seat. In a moment she revived, but it was only to burst into tears, and sob hopelessly—she was plainly unconscious of any one's presence. Mr. Argal gazed at her for a few moments, with an expression of wretchedness, mixed with tenderness unutterable: then he turned and approached the young man.

"You are shocked at this terrible scene, I see plainly, sir," he said in a low, collected voice; "and there is little cause for wonder in the fact. Pray retire with me—I have a few words to say to you."

As he spoke, Mr. Argal summoned a maid, who went quietly to the side of her mistress with the air of one who was quite familiar with such scenes, and then the two men went out into the small porch. The youth walked in a dream as it were—his mind was struggling—he could not think connectedly. Mr. Argal placed his hand, by an unconscious movement, upon his heart, and mastering his agitation, said in a low voice, full of gloomy sorrow :

"Mr. Falconbridge, you have become the depositary of a terrible secret of my family. Do you understand what you have just witnessed, sir?"

"No," came from the white lips, in a tone almost inaudible, "I do not, sir."

"I will explain it. My daughter is mad."

The words sent a shudder through the frame of Falconbridge, and his face turned paler than that of a corpse, but he said nothing.

"The fit seized her to-day, sir," continued Mr. Argal, suppressing a groan; "it was probably occasioned by the affair between yourself and Lord Fairfax, which the servants repeated."

The young man drew a long, deep breath, but was still silent.

"And now, sir," continued Mr. Argal, slowly recovering his calmness, but speaking in a voice of heart-broken woe; "and now, sir, I owe you a few words of explanation, if only to vindicate my own character in this affair, from the imputations which must otherwise rest upon me. I will be plain, I will conceal nothing—for I speak to a gentleman, and a man of honor. I will keep back no particular. My daughter has been subject to attacks of insanity, sir, from her childhood. It was not a defect of her birth, but occasioned by a dangerous fall from a fruit-tree, which inflicted a deep wound upon her head, and affected the brain. Soon after this incident, I observed the indications of mental disease. Her character, which had before been as open and ingenuous as the day, became secretive and subtile. She would look sidewise and watch the persons with whom she conversed, and store away in hidden places little objects which she had taken. Then, as the years passed on, she changed more and more—she became cruel and pitiless, she, my own child! who had been a very angel of goodness and tenderness—whose heart would have bled at the suffering of the least insect—she grew hard and unpitying!"

A low moan accompanied the words of the poor father; he controlled his agony with difficulty, but resumed:

"The strange lustre you must have seen in my child's eyes, sir, then appeared. They glittered with a morbid light—an unnatural, insane light! It was the misfortune of a poor youth to be attracted by their brightness—he loved her, and when she dismissed him, at the moment when one of her paroxysms was approaching, he put an end to himself!"

Again the speaker paused, and a woful contraction of the lip showed the struggle which he had passed through before revealing these things.

"Well, to go on, sir. When she heard of the youth's death, she was seized with a fit of madness. I passed through a scene like that which you have witnessed to-day; it made me twenty years older. But it ended: and my child returned to herself again; to wring her hands and weep, and exclaim that his death was caused by her act. She wrote to the youth's brother and rival, a full history of her mental aberration, and requested him to never approach her again. So that terminated, and soon afterward I removed hither. I now come to the scenes connected with yourself, sir; and I acknowledge in advance that I have been guilty of a criminal weakness. I saw your attentions to my daughter, and feared the result. But I could not speak! I should have done so, as a man of common honesty—that is true, sir—but I could not! Look at my face, Mr. Falconbridge! See the vulture that is gnawing me! I have been false to you—but I could not speak! Oh, sir! may you never know what it is to feel this awful shame!— to be drawn one way by your honor, and another way by love for a poor insane child! I could not reveal her awful secret, degrade her in all eyes, make her name the laughing stock or the horror of every one! I could not brand my own child in your eyes with the stigma of madness! So I paltered, sir, with my terrible responsibility. I said to myself that you were only a youth, in the region for a short time; that you would soon go, and our existence be forgotten. My poor child denied any engagement between you— I know not with what truth—I do not ask, sir. Then Lord Fairfax appeared: she attracted his attention, and his admiration. This very day I had intended to go and tell him what I have told you, sir, if it killed me. That is all. I have spoken, Mr. Falconbridge, with an effort, and laboring under an agony of feeling which no words can describe! It is little to declare to you that my heart is broken—but that is beside the question. I know not whether I should ever have found courage to tell you all, if you had not chanced to come when you did. But you know all now. I have striven to show you that in concealing my child's condition I did not act with deliberate dishonor, to entrap you. Before my Maker, sir, I solemnly declare that I am guiltless at least in this. I was weak, my heart was torn with shame and anguish—I could not speak! I should have fled from the country with my daughter on the eve of her nuptials— that is all!"

With heaving bosom and quivering lips, Mr. Argal was silent for some moments. Then he added:

"I have now told you everything, sir, and I feel less shame than before. In a few weeks I go with my poor child from this region—in some distant land we may bury our shame and suffering. Without her, I should have no life—she is dearer to me than all the world. Speak well of her, Mr. Falconbridge—she is weak, not sinful!—or if that is impossible, say nothing! God has heavily stricken her, and her lot has been a terrible one—do not add to its darkness by your enmity or contempt! After all, sir, however much she may have wronged you, she is a woman, a mere girl, and should excite your pity! You heard her broken words—in her madness—she loved you—I pray you, sir, to forgive my poor child and me."

The broken and agitated voice died away, and no sound was heard but the flutter of a single leaf, which parted from a bough of the oak above, and pattered down. The young man remembered that sound afterwards, and shuddered at it. To the struggling words of the sorrowful speaker he made no immediate reply; his eyes were full of tears, his lips refused their office. At last he mastered his emotion in a partial degree, and in a tone almost inaudible, said:

"Thanks for your confidence, Mr. Argal. I am so far from blaming you for not revealing all before, that I honor and respect your deep love and tenderness, and think I would have acted as you did. You know me well enough to believe me when I say that all this shall be locked up forever in my breast. I need scarcely add that no word against you or your daughter shall ever pass my lips. From my heart, from my soul, from the depths of my soul, sir, I pity and sympathize with you! Your daughter is sacred to me—it is as a child that I shall regard her—my heart is broken like yours, but I blame no one. In the presence of that God, sir, who afflicted your child, I swear to guard her name from reproach or wrong. 'I have nothing to forgive; if I had, I should forgive her."

He held out his hand as he spoke, and a long pressure was exchanged. As the two hands were thus clasped, a low sob at the elbow of the young man made him start and tremble. He turned and saw Miss Argal standing motionless in the doorway, and holding toward him his mother's ring. Her face was wet with tears—her eyes swam as she gazed at him; she murmured, rather than said:

"This is your ring, sir—I have deceived you. Will you forgive me?"

The words were followed by a quiver of the bleeding lip, and bursting into tears, the young lady placed her handkerchief to her eyes, and went hastily to her chamber.

Falconbridge stood looking after her, with the ring in his hand, and never did the countenance of a human-being express more unutterable anguish. He leaned against the pillar of the portico for support, and uttered a groan of such despairing wretchedness, that it seemed to tear its way from the very depths of his being, and compress the woe of years into a second.

Then, making a slight movement with his head toward Mr. Argal, he slowly went and mounted his horse. The bridle lay untouched upon the neck of the animal, and Falconbridge did not speak to or direct him.

Sir John took the road at a gallop toward the Ordinary. The rider seemed to be dreaming. His shoulders bent forward; his chin rested on his breast; from time to time he passed his hand wearily across his forehead, and gazed absently around him.

The animal continued his headlong gallop.

Half a mile from the Ordinary, the young man reeled in the saddle. Overcome by vertigo, he would have fallen the next moment from his flying animal, when the bridle was suddenly seized, the horse thrown on his haunches, and the arms of Captain Wagner caught the drooping form.

12

"So it ends!" cried the gloomy and sneering voice of the soldier, "all is over!"

Two words replied to him, as Falconbridge fainted—two words, in an accent of unspeakable pity :

"Poor child!"

LI.

THE APOLOGY.

TWO or three days have passed. It is a beautiful morning of the "Indian Summer" as before. The landscape of mountain and valley is reposing beneath the mellow haze; and the air has that dreamy and delightful softness which inclines the heart to reverie.

In the large room of Greenway Court, Lord Fairfax is conversing with George and Cannie. The youth had brought the girl behind him from the Fort on the preceding evening—they had spent the night—and before setting out to return, Cannie examined the objects around her, with evident interest.

George was gazing at her with unconscious earnestness. His affection for the girl had grown deeper and stronger. As he came to know her better, the rare charms of her mind and heart had enthralled him. Her goodness and simplicity, and absence of all littleness, irresistibly attracted his frank nature; and the unconscious refinement and grace of the little maiden, riveted the influence which her character had exerted upon the boy. He thus gazed at her with a fondness which was plainly uncontrollable, and the Earl smiled with melancholy pleasure as he saw the youth's secret. His countenance wore the old expression of sorrowful thought, but there was nothing cynical in it now. The grim look had disappeared, and though cheerfulness was not there, still the face was more pleasant for the change. He leaned back in his arm-chair, caressing with one hand the solemn head of a huge deer-hound at his side, and his gaze wandered absently but pleasantly from George to Cannie.

"So, you like my house, Cannie?" he said; "my old hunting-lodge?"

"Yes, sir—oh, yes, I mean my lord," returned the girl; "I have been looking at the books and the pictures and all. They remind me of home."

"Of home? Do you remember your home? Where was that?"

"In the Low Country, sir. But I was born in England."

"And you do not remember England?"

"Very slightly, sir. I look upon Virginia as my home, and love it—because grandpapa is with me. He is all I have."

The eyes of George seemed to contradict this statement, but he said nothing. Then a sigh from the Earl made him turn his head,

"You are right, my child," said the old nobleman, gazing at Cannie with wistful tenderness; "our real home is the land where the heart finds its rest. 'Tis a terrible disease, what is called home-sickness, Cannie, and I've felt it, as many others have done."

The quick look of sympathy in the eyes of the girl seemed to touch the Earl, and he continued in the same tone of melancholy softness:

"I was born and reared in England, and you see that I am living now in another land. I long sometimes to look upon the familiar old scenes, and pluck a daisy from the sod of old England, my mother soil. I remember the same feeling in a nobleman of my acquaintance who was exiled by political troubles to France. His name was Henry St. John, a very brilliant person, whom you, George, have read of, I am sure, and it may be Cannie, also, though he's long dead, and she's very young. I had known him in London, and spent many delightful hours with him—for his conversation was wonderfully attractive. His favorite topic was the superiority of a strong mind to misfortune—the strength he possessed to bear up against obloquy and exile, sustained by his own thoughts and his philosophy. Well, see how it ended. I went to visit him in France, and a more unhappy personage I have rarely seen. All his philosophy was gone—he had yielded. 'The burst of the cloud had gone near to overwhelm him,' he said one day: and he looked as he spoke toward the cliffs of England, as a child does toward its mother. He never rested in his efforts to regain his home—and sometimes I think I am his shadow in the New World. I would return, and lay my bones in the soil where my forefathers sleep."

The Earl was silent again, absently caressing the head of the great deer-hound.

"All is the same, however, my dear," he added, in a moment, "under the blue skies of home, or the stormy clouds of distant countries, the one thing is to be honest and true. One looks down on us who governs and directs for the best—do you not feel that?"

"Oh, yes, sir—my lord," returned Cannie, to whose eyes the sad tones of the old cavalier had brought tears, "indeed I do, and that is enough to make us happy, I am sure! In the mountains or the lowlands, He is still beside us. Whether we are buried in the sands, or the ocean, it is still the same—as Mr. Falconbridge said, you remember, George."

"Mr. Falconbridge?" murmured the Earl; "do you know him, then, Cannie?"

"Oh, yes, sir—he has been to see us, and I could not help loving him. His face is so kind and true-looking—and when he smiles I feel as if it was sunshine."

"That is true," said the Earl, with a bright light in his eyes which made his face pleasant to behold. "Mr. Falbridge is truly a gentleman."

"Oh, I'm sure he is. I loved him from the first moment I saw him."

"He loved you as well," said a voice behind the speaker.

And Falconbridge, who had entered without attracting attention, inclined his head to the company. In a moment the girl, by an irresistible impulse, had risen to her feet, and caught in her own warm little hand, the thin hand of the young man. Then she gazed into his eyes with a wistful look, and said:

"You are very, very pale, sir."

Indeed the young man resembled a ghost rather than a human being. All the laughing pride of the eye and lip had vanished; his cheeks had lost their bloom, and were falling away; an unspeakable sadness stamped his entire countenance and bearing; in a few days he seemed to have lived twenty years. As he smiled now, and pressed the little hand in his own, there was something so touching and pathetic in his appearance, that Cannie could not restrain her tears.

"There, there, don't cry, my dear," said Falconbridge; "you distress me. The change in my appearance moves you, I suppose—but 'tis nothing. I have been somewhat unwell, but am better. I trust your lordship is well."

And the speaker inclined low, with stately courtesy, before the Earl.

"Thanks—yes, sir—very well," replied Lord Fairfax, who had scarcely moved, and still regarded his visitor with evident agitation. But there was nothing hostile in his emotion. On the contrary a strange earnestness and softness characterized his bearing, as he pointed to a seat, and bowed low to his guest.

"Many thanks, my lord," returned Falconbridge, "but my visit must be brief. In three days I shall leave this region, and I come to make an explanation to your lordship."

The Earl, still singularly agitated, glanced uneasily at George and Cannie. The two young persons rose with quick courtesy, and would have retired, but Falconbridge arrested them by a movement of his hand.

"No, do not retire," he said; "my explanation is not a private one—and I have entire confidence in you both, George and Cannie. Pray remain, then—and now, my lord, for my business. I have come hither to say, like an honest gentleman, that I have wronged you, and to beg you to pardon me. I will imitate the reserve of your lordship on the mountain yonder, and add in general terms what I mean. I accused you, in my heart, and to your face, in the forest there, of an unworthy and dishonorable action. I insulted and outraged you, and forced you to meet me in single combat. I am truly glad at the issue of that business, for I wronged you, not intentionally, but no less really. Since that time, I have discovered my error, and your innocence. I have been ill, and had time to reflect. I have risen from my sick couch to come and say to your lordship, that I am sorry for my words and for my actions—to declare my conviction of your irreproachable honor—and to entreat your pardon and forgiveness."

With these words Falconbridge bowed low again, and was silent.

"I have nothing to forgive, sir," replied the Earl, almost eagerly; "I should rather sue to you—for I have wounded you, I fear, deeply. On my honor, sir, the act was not malicious—I pray you to forget all, and receive my hand."

There was something earnest and noble in the voice of the Earl as he thus spoke, and a slight color came to the cheek of the young man. He took the proffered hand, and the eyes of the strange rivals met in one long look of deep meaning.

"I shall now beg your lordship's permission to retire," said Falconbridge. "I am not well, and the ride hither has fatigued me. As I have declared, in three days I leave this country. This will be my farewell to your lordship."

Then turning to George and Cannie, he held out his

hand, with the melancholy smile which had excited the child's tears. She cried again as she took it, and George bit his lip to conceal his emotion.

"I am glad to have seen your kind face again," he said to Cannie; and yours, George, though I trust you'll come to see me before I go. And now, good-bye. I salute your lordship, and bid you farewell."

In spite of the Earl's hospitable invitations to remain, which were uttered with great earnestness, the young man then departed; and soon afterwards George and Cannie set out on their return to the mountain.

"In three days!" murmured the Earl,—"then he goes in three days! But he shall not!—no, he shall not! How noble he is, and how pale! Poor boy, my heart ached when he smiled as he did. In three days? We shall see!"

As the Earl spoke thus, Captain Wagner hastily entered the apartment.

LII.

THE COURIER.

THE appearance of the Borderer indicated news of importance.

"What has occurred?" said the Earl.

"The rascals are coming!" returned Wagner, throwing his hat on the table. "At least they are on the way, my lord—the Injuns!"

"Ah! What of them? What news of them?"

"A plenty, and too much. A courier is following me, and he'll soon relate all to your lordship. Well, I think we'll have stirring times at last. We'll eat 'em, or be eat by 'em, or I'm a dandy!"

As the Borderer spoke, the sound of a horse's hoofs was heard, and in a few minutes a roughly-clad settler from the frontier entered, and bowed low to the Earl. His tidings were soon imparted. The Indians had crossed the Alleghanies two days before, in large numbers, and had laid waste the entire South Branch manor, killing women and children, and even attacking Fort Pleasant and Edwards' Fort, on Cacaphon. In all directions, homes were blazing, fields on fire, the dead bodies of the settlers and their families were stretched across a hundred thresholds, along the line of march of the savages. The incursion had been so sudden that no preparation, on the part of the borderers, had opposed it; and the whole region west of the town of Winchester was helpless at the feet of the advancing enemy. Such was the information of the courier, who gave his account with long-drawn breaths, as one laboring under great exhaustion. In fact he had ridden night and day, and was worn out. Old John speedily took charge of him, in obedience to the direction of his master, and the Captain and Lord Fairfax were left alone together.

"Well," said the Earl, his swarthy face glowing; "well, Captain, there seems every probability of your prediction being verified. We'll have fighting, and that speedily. What are the defences of the region immediately west of Winchester?"

"Few or none," returned the soldier, knitting his brow and reflecting: "there's Pugh's, and Enoch's and Parker's Forts, with Edwards', the strongest. Further west, toward Fort Cumberland, are Pearsall's and Sellar's, and Fort Pleasant, which is well fortified. But these are passed. Its dooms unlucky, my lord—but these worthies seem to have heard nothing of the inroad until it was on 'em, and the very devil will be to pay, or I'm a dandy! Where's the map? I know the region by heart, but may forget some places?"

The Earl drew it out of the drawer, and they were soon poring over it. The result was discouraging. The forts mentioned by the Captain were all regularly laid down, but no others.

"There are plenty of cabins," said the Borderer, frowning thoughtfully; "but they are shells that the first blow will smash. What remains? I tell your lordship I have never been taken more aback. Messengers must, however, be sent immediately throughout the river counties. I'll assemble the hunters and settlers around here myself, and then let the bloody scoundrels look out. I have said I'd eat their carcasses, and I'll do it, or my name's not Wagner!"

A quick discussion of the details then took place, and the plan of operations was agreed upon. In two hours couriers were departing in all directions, and Captain Wagner himself was scouring the country, to assemble the settlers in the immediate vicinity.

On the next evening a messenger arrived with the intelligence that the band of Indians had gone in an opposite direction, toward the Potomac, plundering and burning on their march.

"I'll go after 'em," said the Captain, who had returned from his long ride; "the boys will assemble at Winchester to-morrow, and I'll take command, as your lordship has directed."

"Such is my wish, Captain," returned the Earl, "and thus we may take breath for a moment."

"And I'll take some Jamaica, with your permission, my lord, or zounds! without your permission, for I'm broke down! I've been in the saddle till I feel as if I grew there. I'm bow-legged, or the devil take it!"

Having swallowed his Jamaica, the Captain became more tranquil, and listened in silence to the Earl.

"And now for a private matter of my own," said the Earl. "Where is Mr. Falconbridge, Captain?"

"At the Ordinary, my lord."

"Does he return to the Lowland?"

"He! return to the Lowland! Who? Falconbridge? You don't know him, my lord. He's a good heart of oak, and you ought to have see his face when he heard of the killing of the women and children! It was a glorious face, or I'm a dandy! The very devil in his eyes. You don't know that man as I know him. He is one of the kindest and softest-hearted fellows in the world, but I'd rather go through fire than arouse him! He go to the Lowland, with those women and children kicking and squalling over there, as the bloody scoundrels slit their windpipes? I fancy it! No! He'll be duly in the ranks to-morrow, and I wouldn't give a sixpence for the red devil that meets him!"

"Good, good!" said the Earl, with glowing cheeks. "That is like him, Captain. I knew it—I was sure of it; but he is weak, you know—he has been sick."

And a strange pathos was discernible in the tones of the Earl.

"Sick or well, he is with us," returned the Captain. "Your lordship seems really interested in him."

"I have reason to be."

"How so?"

The Earl did not immediately reply. He mused and hesitated. Then suddenly his irresolution disappeared, and turning to the soldier, he said:

"Captain, did you not think the scene on the Fort Mountain, on the day of our duel, a very strange one?"

"A perfect puzzle!—a mystery! I've been racking my brain to understand it ever since."

"Well, I'll tell you what it meant," replied the Earl, "if you will make me two promises."

"Two promises, my lord?"

"Very simple ones. The first is to guard sacredly what I tell you, and the other is to go this evening, in spite of your fatigue, and bring Falconbridge hither to sleep. I must see him."

"I promise both, my lord—and you know me. When a thing is told to me, I put it under lock and key, and the rack couldn't get me to tell it. I don't talk in my sleep, and I've carried this hatred of the practice of gossiping so far that I've often forgot things on purpose. I knew a man once who always, when he got a letter headed 'burn this,' lit one corner of it to read by. He read the last line as the flame burnt his fingers. That's my habit. I don't repeat—I forget."

The Earl nodded, well satisfied, and said:

"I can trust you, Captain Wagner. I give you a mark of this entire confidence now. I wish you to watch over and guard the person whom you know as Falconbridge, and to explain this request, I am about to give you a brief history. Are we wholly alone?"

The Captain rose and examined the doors and windows, then returned to his seat.

"Completely, my lord; and now I listen. 'The person I know as Falconbridge?' Hum!"

The Earl looked into the fire for some moments, with thoughtful gravity; then fixing his melancholy eyes upon the Borderer, commenced the narrative which he had promised.

LIII.

THE BALL IN THE RIGHT SHOULDER.

"CAPTAIN," said the Earl, with that look of deep sadness which made his countenance at times so touching, "my life has been more or less unhappy from its commencement, but I think I have suffered, within the last month—nay, within a few days—as much as, or more, than in many years before. I have learned what is one of the most sorrowful things in all this world—that much happiness has been wrongfully denied me by one of my fellow-creatures—that I have sighed where I might have smiled—that the heaven above me has been obscured and gloomy, when the simple act of a simple mortal might have dissipated every cloud, and made the sun shine brightly for me.

"But to drop these generalities and come to my narrative. It will not be long, but shall contain the truth and the whole truth. Men at my age do not make intimate confidences for the pleasure of talking—and yet I experience something like pleasure, sir, in the thought that I am about to unburden my mind of some events and thoughts which have long oppressed it. I do not conceal, nevertheless, that I have my own personal object in this matter; I repeat what I said but now, that I wish you to watch over the person whom you know by the name of Falconbridge—with him is connected all that I shall say.

"Listen, sir. I was born at the end of the last century, at my father's house of 'Denton,' in Yorkshire, and grew up in sight of the patrimonial oaks of my family—in the familiar, rustic scenes of English life. My father, Thomas, Lord

Fairfax, the fifth of the name, was a cold, but not an unkind man; my mother, Catherine, daughter of Lord Culpeper, was a very saint on earth. Under the tuition of these beloved parents, and a worthy old gentleman who lived at Denton, I grew to the age of seventeen; when I was sent to the University of Oxford. There, I passed through the ordinary routine of study, and neglect of study, and on leaving the University, obtained a commission in the royal regiment of the 'Blues.' This, however, did not hold me long. I resigned my commission from distaste for the life of barracks, and plunged into the whirlpool of London. My rank gave me access to the finest society of the time, and at nineteen I had become, my friends informed me, one of the most perfect specimens of a maccaroni to be found in the club-houses and drawing-rooms of the capital. I enjoyed this dissipated mode of life for some months, mingling with delight in the political and literary circles which were ornamented by the presence of Bolingbroke, Addison, and other lights of the day; and then, wearied out with play, with the theatres, with fine ladies, and simpering beaux, I retired to Denton, and became a country gentleman again.

"And now commences the series of events which I design relating. My life hitherto had been gay and splendid—no cloud had crossed the bright sky of my youth; in the brilliant circles of London, as in the jovial scenes of Oxford, I had basked in uninterrupted sunshine, and never given a single thought to care; never indulged in one violent or discordant emotion. I was ere long to learn that human life cannot glide away in one unbroken current of limpid smoothness; that there are breakers and reefs on the most smiling coast, which the most experienced pilot cannot always avoid. I was no such experienced person, I need not tell you. To great ignorance of the world, in spite of my years in London, I added an excitable and headstrong temper when aroused: and this defect of my blood was not long in revealing itself. I had never quarrelled with anybody at

Oxford or in London: in both places I had lived among scenes which are often disturbed by evil passions; but I passed through intact. I had gone to the theatres, and supped with wits and gallants, played tric-trac, and wandered forth with the Mohocks at three in the morning, on their revels and absurdities, perpetrated at the expense of the watchmen of the city; all this I passed through without once drawing my sword, without a single affair; how was I to have an affair, in the apparently sluggish scene of Yorkshire.

"There was a gentleman of the neighborhood about forty years of age, whose name was Sir William Powys. He had once possessed a very fine estate, but owing to his want of management, and the extravagant mode of living which he pursued, this great property had gradually melted away. It was covered with mortgages, by means of which Sir William had, from time to time, raised large sums of money to sustain him in his mode of living—and among the holders of these mortgages was my father. He was neither by habit nor inclination a money-lender, and long resisted the request of Sir William, to advance him a large sum of money which had gradually been saved from the proceeds of the Denton Estate. At last, however, he yielded to the solicitations of the knight, and delivered to him the sum, taking a mortgage on the bulk of the Powys Court manor. This had happened a year or two before my arrival—and just before I came, my father had foreclosed the mortgage, and forced Sir William to alienate almost his whole property. I know not if this action of my father was harsh. From my knowledge of his character, as from the general tenor of his life, I am convinced that he proceeded to this apparently unkind act, in the purest defence of the interests of his family. My sister, since dead, was about to be married, and a settlement was absolutely required on the part of the Fairfax family. Sir William could not, or would not, repay the money borrowed —and as I have said, the mortgage was foreclosed. He parted with his property without any overt act of enmity; but it was soon whispered throughout the shire, that the knight denounced my father at his own table and elsewhere, as a usurer, a Shylock, a Jew money-lender, and in other terms equally insulting.

"I need scarcely say, sir, that this intelligence set my blood on fire. My father was then a gray-haired man, full of years; and I knew that he was physically unable to right himself. A long, well-spent life, it is true, gave the lie to these base insinuations and calumnies; but in our family we are restive under insult, no matter whether it injures or not. I saw my father's face flush more than once, when these expressions were unguardedly alluded to in his presence—and I longed for an opportunity to revenge upon the calumniator the wrong which he had perpetrated toward Lord Fairfax. I was determined to seek him, and pick a quarrel upon some indifferent ground: and then—I said with clenched teeth—I will put an end to him, or he shall put an end to me.' An opportunity of carrying out my design soon presented itself. In the vicinity of Denton, and not far from Powys Court, was the race-course of the county. Here, upon a certain day, were assembled all the gentlemen and ladies of the region around. I repaired to the race-course early, but not with any design of betting. I sought Sir William Powys, who would attend I heard—and I was soon gratified. I descried his tall form approaching upon horseback, in the midst of a number of his friends; and I even now recall his athletic and powerful figure, which in bulk of muscle, pride of carriage, and its haughty air of superiority, threw into the background every personage about him. He dismounted and gave his bridle to a groom. Then, accompanied by his friends, he approached the open space beneath the balcony, which was filled with ladies and gentlemen, intent on the coming festivity. The horses, in their sweat-cloths, were being led up and down; a hundred comments were made by the crowd who inspected them;

and bets were every moment offered and taken by the gentlemen on the various racers which had been entered.

"I approached the group, in the midst of which Sir William was standing and expatiating upon the merits of the horses. As I drew near I heard him say;

"'Three to one on the bay—in tens or hundreds.'

"'Done, Sir William,' responded the gentleman to whom he spoke, and who was an acquaintance of mine. His name was Sir John Colburn.

"'I congratulate you, Sir John,' I said, laughing; 'the bay's a miserable hack, and will probably be distanced the first heat.'

"I saw Sir William Powys turn as if an adder had stung him. He was proud of his knowledge of horse-flesh; indeed, it was one of his weak points—and to have his judgment thus sneered at, and by a mere boy, such as I happened to be, enraged him profoundly. His eye flashed, and he surveyed me from head to foot with a glance which was intended to annihilate me. It failed, however. I have a faculty of my blood in a very marked degree—I grow cooler as I become more exasperated. I hated Sir William at that moment, mortally—and I replied to his insulting look by a satirical smile. This heated him more dangerously—I saw his cheek turn crimson with anger.

"'And who are you, sir!' he said, in a tone of excessive rudeness, 'who are you, that presume to put your opinion against mine?'

"'I thought you knew me, sir,' I said, with perfect coolness, 'as I remember meeting you some years since. But no matter. My name is not important—and I presume, in spite of your extreme dissatisfaction, to say that in my humble opinion the bay is the poorest and most ludicrous horse entered; it is hard to look at him without laughing in fact—and no one but a tyro would bet on him.'

"'What do you mean, sir!' said Sir William, turning white with rage at my tone of disdainful indifference, and advancing close to me as he spoke, 'your meaning, sir!—if it is an insult you intend uttering, this horse-whip shall teach you—!'

"In an instant we had grappled. I had designed nothing of the sort; but the sight of the degrading instrument raised above my head, aroused the devil in me, and made me wild. I caught at it, fully intending to wrench it away, and apply it to his own person—and in a moment we were locked in a furious embrace. We were parted immediately by the bystanders, who rushed to us with loud exclamations —and a glance at the balcony above showed me that a young lady had fainted, and was being borne out.

"'Who—is—this person?' panted Sir William, with powerless fury; 'had my right arm been unmaimed I would have punished his insolence!' And he glared at me wildly, and would have tried to strike me again, had not his friends restrained him and told him my name.

"'Tom Fairfax! Tom Fairfax!' he muttered, with clenched teeth; 'very well! this may be arranged elsewhere! Ah! a Fairfax, is it?'

"'Yes, sir,' I replied scornfully, 'my name is Fairfax, almost or quite as good a name as your own, and you shall not have to wait very long for the "arrangement" you desire!'

"With these words we exchanged ceremonious bows, and separated—Sir John Colburn accompanying me. In three hours all was 'arranged' as I had promised. We were to meet with pistols, at a spot near the race-course, which had been agreed on. The objection to the use of short-swords lay in the condition of Sir William's right arm—he had been kicked a short time before by one of his horses, and somewhat disabled. He insisted very generously and fearlessly upon swords, but his second overruled him, and pistols were decided upon.

"Well, not to lengthen my narrative unduly—we met: at the first fire my ball penetrated his right shoulder, and so great was the agony which it caused him, that he fell, and fainted from loss of blood. His ball did not touch me. The duel ended thus, and Sir William was borne home in his carriage. It was his daughter who had fainted in the balcony.

"So terminated," continued the Earl, "an affair which was recalled to my recollection in a very strange manner some time since—in the Ordinary yonder. But to resume. I returned home only half pleased with the issue. Such is the depravity of the human heart, and to such a height had I been aroused by the wrong done my father, that—I am sorry to say it, but I must be candid—I thirsted for my enemy's blood. For the present, however, this desire was doomed to disappointment. I reflected—but on the very next day a new means presented itself. Sir William's family consisted of a son and a daughter—Edith and Arthur, who were twins:—well, Arthur, on the morning after my duel with his father, sent me a challenge, which I accepted at once. He was a few months younger than myself, but was reputed to be an excellent swordsman. I referred his friend to Sir John Colburn, and everything was soon agreed upon—but the matter was all at once arrested. My father had remonstrated with me strongly for my affair with Sir William, and begged me to avoid in future any occasion of renewing the quarrel. If I insisted upon fighting he would meet Sir William himself. He soon found out my design of meeting Arthur Powys, and rode hastily to Powys Court. There had never been any open quarrel between the two— and their meeting, I afterwards heard, was amicable. The consequence of the visit was, that the elders forbade the juniors, on pain of their displeasure and forfeit of affection, to proceed in the matter. In the end, both Arthur and myself were summoned to the side of the sick man—and Sir William very nobly apologized for his insult to me on the race-course.

"'Had I known you, sir,' he said, 'I should never have

been guilty of the act of raising a horse-whip to strike you —that, I need not say. I saw no indication of your rank or family—and now beg to say to you, that I deeply regret the whole occurrence, as I regret some very inconsiderate and ill-advised expressions which I doubt not, really led you to provoke me into a quarrel. There must be no more contention, Viscount, and if you refuse me this request, I shall rise from my sick couch and meet you when you will —if you require me, this moment.'

"This speech ended all. The apology for the hasty reflections upon my father calmed me somewhat, and the matter terminated by the withdrawal of Arthur's challenge.

"Ten days afterwards I was out fox-hunting with a number of gentlemen, among whom was Arthur Powys. We were separated from the rest, and rode side by side at a great pace. We came to a bad fence—Arthur's horse rolled into a ditch, and he fell beneath. I drew up quickly, and dismounted. His leg was cruelly fractured, and taking him in my arms like a child, I held him on the saddle, and slowly conveyed him to Powys Court. As I entered the last gateway, the insensible figure resting upon my bosom, the pale face near my own, I saw a young lady rush out, wild with terror, and hasten toward me, weeping. It was Edith Powys, who received from my arms the unconscious form of her brother.

"Our hands touched: it was the first time.

CHAPTER LIII.

THE ORIGINALS OF THE PORTRAIT.

"WITH this incident," the Earl gravely continued, "commenced my new life. From that moment, when she came crying to take the young man upon her bosom, I loved Edith Powys with all the ardor of youth and romance. I do not scoff at it, or laugh, as some persons I think do; love to me, sir, has been a blessed reality, and solace—the supreme comfort and charm of my existence. I have known many sneer at women, and at the passion of pure love—for myself I regard it with a sacred wonder, and kneel almost humbly before a true-hearted girl, be she the peasant maid or queen on her throne. Oh no, sir! women are capricious—they are fanciful—they have many great weaknesses—but at the bottom of all the folly which appears in many of them, there is purest gold!

"Well I loved Edith Powys—she is with me still, though long years have fled over me, and dulled my heart, since the day when I buried her beneath the spring violets at Denton. It was the decree of an All-merciful being that she should love me too—in spite of all her prepossessions against me. She often told me afterwards that her sentiment toward me, on the day when I grappled with her father in front of the balcony on the race-course, was pure hatred—and that she had registered a vow never to have any other for me. But the sight of her brother bleeding in my arms—pressed to my heart—this touched her and paved the way for the entrance of less bitter feelings; and then love came to answer the love I felt for her.

"Powys Court was no longer closed against me now. Thanks to the incident which I have related, entrance was freely accorded me. I had really conceived a strong friendship for Arthur—first from the fact that we never afterward look indifferently upon a person whom we have been kind to—whose weak form we have carried in our arms—and secondly, from another and equally natural circumstance. The brother and sister were not only twins—they were the most extraordinary copies of each other. Both had delicate features—the same clear, frank eyes—the same lips full of laughing pride—the same soft brown hair. Had Edith assumed the costume of her brother, you would have said, that a miniature Arthur Powys stood before you. Had the brother donned a female dress, Edith, larger it is true, and more masculine, but still Edith, would have looked at you with the smile of her brother.

"I have a portrait of the young man, painted some years after these events—'tis up stairs over the fireplace of one of the bed-chambers. I scarce dare to look at it when melancholy oppresses me—for the resemblance to Edith Powys sends a thrill of bitter anguish through my heart, and I recall all the past, as I gaze! To continue: I say that this singular resemblance between the young man and the young lady, insensibly drew me to his side. In his company I was almost enjoying the society of his sister. I availed myself of the incident which had bound us together, and went regularly to ask after his health. He soon improved. The fracture was painful, but yielded to the treatment of the physicians, and he was soon limping about the house again —leaning on my shoulder or his sister's, and smiling as before. He was a noble youth—one of the truest hearts I've ever known. He soon came to look upon me with affection and confidence, and the feud between the houses of Fairfax and Powys seemed destined to terminate with the elders.

"But I had calculated *without my host*. Sir William Powys was one of those men who never forgive. He might waive his enmity, for the occasion, and even utter words of courtesy and good humor—but beneath all this was the implacable memory—the rooted and incradicable recollection of his real or fancied wrong. It thus happened that the keen-eyed knight watched the growing intimacy between myself and his daughter with ill-disguised disapprobation and opposition. He was too well bred to refuse her hand before I had asked it; and evidently writhed with secret anger at the past. As my object in visiting Powys Court became plainer and plainer, and the artless affection of the young lady was less disguised, the Knight's dissatisfaction grew more intense. I saw it, and ground my teeth as I thought of it, often—but that was all. In the depths of my heart I think I really respected him more for it—for his loyalty to the family feud and the dislike he exhibited and plainly experienced, to a match between his daughter and a person, his social superior. He was only a baronet, and his possessions were reduced to nothing nearly—but he nevertheless opposed bitterly the union of his child with one who would soon be Earl of Fairfax and Baron of Cameron, with ample means of keeping up both titles. Indeed there was nothing small or mean about Sir William Powys. If he ever committed an action which seemed to indicate those qualities, you had only to search deeper, and a more noble passion would reveal itself. The craving for vengeance might induce him to act basely—but mere paltry love of gain never could.

"Thus, to return, I was obliged still to respect the knight, in spite of my bitter feelings at his manifest opposition. I tried to soften him—it was all in vain. Edith and Arthur became my advocates, and would sound my praises. The baronet only sneered, and asked if *both* of them were in love with me. Thus things went on until I could no longer control myself. I went to Sir William one day—confessed my affection for his daughter—and requested his permission to pay my addresses.

"'My permission, sir!' he said, with a bitter laugh, 'why truly you are a very entertaining person.'

"'Sir William!' I exclaimed.

"'Oh! don't let us argue,' he replied, 'I'm not such a dunce, sir, as not to see beyond my nose. I have observed what has taken place in my house for some months past, and I therefore say that your addresses have been paid without ceremony, and without my leave, sir! You will judge yourself if the act was not dishonorable!'.

"His face began to flush—and my own as darkly.

"'Sir William,' I said, 'you have wronged and insulted me! It is not becoming to do so, when I hold the position toward you which I do. And permit me to say, sir, that I have done nothing unworthy of the name I bear—of the name of Fairfax, which is as old and as honorable as that of Powys!

"His reply was a burst of rage. The comparison of the two names seemed to arouse all his old enmity. He gnashed his teeth, and seemed about to offer me some outrage.

"I had dared to come into his house, he said, and wile away the heart of his daughter—and his son. Under the mask of friendship I had beguiled her affections, and now came impudently to ask permission to pay my addresses. No! I should not have his consent! I should never marry his daughter! No person who bore the detested name of Fairfax should wed with one of the family of Powys! He had intended to express to his daughter plainly, his feelings on the subject long before—but pride restrained him. He had hoped that her sense of what was due to himself, as well as the blood which ran in her veins, would preserve her from yielding to this miserable infatuation! But he would no longer preserve silence! He would speak his mind plainly! Then, if she chose, she might marry me and welcome! She would at least have his curse for a dower!

"The baronet uttered all this and much more with a fiery wrath and indignation which seemed to increase as he proceeded. When his speech ended, he was furious, and red with anger. I was pale.

"'Sir William Powys,' I said, with a sinking heart, but a collected voice, 'you have done what gentlemen seldom do—insulted a visitor in your own house! But I have no insult to hurl back in return. You know well that I cannot answer you—you know why. I scorn to reply to your charges of dishonor—they fall harmless, for they are unjust and unfounded, as you know. I shall now go, sir—this interview ends all, as you desire. I will intrude myself upon no family which scorns me—you need fear nothing, sir—it will not be necessary to curse your daughter.'

"And I bowed and went away. On the portico I met Edith. She was as pale as death. She had heard all through the open window. With a quivering lip she held out her hand. I pressed it to my lips with a groan, and rode away, at a gallop, with a choking sensation in my throat. I had acted as a gentleman of the house of Fairfax should act—but my heart was almost broken in the struggle.

"I will hasten on in my narrative. When old events return they beguile me into unending details."

LV.

WHAT THE PACKAGE TORN BY THE BEAR CONTAINED.

 FEW months afterward, Edith Powys had become my wife:—my father and mother were both dead:—I was the head of the house, though I had not reached my majority."

The Earl paused as he uttered these words, and a deep sigh issued from the depths of his heart. These memories evidently agitated him profoundly—but controlling his emotion, he continued his narrative.

"I shall not pause to speak of the grief I experienced at the loss of my parents—upon that subject I do not like to say anything. I shall confine my attention to the events which I wish to relate. The explanation of my marriage will not be either difficult or lengthy. From the day on which I held the angry interview with Sir William Powys, the relations between himself, and his son and daughter, had greatly changed. A mutual coldness sprung up. The father regarded the daughter as a rebel against his authority—an unworthy scion of the house of Powys. The daughter—with what justice you must decide—considered her father harsh and unjust. The insults which he had heaped upon an unoffending gentleman, aroused her nice sense of fairness and justice, and his coldness toward herself revolted her pride and self-respect; in a word, the family at Powys Court were divided, and marshalled on opposite sides. Arthur sided with his sister. He was never, in the remotest degree, discourteous to his father; but a thousand trifling incidents indicated his opinion of the amount of blame attaching to each. Under this household discord, the baronet writhed vainly. There was nothing to find fault with, no disrespect ever was shown him, much less any disobedience; his orders and requests were all sedulously complied with, and no word of complaint was uttered. But the skeleton was there. In the eyes of the young man and his sister, the knight read as plainly as in a printed book, changed feeling, coolness, the revolt against injustice. The baronet endured it in wrathful silence—but he endured it. It broke the health of his daughter. She could not preserve her feeling toward her father without bleeding inwardly—her cheek became paler and paler—she grew ill. Then she did not rise from her couch, and the tragedy approached its catastrophe. The baronet went to see her one morning, and she threw her arms around his neck, and burst into tears. She could not go on feeling thus toward him, she said: it would kill her; she loved him more than her life; he was her own dear father, and she had been sinful.—Then her voice was choked with sobs. All the tenderness so long pent up in the heart of the baronet responded. He took the girl to his heart, gazed with apprehension upon her white worn cheeks, and groaned aloud. An hour afterward he had passed through the great struggle between his affection and his pride. He came to Denton and begged me to pardon his harsh words. Would I ride back to Powys Court with him? He set his teeth close as he spoke, and breathed heavily.

"I need scarcely say that I acceded to the invitation. The weeks which had elapsed, had nearly killed me—my health and strength were gone—I was the mere shadow of myself. The loss of Edith had nearly broken my heart, and I moped like an octogenarian. Thus I had no pride to oppose to the baronet. I think my face flushed with delight. His horse scarcely kept up with my own as we rode toward Powys Court.

"I did not see Edith, of course, but I saw Arthur. He

dined with us; and I could read in his frank face the happiness he felt at the event of the morning. The baronet was sedulously courteous and attentive to me during dinner, and we sat long at the table, drinking wine and talking on a variety of topics. We both understood that the whole scene was a piece of acting—but when two men desire mutually to carry on a drama, there is no failure in the dialogue or the gesture. I knew that the obdurate father had relented; that he intended Arthur to relate everything to Edith; and he doubtless knew that I rated his sudden courtesy at its just value, and comprehended its design. When I left the house, I had promised to return in a few days. When I again entered the old hall, I was told that Edith awaited me in the drawing-room. Arthur handed me a paper as he said this, smiling; and I read the words:

" 'I consent that Viscount Fairfax shall proceed in the matter upon which we had, some months since, a discussion, if it still be the desire of that gentleman. WILLIAM POWYS.'

"I blushed with delight, and placing the paper in my bosom, hastened forward toward Edith, who came to meet me with a faint color in her cheeks. Let me not speak further of this scene, except to say that when I left Powys Court, late in the evening, the young lady was affianced to me. Six months afterward we were married.

"I now speak of a portion of my life, which stands out clear and distinct from the rest, as one of the great mountain headlands here, lit by the sunset, raises its head above the gloomy valleys. For a time I was happy—wholly, perfectly. The days glided away like hours, and they were days of unalloyed sunshine : for I loved my wife with a depth of tenderness which is indescribable. She bloomed in the great old hall at Denton, like a flower of the spring; blessing me with her sweet smile, and tender eyes, and adding a new lustre to my life. Those months are now my most cherished recollection; I go away from the lonely present, and live again in the past. I feel her heart beat against my own, and—I wake from the dream to stretch out my widowed arms and utter a groan—for she is past the stars!

"My narrative is nearly ended. I proceed now to relate events which have been a mystery to me for more than a quarter of a century—which I came to comprehend but the other day—on the mountain there, when I retired with the personage who passes under the name of Powell, but who is no other than the Sir William Powys, of whom I am speaking. You start, but do not interrupt me. To continue: Left alone almost, at his old country house, the baronet became silent and gloomy. His daughter had been more to him than all else in the world, and by removing her from his side, I had added another to the long list of wrongs which he had scored up in his brooding memory against the name of Fairfax. Arthur was good company, and had been the pride of his father; but the young man's espousal of his sister's cause, had created a coolness toward him on the part of the baronet; and the old familiar relations between them were thus interrupted. Another cause of complaint against the young man was the frequency of his visits to Denton, whither the baronet himself very seldom went; and thus the days of the master of Powys Court were lonely and unhappy. Upon my head, as I now know, all the pent up storm was secretly discharged. He had been forced by circumstances to sanction my union with Edith, but his repugnance to myself remained undiminished; and this feeling ripened rapidly into a sentiment of actual hatred—smouldering silently, and only awaiting an opportunity of striking its object. This opportunity soon came. The Countess of Fairfax returned, after the English custom, to the mansion of her parents, to pass through that ordeal of suffering, which God has imposed upon women as the penalty of their entrance into the sacred world of maternity. True, Edith's mother was not living, but at Powys Court, she might fancy the presence of the dear form at her bedside; and to Powys Court she accordingly went.

"A month afterward, an heir of my name was born; but died in twelve hours. My wife was already dead—she had surrendered her existence in giving life to another human being. She died with her hand in my own, smiling sweetly as she always smiled when she looked at me; as she will smile, I trust, when we are reunited in heaven, where sorrow and tears come no more."

The Earl pressed his hand to his forehead, and his weary eyes moistened as he thus recalled the scenes of the past. His brows contracted with a weary shadow, and a groan which issued from the bottom of his heart, revealed the extent of his suffering. He remained thus silent, and overcome by emotion for some moments, then his eyes suddenly became dry again, and a flash darted from them. A cold and menacing expression came to the quivering lip, and he continued:

"I said that my son died twelve hours after his birth. In so declaring, I gave the statement of his nurse and Sir William Powys—a falsehood! Yes, a horrible, base falsehood, unworthy of a menial, much more of a gentleman! The truth will serve to display the awful depths of depravity, to which a man who profoundly hates another will descend, under the influence of a thirst for vengeance. It was not my son who died; it was the child of one of the maids, born almost at the same moment, and substituted, in its death-throes, in place of my own. The unhappy man confessed all to me on the Fort Mountain in our interview—confessed with shame and repentance, and shuddering humiliation, the means which he had made use of to rob me of this solace of my widowed heart. By a large bribe he induced a woman of the household to make the change; the child of the servant thus died in the chamber where my dead wife was lying; mine was placed in the arms of the servant as her own.

"Thus, under the stimulus of a horrible sentiment of hatred, and thirst for vengeance, did Sir William Powys commit an action which has made him, he declares, supremely miserable for more than a score of years. His object was a double one. He aimed at depriving me of an inexpressible consolation, and at securing to himself the child of his daughter. It was almost with burning jealousy, he declares, that he thought of me, in possession of this memorial of his child, whom he loved so tenderly, and relinquished to me only to make her happy. His scheme, he declares, was to rear the boy carefully, to make him heir to his entire possessions; and before I died to reveal the whole matter, and further secure for him the earldom and wealth of the house of Fairfax. Such was his design—a portion of it woefully succeeded. But to return.

"I followed the dead bodies of my wife, and my supposed child, to the Denton churchyard, and saw them placed in the earth. Then I mounted my horse and returned to my desolate home, broken-hearted and longing for death to put an end to my misery. I was destined to be struck again heavily. A servant handed me a package as I dismounted; I opened and read it with a quivering lip; then I fell into a seat, almost prostrated. My guardians had cut off the entail of Denton, in order to preserve the great Leeds Castle Manor, derived from my mother, the daughter, as I have said, of Lord Culpeper: the house of my forefathers was no longer my own; I was tenant at Denton by sufferance. I despair of conveying to you any adequate idea of the weight of the blow which thus struck me. It is true the project had long been under consideration, in spite of my remonstrances and protests; but I was now so near my legal majority, that I had abandoned all fears upon the subject. I was tottering when the stroke came; it almost prostrated me. Denton was lost to me! It was no longer my own! The house which I was born in, which recalled to me every happy moment of my youth, which my wife had lived in, and made sacred in my eyes—Denton was the property of strangers. To my overpowering pain, succeeded a mad, speechless rage; and I stormed like a child at the men who had done this. I went to them and told them I would never forgive them; but it was a pitiful conclusion after all. I was powerless—finally I yielded, and grew calm. I surrendered the house and went to London. I lay there for months tossing with fever—then I rose, an old man at twenty-one.

"Such were the events of my early years in England."

LVI.

CONCLUSION OF THE EARL'S NARRATIVE.

"THE rest of my narrative," continued the Earl, "may be related briefly. But, first I shall tell you what you have no doubt understood ere this, that the young man who passes here under the name of Falconbridge is my son. Let me go on.

"After his terrible, and successful plot, Sir William Powys proceeded quietly to adopt and rear the child, of whom he had deprived me. But events soon occurred which overthrew all his calculations. A creditor who had a claim upon every foot of land which the baronet possessed, forced the payment of the debt, and thus Powys Court passed from its owner's hands, as Denton had escaped from mine. The baronet was thrown upon the world, and had it not been for his son, Arthur, would have had nowhere to lay his head. The young man had married some time before, and now received his father and the child under his roof.

"But Sir William was haunted eternally by a single thought. He dreaded the discovery by himself of the infant's identity, and the thought of being compelled by law to part with him, aroused all the old hatred and jealousy in his heart. The boy already began to display unmistakable indications of his origin. He was the image of his mother, and no one who had ever seen Edith failed to note, and refer to this resemblance. People began to inquire why the haughty and aristocratic Sir William Powys had adopted and received as his own child, the son of a servant in his household. The gossips of the neighborhood duly seized upon the matter, and began to shake their heads, and ask if that poor young Lord Fairfax had really lost his child. It was a vague and undefined idea in all minds; but the question was not permitted to rest.

"This state of things became at last so troublesome, that Sir William cast about him for some means of quieting the gossips, and at the same time securing the infant from ever falling into my hands. The means all at once presented themselves. A Mr. Falconbridge of the region was about emigrating to the Virginia Colony—and his wife, who was childless, had taken a great fancy to the boy. Sir William was not long in making up his mind. He sounded the parties, and discovered that they would willingly adopt the child as their own, and take charge of his future. The bargain was soon agreed upon, and when Mr. Falconbridge sailed for Virginia, he took my son with him, as his own child, and bearing his name.

"Thus had crime reached its punishment. This man who had inflicted upon me such a cruel vengeance, was as cruelly wounded himself. He loved the boy dearly, and was compelled to part with him. He continued in England, dependent upon the bounty of his son—but after some years even this was denied him. Arthur died, and his wife followed him. The family had subsisted upon the salary of a county office which the young man held: and thus Sir William found himself without means of support, with a further cause of disquiet and apprehension. Arthur had left a little daughter. You know her, under the name of Cannie Powell. This daughter the poor man came to love with a doting affection; and to rear her in a manner suitable to her origin and rank now became the most cherished desire of her grandfather. Without means of doing so in the Old World, Sir William came to the New. He crossed the ocean, and settled upon a small tract of land on the shores of the Chesapeake; and thence came here to the mountains, for the health of his granddaughter. Soon after his arrival, he discovered a mine of silver and gold, and in working this mine, impelled by the desire of amassing money for his child, he secured that reputation for witchcraft, which ended in his arrest and trial. He had frequently seen his grandson, young Falconbridge, in the Lowland, but shame had prevented him from revealing their connection, and even from making his acquaintance, as a stranger. Assured of the fact that the elder Falconbridge loved the young man, and regarded him as his son, he yielded to the hard fate which kept them asunder, and dedicated his life to little Cannie. When I came to Greenway, a year or two since, Sir William was residing in the mountain. Why I emigrated to America, you doubtless know. Stripped of Denton, and longing for new scenes, I came hither, and took possession of my property, like Leeds Castle, derived from Lord Culpeper through my mother. I never met Sir William, though I often hunted in the Fort Mountain—and a strange Providence threw us, for the first time, face to face, in the attitude of criminal and judge. By the side of the old man I saw my son, and my son's cousin ; his grandchildren, both ; and all strikingly alike. The strange resemblance which Falconbridge, as I shall call him still, bore to Arthur and Edith, impressed me powerfully on our first meeting, and one night, when he slept here, I stole at midnight to his chamber, led thither by an impulse which I could not resist.

"You know all, now, Captain Wagner. I have related my whole life. You are acquainted with the events which have occurred since the young man's visit fo this region ; I scarce dare to refer to them. An inscrutable Providence decreed that father and son should be rivals, in a mad infatuation for a woman ; that they should oppose each other sword in hand ; that they should shed each other's blood, though God be thanked, not to the death ! The man whose act placed us in this unnatural attitude, revealed all before it was too late. In our interview on the mountain, he confessed his crime, and prayed me in a trembling voice to forgive him. He had delivered, some time before, a package to the youth for me, containing the whole explanation, which was strangely lost. But at least it came in time. No power can now arm us again. I shall never look more upon the woman whom my boy loves; I will warn him against her, for I feel that she is false and dangerous.

"That is all, Captain," said the Earl, raising his head, and sighing deeply, but no longer with the old painful expression. "I have related a strange history—'tis such, is it not?—and you have listened as friend listens to friend. The narrative has been a singular relief to me; I feel light-hearted almost. I end by a serious and earnest petition. I impose upon you a duty which I know you will gladly perform. In the scenes of danger which my boy is about to enter, watch over his life, and bring him back safe to me. On the day of his return I will tell him that his name is not Falconbridge; that his blood is *my* blood; that I thank the Supreme Lord of this world, and all worlds, that Edmund Lord Fairfax, the *seventh* of the name, and Baron of Cameron in the kingdom of Scotland, for such will be my boy,—is better than a mere noble, better than the greatest lord—a noble and true hearted gentleman!"

The face of the glad father glowed as he spoke, and his form rose erect, with a pride and happiness which is indescribable.

"Yes, Captain!" said the Earl, with flushed cheeks, and brilliant eyes, "yes, Falconbridge is a gentleman every inch of him! a nobleman by God's patent, as by the king's! In his presence, as I gazed at him, and listened to his voice, I have said, "This is a chevalier of old days!" In his persuasive tones, in his clear, frank eyes, in his lips, in his whole bearing, in his rage, as when he smiled, I have seen the great soul of the boy, the pure gold of his nature! I have thrilled with a nameless delight, when he spoke; I have gazed with longing into his deep, true eyes; I have said, 'What pride must this youth's father feel!' and you may understand now the emotion which I experience when I can add, 'This is my son.'"

The Earl was silent, and Captain Wagner did not immediately reply. Leaning his head upon his huge hand, he reflected with absorbing interest upon the remarkable history which he had just heard. He remained thus absent and buried in thought, for a long time after the Earl ceased speaking. Then he raised his head, and uttered the characteristic words:

"Yes, a trump, or the devil take it!"

The Earl smiled at the sonorous voice of the worthy soldier, and said:

"You mean my son?"

"Yes, my lord. And I beg you to observe one fact—that when I say a man's a trump, I mean the trump of *hearts*, that being the finest card, to my thinking, in the pack. I have always regarded your lordship as a man of discrimination; I think so now more than ever, or I'm a dandy! Yes, this Falconbridge is truly a gentleman, and that's better, as you say, than being a nobleman. I am not myself a gentleman—don't be waving your hand, my dear friend—I *would* have been, with training, if that satisfies you. I think in fact that a real marquis was spoiled when Captain Julius Wagner took to the border. Nevertheless, in spite of this unfortunate state of things, I am acquainted with the article, and recognize it. I say Falconbridge is made of real gold! Let me hear anybody deny it! I'll slice 'em! Zounds! my lord! I loved him at first sight! I couldn't keep my eyes off that proud-looking face of his—and when he dangled after that woman, I nearly cried! From the first, this young fellow bossed Wagner, or I'm a dandy! I am fond of your lordship, but I honestly declare that yonder on the Fort Mountain, I hoped he'd make a hole in your coat—that is to say—hum! rather than be drilled himself! Friendly, that, eh, my lord? But it's true. It will show you how that boy has wrapped himself around my old heart: I growl like a miserable old bear, when he groans—he's as much my son as your lordship's!"

The Captain accompanied the words by a blow upon the table with his fist.

"There, there," he said more calmly, "I've made a fool of myself—if I haven't done a disgraceful piece of courting. The fact is, my lord, I wan't a manor on the Opequon, and it occurred to me that this was the way to get around you, I have no sort of liking for this lofty headed youngster, but I praise him, you see, to arrive at my own ends. Is the 'Redbud Manor' still unoccupied, my lord?"

And the Captain gazed with a look of earnest inquiry into the countenance of Lord Fairfax.

The Earl smiled. It was a happy smile—no longer grim and melancholy, as on former occasions.

"You are a bungling courtier, Captain Wagner," he said, "and I predict will never become a very distinguished diplomatist. But I'll make a contract with you. Bring my boy back safely, and I'll make you a deed to twice as many acres as the 'Redbud' tract. Is it a bargain?"

"No, my lord," returned the Captain, "it is nothing of the sort. The fact is, the 'Redbud' land is miserably barren—not half equal to my wife's property which joins it. No, your lordship, and at present Captain Wagner is talking seriously—by the book—I'll receive no pay, for looking after the youngster, any more than I would for guarding Julius, Lord Wagner, the second of the name and Baron of Winchester in the Kingdom of Virginia! I'll be by him, and keep the balls off him—if I don't I'm a dandy! And so that's all. Let me now go and carry out my other promise —that of bringing Lord Fairfax, the younger, to Greenway. The sun is getting low, and it is time to be on the road. Your lordship wishes him to come sleep here?"

"Yes, Captain. You will pardon the weakness of a father

whose son is going on a perilous expedition to-morrow; I would see him once more."

"Right, right! I've had boys myself, and I know what that means; you want to have the youngster here close to you."

The Earl smiled and inclined.

"It is one of my chief happinesses in this lonely region to have by my side a friend like yourself, Captain, who understands me. Go then—'tis another obligation still."

"Stop that talking, my lord. Julius Wagner's a good fellow, but no such great things after all. I'll go bring him—whether he wants to come or not—or I'm a dandy!"

With which words, the Borderer issued forth, and mounting Injunhater, hastened to the Ordinary. Two hours afterwards, Falconbridge, as we shall continue to call him, was seated in the great apartment at Greenway, conversing with George, the Earl and the Captain.

LVII.

THE CONFLAGRATION.

WE might pause here to note the strange and moving attitudes which some of the personages of our narrative sustained toward each other. We might exhibit the good Earl in the presence of his son, listening with smiles as the young man talks:—or returning to the day when Falconbridge visited the Fort Mountain, we might dwell on the secret attraction which he felt toward his little cousin, and the sympathetic affection of child in return.

We might dedicate some pages to this series of reflections, but it is not necessary. It is well that such is the fact. Our narrative is not ended. It must depict more than one additional scene of passion before it concludes. The hours are even now descending upon the actors in the valley and the mountain, at the Ordinary, and Greenway.

For a long time the occupants of the old border mansion continued to converse upon a variety of topics. Falconbridge was gloomy and the victim evidently of an incurable sadness—but he no longer cherished any ill-will toward the Earl. It is true, he still wondered at the scene in the Fort, and vainly racked his brain to account for the action of Lord Fairfax: but a more absorbing thought filled his agitated mind; the terrible secret which had been revealed to him by Mr. Argal.

He looked older. His countenance, which before had been the model of youthful beauty, began to shrink away, and present the traits of age. His cheeks were hollow, his eyes dim—his lips were filled with inexpressible sorrow; or wore a smile of such sadness that the Earl was moved almost to tears as he gazed.

As the hours drew on, however, something of this gloom disappeared. Captain Wagner directed the conversation toward the events of the morrow—the march on the Indians —the fated struggle. Then Falconbridge aroused himself. His eyes glowed, his cheek flushed—when the soldier drew a picture of the murdered women and children, the face of the young man became menacing and dark—the war fever began to replace the sombre brooding.

George never moved his eyes for a moment from Falconbridge. The youth seemed to be drawn to him by an irresistible attraction. The manly eyes of the boy uttered plainly the emotions of his heart—the deep affection which he felt toward the other. Indeed, this feeling amounted to a passion almost; and if, amid the advancing scenes of our narrative, we have not paused to dwell upon this beautiful friendship, it was not because it did not possess all the elements of an exquisite picture. From the first day of their meeting, these two natures had embraced each other. Heart spoke to heart, with the frankness and sincerity which spring from nobility of soul. With the elder it was a sentiment of affection, almost tenderness—with George not only that: he looked up to his friend as to one who should be taken as a model—as to his superior, and bright exemplar in all things.

Long afterwards, when a new world had risen from the ruins of the old—when a long stormy life had thrown the youth into contact with all varieties of excellence and nobility and moral grandeur—when, a gray-haired man, George returned to this region—he gazed on the scenes amid which his friend had once moved; and said with a sigh, which sounded strangely from him, "There never was another human being like him!"

So the long hours fled away into the darkness of the past—and at night the occupants at Greenway retired. It was the last time they ever met, all together in the old apartment.

In an hour they were slumbering quietly—but they were destined to be awakened.

Falconbridge was sleeping as tranquilly as an infant, when suddenly he felt a violent grasp on his arm, and the voice of Captain Wagner thundered:

"Wake, comrade! They're on us at last!"

The young man sprang from his couch and rapidly dressed himself without speaking. George, who slept in the same room, did the same.

"They're on us, or the devil fly away with it!" cried the Captain; "come, hurry! His lordship's waiting by this time. I sent the messenger to his room!"

"The messenger?" asked Falconbridge, coolly.

"Yes! Just look out and you'll see what news he brought!"

As he spoke, the Captain raised the curtain of the window and pointed to the west. Above the belt of forest soared a tongue of flame, and the country was illuminated for miles by a great conflagration.

"The Ordinary!" said George.

"Yes, the Ordinary! By the horns of the devil! You are right! Come, friends! There's not a moment to lose!"

And the Captain hurried down to the large apartment where, while sleeping as his wont was on one of the couches, the messenger from the tavern had aroused him.

Lord Fairfax was already dressed, and speaking rapidly to the man who had brought the intelligence. George and Falconbridge entered, as he was doing so.

The news was quickly communicated to all. The band of Indians who had made a feint of directing their march toward the Potomac, did so only to mask their real plan. They had turned back suddenly and descended upon Winchester, and the Greenway Court manor, burning and murdering as they went. They had come thus, duly to the neighborhood of the Ordinary, and at once proceeded to attack that mansion. The occupants could make little or no resistance—the savages had taken the place and set it on fire an hour before. The fat landlord, Van Doring, had been killed on his threshold—every servant but the one who related these events had fallen victims to the assailants; and the savages had finally hastened away, in a southern direction, carrying with them as prisoners, Mrs. Butterton, Monsieur Jambot and Major ·Hastyluck, who had slept at the tavern—as beasts of burden to bear the plunder on their shoulders.

The Captain bounded again as he heard this, and growled rather than said:

"To horse!"

With which words he rushed from the apartment. In ten minutes every one was mounted, and a hurried consultation was held as to the propriety of leaving Greenway undefended.

"They're gone southwest! I know 'em," growled Captain Wagner; "the attack on us here would have been made before this if they had not been afraid that the house was regularly garrisoned!"

The servant who had brought the intelligence corroborated this view, and stated that he had heard the Indians discuss, in broken English, the question of attacking Greenway. They had given up the idea, upon the identical grounds mentioned by the Captain—and had hastened toward the south, leaving him tied in the burning house, from which he had managed,·however, to escape.

This settled all doubt: and in a moment the four men were spurring rapidly to the scene of the catastrophe.

A horrible spectacle awaited them. The mansion was wrapt in flames, and in front were lying no less than six dead bodies, among whom was seen the portly form of Mynheer Van Doring, scalped and bleeding from many mortal wounds. A sight if anything more terrible was presented a few paces off. Several infant children, belonging to the dead servants of the establishment, were hanging in trees, transfixed with arrows. The Indians had evidently perpetrated this shocking tragedy in sport; and while the Earl and his companions were gazing at the contorted forms, another barbarity still was revealed. The stable of the Ordinary was burning like the mansion, and the cries of some cattle and sheep which were shut in, made the night hideous to the listeners.*

The first act of the party was to drag the dead bodies out of the flames, and liberate the cattle which went bellowing with terror into the forest. Then the Captain leaped into the saddle and cast a rapid glance around him. A number of settlers, for the most part hunters, had assembled, attracted from their homes by the flames of the burning mansion. To these the Borderer, who seemed on fire with rage, addressed himself in quick, brief words. His directions were succinct and simple. They were to disperse in all quarters and arouse the inhabitants—the men would meet at the "Three Oaks," near the house of Mr. Argal—a point in the prairie which every settler was acquainted with. He himself would spend the night in scouring the country. The various parties would assemble at daybreak, or sunrise at the latest.

These directions were rapidly obeyed. The hunters dispersed and hurried away, disappearing with long strides in the gathering darkness.

---

* "The Indians dragged the dead body back to the house, threw it in, plundered the house of what they chose, and then set fire to it. While the house was in flames, consuming the body of Mr. Painter, they forced from the arms of their mothers, four infant children, hung them up in trees, shot them in savage sport, and left them hanging. They then set fire to a stable in which were inclosed a parcel of sheep and calves, thus cruelly and wantonly torturing to death the dumb animals. After these atrocities, they moved off with forty-eight prisoners, among whom were Mrs. Painter, five of her daughters and one of her sons; a Mrs. Smith and several of her children, among them a lad of twelve or thirteen years old, a fine, well grown boy, and remarkably fleshy. This little fellow, it will presently be seen, was destined to be the victim of savage cruelty. . . . . One of the Painters, with Myer, ran over that night to Powell's fort."—KERCHEVAL, Page 105.

"Now friends!" said Captain Wagner to the Earl and his companions, "let every man imitate me. There's no time for ceremony! I could bite off my head for this hoggish stupidity of mine! I trusted that fellow who brought me the news that the band had gone back, and would slay him where he stood if he were here! To work! I will go and bring the boys from Winchester, where they were to assemble to-day—for days coming. Go arm, gentlemen! arm; this is only the beginning of the sight you're going to see!"

And saluting, the Borderer put spur to his huge animal, and took the road to Winchester at a thundering gallop.

"I will return to Greenway Court, gentlemen," said the Earl, with his old grim expression, "I will send all my servants in every direction—and then join you at the 'Three Oaks' at daybreak."

With these words he left the room and soon disappeared like the Captain, at a rapid gallop.

George and Falconbridge looked at each other. The same thought had occurred to them at the same instant. The Indians had gone southward—in the direction of Mr. Argal's—in the direction of the Fort Mountain!

No word was uttered: a simultaneous movement of the head—the spur in the sides of the horses—and they separated and were lost in the darkness.

LVIII.

THE SEARCH.

FALCONBRIDGE pushed his spirited animal until the courser rather bounded than ran.

The great trees flitted by like spectres; the prairie glimmered, and fled behind him; darting onward like some phantom of the German poets, he resembled rather the wild image of a feverish dream, than a real man of flesh and blood.

A terrible dread had seized upon him. The Indians had gone directly toward Mr. Argal's. She was slain perhaps— even now she might be weltering in her blood! That tender and beautiful face might be gashed by the tomahawk— the scalping-knife might have encircled the white temples, —and the mass of raven curls which he had often twined around his fingers might be hanging at the belt of a savage!

The thought maddened him almost, and he felt, with something like a dreadful shudder, that he loved this woman still.

All the nobility and pity of his high nature was aroused. She had trifled with him perhaps—she had played with his deep love—but after all, she was a woman, a weak woman! She was even more than that! She was a poor feeble girl, smitten by the hand of the Almighty, and irresponsible! Could he think of her lying in her blood on the threshold, and turn away coldly with the thought, "She has deceived me—I care nothing?"

No, that was not possible. She was sacred to him still— if all was ended between them. His life was a bauble; of no value; he cared naught for it: he would fulfill that promise which he had made to her father. He would still guard her from harm, and if necessary, die for her.

He fled on more rapidly. Sir John panted, and the foam flew from his jaws. Then suddenly the house rose in the darkness.

All was silent. The young man leaped to the ground and rushed in.

As he entered he stumbled and almost fell over a dead body. An awful shudder convulsed him. He scarcely dared to look down. Leaning for an instant against the framework of the door, a sort of mist passed before him, and he shook from head to foot. Then he summoned all his strength, and knelt down, passing his trembling hand over the figure. It was a woman, but not the form of her he sought. A deep breath filled the bosom of the young man as he rose erect. Stepping over the corpse of the servant, he hastened in, and going to the fire-place, struck a light. The apartment was all at once illuminated. An awful spectacle presented itself.

All around lay the corpses of the servants of the establishment, in attitudes of indescribable agony, as they had died. The room was rifled, the furniture broken. On more than one object was a bloody stain which indicated a desperate struggle. This, however, was the least of the spectacle. There was another element—an object, or rather five objects which sent the blood to his breast, and made him turn sick with horror.

To the four corners of the room were affixed, by knives driven through them into the wall, the quartered body of Mr. Argal. On the summit of a stake which leaned against the mantel-piece, the bleeding head of the unhappy man looked, with a ghastly grin upon the features, at the intruder.*

---

* "The remaining two" Indians, "resolved not to give up their prey, found it necessary to proceed more cautiously; and going to the least exposed side of the house,

The young man recoiled before the terrible sight, step by step, until he touched the opposite wall. He seemed endeavoring to fly from the grinning mouth, the lack-lustre eyes.

Then suddenly he remembered the object of his visit, which had disappeared from his mind for an instant. *Her* figure was not among the corpses on the floor—was it elsewhere?

With the flaring light raised above his head, he rushed through the house from top to bottom—with clenched teeth —breathing heavily—searching for what he dared not to think of.

It was not visible. Then she too had been carried away prisoner—every moment that he tarried, increased the distance between them. Hurrying back to the main room, he passed through it with averted head and shuddering limbs. Stepping over the dead body of the woman at the threshold, he ground the light beneath his heel, and leaving the accursed mansion with its horrors to darkness and silence, leaped into the saddle and darted off in the direction of the "Three Oaks."

---

one was raised upon the shoulders of the other to an opening in the logs, some distance above the level of Mr. Williams, who did not consequently observe the manoeuvre, from which he fired and shot Mr. Williams dead. The body was instantly quartered and hung to the four corners of the building, and the head stuck upon a fence stake in front of the door. This brave man was the father of the venerable Edward Williams, the clerk of Hardy County Court."—KERCHEVAL.

14

LIX.

AT THE HOUSE IN THE MOUNTAIN.

GEORGE had meanwhile directed his course as rapidly as Falconbridge toward the Fort Mountain. The same terrible fear made his heart turn cold, and his temples throb with fever. His imagination also made a picture for itself—the form of a young girl stretched dead upon the ground, all mangled, and bloody from the blows of the savages.

They spared no age or sex—hence they could not have passed over Cannie, if they had gone, as they probably had done, to the Fort Mountain. The child whom he loved more than he loved his life, was dead—she would smile for him no more—all his future was to be darkness and despair.

With a quivering lip, and eyes moist yet fiery, George fled across the prairie at a desperate pace, driving the spur, cruelly, into the sides of his animal.

More than once the horse stumbled and nearly fell in the tall grass, but a powerful lift of the bridle held him up:—again he fled onward, like the shadow of a darting bird across the wide expanse, toward the river.

The stream was reached, and soon crossed. Into the frowning gorge, up the winding road, over rocks and fallen trees which the animal cleared bound after bound, the boy rushed on.

His horse reared and almost fell at the door of the mountain dwelling—the ascent had been cruelly exhausting.

George entered. An old servant was holding Mr. Powell in his arms, and staunching a deep wound in his temple.

The old man was insensible—the servant was groaning and uttering exclamations.

It was some time before George could extort anything from the servant, who only cried, "such a country! such a country! Oh! for England again!"

At last he was mastered by the stern tone and resolute command in George's voice—he related what had happened.

An hour before, the Indians, in large numbers, had surprised the dwelling, and carried off Cannie. His master had fought desperately, but was soon overpowered—a blow from a tomahawk had struck him down. Then the house had been rifled, and the band hurried away, right over the summit of the mountain.

"And where were you?" thundered the youth, in a tone which made the servant quake; "cowardly wretch! Why are you alive, to speak to me—when your mistress is a prisoner of the Indians?"

The truth soon came out. The servant had fled into the woods, and returned only when, from his hiding-place, he saw the band depart.

As he finished his reluctant explanation, the old man opened his eyes, and looked vaguely around.

"George," he murmured, "where is Cannie?"

And with a violent movement he strove to rise to his feet.

"Sit still, Sir William! there, sit still!" said the servant, holding him.

"What have you done with my child?" cried the old man, flushing to the temples, and speaking in a tone of such terrible anguish that it made the hearers tremble; "where is my child? Bring her hither!"

He resembled a lion at bay as he thus spoke, with glaring eyes; but his strength suddenly failed him. The blood gushed from the deep wound; and stretching his arms out wildly he exclaimed, as he fell fainting:

"My child! my child!"

George's face had turned so pale that it frightened the

servant and made him recoil. His teeth were clenched, and his eyes burned with a steady and meaning flame, which indicated the depth to which his nature was aroused. No one would have recognized in the man of resolute coldness, who stood gazing at the inanimate form, the gay and smiling boy which he had always appeared to be.

George was passing through that ordeal which tempers the metal, and makes the soul steel for the real struggles of life.

"Take care of your master, and bind up his wound," he said hoarsely, "I leave him in your charge. If he asks for his daughter, or for me, when he revives, say I told you I had gone to bring her back or to die with her! Remember!"

And leaving the room, he mounted his panting animal and pushed down the steep declivity as he had ascended.

The gorge was passed—the river crossed—through the prairie, which began to glimmer in the first light of daybreak, he rapidly advanced toward the "Three Oaks."

Many settlers had assembled, and others were approaching from every quarter. Above the crowd, motionless as a statue, on his white horse, the form of Falconbridge rose clearly against the sky.

From the north, Captain Wagner, followed by a number of hunters, approached at a tremendous gallop.

CHAPTER LX.

THE DEVIL'S GARDEN.

IT is the evening succeeding the scenes which have just been related.

The sun is near its setting.

A stream of crimson light, as red as blood, bathes the valleys and mountains, coloring tree trunks, and mossy rocks and flowing streams, with its ruddy splendor.

As the day declines, the deep flush ascends the trees, and creeps up the precipices—with a stealthy crawl, like some variegated wild animal, disappearing in the depths of the gorges.

Finally it raises the golden crown from the top of the Blue Ridge—fades from the pines of the wave-like Massinutton, and lingers for an instant on the Great North Mountain, and those serried ranges which extend, like the huge ribs of some prostrate giant, through the region which is watered by Lost River.

One pinnacle only at last remains illuminated. It raises its mighty head abruptly from the valley, at a point not many miles south of the spot where Lost River sinks and disappears at the base of the mountain, which vainly seeks to bar its advance.

There is something no less curious than majestic about this vast pile, which is appropriately styled, by one who has described it, a "truly wonderful work of Nature."

Between two ranges of the bristling mountain, a strip of ground, about half a mile wide, commences ascending from the head of "Trout Run," and continues to mount gradually for the distance of three miles. Then it suddenly terminates in a dizzy precipice—a vast Titanic pile of dark granite, such as the giants who warred against the gods might have heaped up as a memorial of one of their slain brethren. The immense mass is entirely separate from the surrounding mountains—yawning chasms upon each hand present an impassable gulf—in front the precipice descends as straight as an arrow to the depth of five hundred feet.

The details of this singular natural wonder, are no less striking than the object itself.

A portion of the summit is covered with flat rocks, forming a natural pavement—interrupted here and there by fissures,—and on the eastern edge stands a gigantic bust in granite—the head, neck and shoulders, clearly defined:—the whole presenting to the eye "a frowning and terrific appearance." Near this figure, which gives its name to the peak, formerly stood a granite pillar, ten or twelve feet high—two or more feet in diameter, and four-square. This pillar has been broken from its base by some convulsion of the earth or the elements, and reclines in the form of an arch across one of the fissures of which we have spoken.

This is the summit. But the strange details of the peak are not exhausted. About a hundred feet below the base of the statue a door leads into deep caverns in the rock. After leaving the entrance, the explorer finds himself in an apartment with level floor and ceiling—from which a flight of stone steps ascend to another still larger. In like manner twelve flights of steps give access to twelve apartments—the last of which is just beneath the pavement of the summit, and is lighted by one of the fissures already described.*

Such is "The Devil's Garden." And to this wild scene we now beg the reader to accompany us.

For a time no living thing is seen, except some huge eagle, sailing by on broad wings, above Lost River, a flying fallow

---

* The description of this singular place is taken, almost word for word, from Kercheval's "History of the Valley."—APPENDIX, page 465 ;—heading "*The Devil's Garden.*"

deer, or a bear, slowly shaking his black head, and vanishing in the tangled thickets of the mountain side.

The sun slowly sinks, and his last beams linger on the weird-looking statue, and the vast mass of piled up granite which soars above.

The wild scene, with its billowy ranges, and glimmering torrents grows wilder—the denizens of the night begin to wake in their lairs and prowl abroad to seek their prey—over the immense horizon, all bristling with jagged peaks and precipices, the solemn grandeur, and rude magnificence slowly yield to a brooding gloom,—the scene is an overturned world, convulsed and shattered—the very genius of desolation descends and reigns, on his blood-red throne of mountains.

The blazing shield at last sinks beneath the horizon, and night stretches its broad pall, prepared to throw it over the whole.

At this moment a slight rustling might have been heard at the entrance to the caverns, on the declivity of the peak, and a swarthy face appeared at the opening, followed ere long by a strange and repulsive-looking figure, which remained for a time motionless in the gathering gloom.

CHAPTER LXI.

THE HALF-BREED.

THE figure which thus obtruded itself upon the wild scene, belonged apparently to no nation or class, if, indeed, to the race of human beings! It was nevertheless possessed of a revolting interest, and a lover of the horrible and picturesque united would have feasted his eyes upon the animal.

He was a half-breed, about five feet high, with a deep yellow, or sallow complexion, a gigantic breadth of chest, long monkey-like arms, and legs which resembled the crooked and gnarled boughs of a distorted oak. His forehead was scarcely an inch in height; his small eyes, as cunning and cruel as a serpent's, rolled beneath bushy brows; his nose was crooked like a hawk's bill, and the hideous mouth, stretching almost from ear to ear, was disfigured with protruding tusks like those of a wild boar. The half-breed was clad as an Indian, with doeskin leggins and breeches, but his rugged chest and shoulders were bare. His enormous flat feet were cased in huge moccasins; and in his belt he carried a knife, a horseman's pistol. and a tomahawk, to the unwiped edge of which still clung a quantity of bloody human hair.

Such was the figure which now cautiously emerged from the cavern, and cast a keen and searching glance upon the panorama of forest, mountain and river. This look seemed to plunge into the obscurest depths of the gorges, beneath the heaviest foliage, and to descry every object within the range of human vision.

"All's safe so far!" muttered the half-breed in a guttural and discordant voice, with a slight French accent; "they have either not followed us, or the trick has deceived them. We may lay low here a day or two safely, until the alarm has blown over—then to work again!"

As he spoke, with a sneering and horrible smile, a light hand was laid upon his shoulder. He started and turned suddenly, half drawing his long knife. Then at sight of the intruder on his reverie, he returned the weapon slowly, as if against his will, to its place, and said sullenly, with an unconscious scowl, full of hatred and menace:

"What does the son of War Eagle want with me?"

"I would speak to the Yellow Serpent," said a grave, collected voice in the Indian tongue; "the day is done, and the hour has come for talking."

With these words the young Indian, Lightfoot, who was the intruder, leaned back against the rock, and fixed his eyes upon the threatening countenance of his companion.

Lightfoot was clad as we have seen him on a former occasion. His slender but nervous limbs, with their rounded but clearly defined muscles, were cased in pliant doeskin; his narrow feet, with the lofty instep, based themselves firmly on the crag; above his forehead waved the variegated plume which indicated his chiefship. There was the same calm air of grave, almost melancholy dignity—the same clear yet mild expression in the eyes; as before, his figure, and attitude, and whole bearing were characterized by the simple and exquisite grace of a nobleman of the great forests.

"And what does Lightfoot come to say?—talk it out!" said the discordant voice, which attempted to assume an accent of friendly interest; "the time is passing, and much must be done."

"Will the serpent return to the war-path again?" said Lightfoot as before in the Indian tongue—then, with a sudden change in his expression, from gravity to scorn, he added, "but there is no war trail! The braves are on the path to the cabins of women and childen. The white warriors are away, and the Catawbas creep over the fences in the night—they are rabbits, not panthers!"

And the lip of the Indian curled. His words produced a strong effect on the half-breed. The snake-like eye flashed fire, and with a guttural sound like the growl of a wild animal, he laid his hand on his knife, and seemed about to throw himself upon the speaker.

The young Indian did not move a muscle, or remove his scornful eyes from the face of his companion. With a movement wholly simple and unostentatious, he rested his hand on the hilt of a long poniard in his belt, and continued to gaze at the other.

"Does Lightfoot know what he is saying?" said the half-breed, growling and letting his hand fall.

".Yes, the truth," was the reply.

"*I* am one of these Catawbas."

"I know that you are."

"And you tell me to my face I am a rabbit: you dare?"

"I dare!" said Lightfoot, with superb scorn, "it is little to dare!"

Again the hand of the Yellow Serpent wandered to his weapon: but he seemed to want courage to attack his adversary. A glance at the precipice near which they were standing—a glance as rapid as lightning, and full of horrible menace—betrayed the thought which passed through his mind. But it was not carried into act. The young man seemed to exert a singular influence over him—he evidently hated him bitterly, but he cowered almost before his eye, and yielded in the contest. The threatening scowl disappeared: the hand fell again: with a grin which was even more repulsive than the frown, he said, in a wheedling and insinuating voice:

"Lightfoot is bold and outspoken as he has always been —as his great father was before him, for whom twelve tribes mourned when the blood ran out of his brave bosom. But let the Yellow Serpent give Lightfoot a piece of advice. These words are dangerous, and the warriors would want to kill him. They are nothing to the Serpent. He is a half-breed, and knows more than the redfaces. He is Lightfoot's friend and would serve him."

"Yellow Serpent," said the young Indian, returning to his calm expression, "do you believe in the Great Spirit?"

The half-breed grinned and replied:

"I believe in the Great Evil Spirit—what the palefaces call the Devil—for he talks to me, and tells me what to do."

I believe that, Serpent. But there is a good Spirit, too, and he is the bad Spirit's master."

The half-breed shook his head.

"Are you certain of that, Lightfoot?"

"I am certain. It is Manitou—the great and good. The Dove of the Mountain told me this long ago."

"Ah! ah! the Dove of the Mountain!" was the grinning and sneering reply; "you are a friend of the Dove!"

"I am. She has made me better. I am evil, but not so much as I was."

"It is a pity that the tribe took her prisoner. But what about the Great Spirit?"

"I would ask if you think you do right, Yellow Serpent, when you put to death women and children?"

"They are whites," said the half-breed with very great surprise; "you see we strangle the brood when they are young, to get rid of them."

"You are cowards! Yes, *lâche! lâche!*" said the young Indian with sudden vehemence, and using a term which he had derived from the French allies of the savages, "*lâche!* You are a dog, Yellow Serpent! But, no, not even dogs would be so cowardly!"

And the young Indian's eyes were terrible for their depth of indignation. The half-breed cowered before him, and dared not speak. He seemed to want nerve. With a dark scowl, which had in it something tragic and dangerous from its subtlety, and veiled menace, he muttered :

Lightfoot is a great sagamore. The Serpent is not as noble as he is. Let Lightfoot speak."

"Listen, then, Yellow Serpent," said the Indian, stretching out his hand, and speaking in a voice of such nobility and solemn earnestness that the furious and shuddering half-breed was subdued by its very tones: "listen, Serpent, and pay attention to what I am about to say. In this world are two tribes of men—they are the evil and the good. There is but one master over all, the Great Spirit. The Evil One is his slave, but is not chained. It is his business to make the tribes commit evil; and even now he is in your heart, though you do not see him. But the Good Spirit is not idle, or indifferent to the happiness of his creatures. He is yonder in the clouds looking down, and watching. He speaks in the thunder of the mountains—the lightning is the flash of his eye; his finger marks the track of the rivers; he is the Father of this world and its people. Not a tribe roams the forest, from the sand hills of the mighty lakes, to the Big Water of the South—from the Minnehaha to the land of Shawandasee—which is not beneath his eye. He sends to all, the bright seasons, the moon of strawberries, and the moon of cohonks;—mondamin grows for all, and plenty crowns the feasts of all the mighty tribes of the beautiful world. But in these tribes there are some whom the Master of Life looks on with smiles—there are others upon whom he frowns. He frowns on the bad, on the cruel, on the oppressors of the weak, on the slayers of women and children? Once these evil people made him angry, and the sea swept over them—but the land was repeopled; then they grew as evil as before. The Master sent his son to heal the sick ones, and to make men pure again. They nailed him on a cross, and killed him! But before he died he told them many things, and among the rest he said, 'Let the children come to me—the Master loves them, and his land is full of

them.' He loved them because they were weak and helpless
—and he told the tribes, not the redfaces only, but all, to
love each other, and forgive even their enemies. The Master said that! And now what are you doing, Yellow Serpent? You are killing the women and the children who
never wronged you; you are not even acting like a warrior,
and meeting the palefaced braves in battle,—you are *lâche!
lâche!* You have said rightly! The Evil Spirit whispers in
your ear, and sets you to do his work! You are his slave,
Yellow Serpent."

And the young Indian, with a cold and collected air,
leaned back against the rock from which he had half risen
in the ardor of his address.

His words seemed to affect the half-breed strangely. A
sullen and gloomy expression came to his hideous features,
and he cowered, almost. The young chief plainly exercised
a singular dominion over the monster. Then this sullen
air disappeared—a flash of concealed hatred darted from
his eyes—lastly, the former crafty and insinuating grin succeeded.

"Lightfoot is a great brave," he said; "the Serpent cannot talk with the son of War Eagle. I think I will tell the
tribe what he says, and in future they shall spare the women
and children of the pale-faces, whom Lightfoot loves better
than his own tribe. Oh, yes! we will not kill any more!"

The Indian shook his head.

"Yellow Serpent," he said, "I know you very well, and I
do not trust you. The word of a brave is his word—yours
is the word of a half-breed. You hate me, and are envious
of me, because when we rise at the same moment to speak
to the tribe, the warriors say, 'Let us hear the son of War
Eagle.' You would destroy me—but I fear you not. Beware! You have said that I love the pale-faces. That is
true. They are the children of the Great Spirit, like the
red-faces. They have been kind to me, and I will speak for
them as I have spoken in council. Enough. They are on

the war-path even now, and the bullet for your heart may be moulded. Yellow Serpent, you are evil; the Devil of the whites, truly, is your friend. Beware of him—he will tear you limb from limb, and devour you. I have spoken!"

And turning away, the young Indian swept the landscape with a comprehensive glance, and re-entered the cavern, in depths of which he disappeared.

The half-breed, who seemed to be agitated strangely, as though under a magnetic influence, remained motionless. This influence was slowly dissipated: his crafty grin returned, and with a menacing flash of the glittering eyes, he followed Lightfoot into the cave.

For five minutes he had been covered by a dozen rifles, from the depths of the opposite mountain, where Captain Wagner and his party lay concealed.

LXII.

THE TRAIL.

THE party had set out from the "Three Oaks" in twenty minutes after the arrival of Captain Wagner. That worthy, who, now that the contest was approaching, grew as cold and deliberate as an automaton, would not wait for Lord Fairfax, and his troop. In brief, quick words, he delivered his orders—explained that he was officially commanding for the Earl, the Lieutenant of the county—and reviewed the arms and equipments of the party. They were hunters for the most part, and carried rifles and powder-horns. Nearly every one had his provision of jerked beef for the expedition.

The rapid examination having proved satisfactory, the Captain took the head of the party, and directed his march straight toward the Cedar Creek Mountain to the west, in which direction his knowledge of the country and of the habits of the Indians told him that the band had gone.

They marched rapidly and silently until noon without finding any traces; but all at once they came upon a cabin, rifled of its contents and half-burned. The fire had evidently gone out, and a miserable-looking woman who had escaped on the appearance of the savages, and only returned when they went off, was crouching by the chimney-corner. Captain Wagner learned from her that his views were correct in relation to the direction taken by the band, and all set forward with new ardor.

They soon entered the wild range of the Cedar Creek Mountain, and here, in the soft earth along the stream, struck on an unmistakable trail. At points also distant only a few yards from each other, the boughs were bent down and broken, and the prints of feet were easily traced in the earth.

Captain Wagner pointed these out to Falconbridge.

"Miss Argal's," he said, briefly, indicating a deep, narrow footprint; "and there's my friend's, broader and heavier."

They pushed forward with new ardor, and followed the footprints for several miles. Then the Captain suddenly drew rein, and exclaimed:

"Stop! what's this? The marks are no longer to be seen."

And the Borderer dismounted and examined the ground in every direction. The female footprints had disappeared; but in place of them were unmistakable indications of blood. An ominous frown passed over the face of the Captain, and he looked at Falconbridge. He was trembling. As to George, he was as pale as death.

"It's nothing," said the Borderer, assuming a stolid look; "see, here are the broken boughs still."

In fact, these indications of the route which the band had taken, as well as heavy moccasin footprints, were still visible. As the prisoners had undoubtedly resorted to this device to direct the search of their friends, those prisoners were yet alive.

"May the devil take me if I understand that!" said the Captain, frowning, "but we'll push on."

The path now lay toward the north. They had followed it for five miles, when it suddenly entered a stream a hundred yards wide. Captain Wagner plunged in and forded. On the opposite shore there was no sort of indication of the passage of the band. The broken bushes had continued regularly to the stream—there they suddenly stopped.

Could they have taken to canoes? No, the band was evidently too numerous, and the savages could have brought none with them. What was the explanation? Why had those marks disappeared? The Borderer knit his brows and reflected; then suddenly he pushed back through the water and went straight to one of the limbs which had been bent down and broken. He examined it attentively for an instant, and then leaped into the saddle again.

"About face, friends," he said, "we are on the wrong trail. Follow!"

And he set forward, quickly, returning over the ground which they had just traversed.

"What is the meaning of this retreat, Captain?" said Falconbridge, who seemed possessed by a sort of reckless excitement, "we lose time."

"We have lost much," was the brief reply.

"Those broken boughs"——

"Are devices. Look at 'em, Falconbridge! Don't you perceive that they are thicker than any woman could break —and more than one higher than any but a man could reach? Then observe how plain they are! As much as to say 'Come on! don't mistake!' Prisoners never could have broken 'em without being noticed—it's a blind, and soon you'll see!"

Without further words the Borderer pushed forward, followed by the party, who knew him well, and did not think it at all necessary to question him. They soon reached the spot where the blood was visible, and the footprints of the females disappeared.

"Friends," said the Borderer, after nosing the ground for some moments, like a dog, and examining the dry grass and twigs in every direction, "we are on the trail again. At this spot the bloody rascals discovered the trick of the women to direct us, and one of 'em was struck with a tomahawk! No blazing eyes Falconbridge, or George!—maybe it was a friend of mine! If so, I'll hew down the devils to the last man, or die! But come! The device is plain! The women were taken up, or their shoes removed here; and the fellows sneaked off with 'em, leaving no tracks, while a part of the band went off north breaking limbs and stamping into the ground to mislead us. When they came to the river, they waded in the shallows for a mile, and then doubled back to join the main body."

"Why, there are no tracks here," said Falconbridge, eagerly.

"That's so—to your eyes, it may be, comrade. But I can see 'em. Look at that sprig of grass broken by a moccasin, and see this stick? Follow, friends! I'm on the track—I can smell 'em!"

And the Borderer set forward rapidly. His predictions were soon verified. At the distance of a quarter of a mile from the bloody spot, the traces of feet again became visible, and the narrow marks of high-heeled shoes. The pursuit was now more rapid and sure. On the banks of Trout Run they all at once found other footprints approaching from the north; and Captain Wagner called the attention of Falconbridge to the circumstance, with a significant look.

At the head of the stream, which the party reached, as the sun began to sink, all the footprints disappeared again ; but a curl of the lip betrayed the feelings of the Borderer.

"They are a bungling set of rascals after all," he said; "and don't know their trade, or I'm a dandy! Come, friends, back!"

"Back, Captain!" exclaimed Falconbridge, with surprise.

"Yes, comrade—you are too curious for a hunter or a war party. Come by my side, and I'll explain as I go."

The hunters had exhibited none of Falconbridge's surprise. They obeyed implicity the directions of the Borderer, and followed silently in the footsteps of his horse. Turning a huge shoulder of the mountain, he said to Falconbridge as they proceeded :

"This is the whole thing, companion. The red snakes have crawled into the caves on the Devil's Garden, three miles from the place we stopped at. If we had gone on they would have seen us, and perhaps laid an ambush for us. At any rate, we could have done nothing."

"Yes, I see, but may I ask your plan?"

"Certainly. You are my second in command, and it is simple. I am going to skirt this big shoulder, and mount the peak yonder. From the top of it you will see the precipice of the Devil's Garden, in which the enemy are concealed, not two hundred yards in front of you. A gulf separates it. But I know a way of passing over—there is a path which is covered with pine bushes, winding down into the gorge. As soon as night comes on, if we see good we'll make the onset. I think the cards are pretty well shuffled, and the game is about to begin, comrade!"

As he spoke, the Captain dismounted, and advised all who were mounted to imitate him. He took the saddle from the back of his horse, and hobbling his legs, turned him loose into a little glen, where there was grass and water. The rest did likewise: and then headed by the Borderer, they cautiously wound up the precipitous mountain, the summit of which they reached as the sun sank from sight.

"Look, Falconbridge!" said Wagner, putting stealthily aside the heavy pine boughs beneath which they were concealed; "there are two of the red devils at the mouth of the Devil's Cave!"

As we have seen, these were Lightfoot and the Half-breed.

LXIII.

LIGHTFOOT AND CANNIE.

THE interior of the cavern presented a singular appearance.

A bright fire was burning, and on all sides were piled up articles which the savages had carried off with them from the plundered dwellings. These objects were indicative of the mingled barbarism and childish simplicity of the Indians. There was much gaily-colored crockery; many bright linsey and other fabrics were seen scattered about; and a few strings of beads, and brass rings, taken from the dead bodies of the women whom they had slain, and brought, not without unwillingness, to the general mass, were the objects of longing and covetous glances.

The Indians were forty or fifty in number, and were scattered about the large cavern in various attitudes, picturesque and graceful, or odd and grotesque. Here a great warrior was broiling a piece of venison at the blazing fire in the centre, the savory odor diffusing itself throughout the cave:—there an Indian boy was striving to put together the broken pieces of a red crockery dish, which he had guarded on the march with a jealous care which indicated the high value which he placed upon it. In a corner a number of the braves were sleeping tranquilly in the red light, the blood of the slain still staining their tomahawks, and more than one gory scalp hanging from their girdles, but slumbering, nevertheless, like infants, under the stupefying effects of a long march, a heavy meal, and some rum which they had taken from the Ordinary.

In an obscure corner to which the light of the fire scarcely penetrated, a number of captives, male and female, with their hands securely tied, were huddled together upon the the floor of the cavern, under a guard, who watched them with grave intentness. Neither Monsieur Jambot nor Major Hastyluck was visible, however :—and we may as well say here that these worthies had been "pricked onward" under heavy loads, by another portion of the band, who had hurried westward, and were never more heard of in that region. Hastyluck, doubtless, drank punch among the Sioux and Catawbas—when he could get it—for the remainder of his life: and Monsieur Jambot taught the minuet and reel to youthful savage maidens.

Lightfoot passed through the group, who made way for the young chief with evident respect, and slowly ascended the rugged stairway into the next cave above.

In this were confined, under guard of a single Indian, who stood outside, Mrs. Butterton, Miss Argal, and Cannie.

The two former were sleeping, wrapped in shawls, near a blazing fire, on piles of dry grass which had been arranged for them—their feet swollen and frayed by the long journey —their skirts cut off below the knees—a necessity to facilitate their movements.*

Mrs. Butterton was slumbering fitfully; her dress was stained with blood, and a wound was visible upon one of her large fat arms; from which wound, indeed, had flowed the blood which the pursuing party discovered at the point of divergence of the two routes. The dame had been discovered bending down and breaking the branches, and one of the chiefs had struck her with his tomahawk. The wound was not dangerous, however. She slept uneasily, but evidently without much physical pain. But, from time to time, her features would become distorted by an expres-

---

* See Kercheval in many places. This was a systematic practice among the Indians, with their female captives.

sion of fear, and she would raise her hands wildly and murmur some broken and indistinct words, which the young Indian sentinel would listen to with grave interest. Miss Argal slept as quietly and sweetly as a child.

Cannie was awake, and when the light tread of the young Indian attracted her attention, the little face became brighter, and she held out her hand to Lightfoot with the air of a child who sees a protector approach. The smile with which she greeted him was inexpressibly sad; but his presence was evidently a comfort to her.

"Oh, I am so glad to see you, Lightfoot!" she said, wiping away two tears which hung like dew-drops upon her eye-lashes; "this place frightens me, and it is like home to see you."

The word *home* seemed to direct the girl's thoughts to her grandfather, and with a sudden rush of blood to her cheeks, she placed both hands upon her face and sobbed.

"Oh, me! they have killed him! they have killed him!"

Lightfoot stood for a moment, silently regarding the girl as she half reclined upon the couch of dry grass, her frame shaken by sobs, her breast heaving, her long chestnut curls falling wildly about her shoulders. An expression of unspeakable love and tenderness came to his eyes; and he seemed unable for the moment to command his voice.

He controlled his emotion, however, with the wonderful art of his race, and made a movement of his hand toward the young Indian who stood on guard.

"Go," he said, in the Catawba tongue, "I would speak with the captive."

The sentinel obeyed with an alacrity which indicated perfect willingness to join his companions below, and disappeared. The cavern was left thus untenanted except by the two persons, and the sleepers, whose heavy breathing invaded the silence.

Lightfoot took the hand of the girl in his own, with an air of the deepest respect, and said, mildly:

"No, they have not killed your grandfather, Mountain Dove. You know that I came from the forest as the Catawbas made their attack. Had I arrived sooner," added the young Indian, raising his head proudly, "it would never have happened, for they obey the son of War Eagle. I came in time to stop the knife which would have scalped the old man:—he is scarcely injured, and will soon walk the mountain again."

"Oh, are you sure, Lightfoot?" cried Cannie, removing her hands quickly, and raising her wet face, "are you sure? Dear Lightfoot! you love Cannie—do you not? Do not deceive me! I am only a child," she added, weeping silently, "and very weak, but I can bear it—I won't cry! Are you certain that grandpa was not killed?"

"He was only wounded, and not badly. I struck down the arm of the warrior who would have scalped him; and you know the tribe directly commenced their march."

There was an air of such simplicity and sincerity about the young Indian as he spoke, that his words carried conviction to his hearer. Her eyes sparkled with sudden delight, her breast was filled with a long, deep breath, which seemed to afford her inexpressible relief, and seizing the Indian's hand, she exclaimed with touching earnestness and affection:

"How can I ever love you enough, dear Lightfoot, for protecting grandpa? I will love you until I die!"

And carried away by glad emotion, before he was conscious of her intention, Cannie raised the hand which she held to her lips, and imprinted upon it a long, lingering kiss.

A shudder of delight ran through the frame of the young Indian. His face flushed, and the eyes which were generally so calm and clear, suddenly filled with impetuous emotion. A thrill of happiness agitated his pulses, at the contact of the soft, warm lips, and he drew away the hand, with a look of such unspeakable tenderness that Cannie colored to the roots of her hair.

That look had revealed to her in an instant, with the rapidity of lightning, as it were, the secret of the young Indian. For years she had known that he had a deep affection for her—from her childhood he had visited the mountain cottage regularly, and always exhibited his fondness—but now she saw plainly that there was a deeper feeling in his heart. The instinct of womanhood explained all this to her—she saw for the first time, with agitated eyes, that the young Indian loved her as a youth loves a maiden.

And Lightfoot was not backward in discerning the new relations which must exist from that moment between himself and Cannie. He saw that his glance had betrayed him, that she had witnessed his tremor of delight—that she had understood at last his real feelings. They had grown up together, as youth and child—they were no longer such. It was a man who was sitting beside the woman whom he loved with a devotion and tenderness which absorbed his very being,

For some moments deep silence reigned in the cavern. Both were too much overcome to speak. A vague pain and pity, not unmingled with tenderness, filled the bosom of the young girl; and from time to time, she stole a furtive glance at the Indian, her cheeks burning with blushes, her lips trembling. Never had she looked so beautiful as at that instant. The curls of her chestnut hair fell in glossy masses around the pure young face with its innocent and grave sweetness—the slender figure inclined sidewise, in an attitude of exquisite grace—the head was bent over the left shoulder, and nearly rested upon it:—in outline and carriage, in the entire character and expression, of the girl, there was no longer anything of the child: it was a woman, and a woman of surpassing loveliness, who had burst into bloom—passed suddenly from the bud to the perfect flower. Had sorrow caused this rapid development? It may have been so. But often a similar phenomenon takes place without any visible reason.

It was then that the young Indian proved the nobility of his nature. Instead of taking her hand, he drew his own away. Instead of gazing into the blushing and agitated face, to discern if his feelings were returned, he lowered his eyes. For some moments his gaze remained fixed upon the floor of the cavern, and the heaving muscles of his chest alone indicated the terrible war of emotion in his bosom.

When he raised his head he had become calm again. There was no longer any light in his eyes, any flush in his cheeks; and the lips were firm again. A grave sweetness and serenity, just tinged with melancholy, had replaced the sudden rush of ardent emotion. It was the face full of serious and noble dignity to which she was accustomed : and Cannie blushed again, as she looked into the clear eyes, as the woman's thought came to her—he is so noble, and he loves me!

For some moments they sat gazing thus in silence at each other. Then the young Indian gravely took her little hand in his own, and pressed it to his lips, with the expression of a devotee at the shrine of his saint.

"Lightfoot is a poor weak boy," he said, in a low voice, which had not recovered its calmness wholly; "he has done wrong. But the little Mountain Dove will forgive him—will she not?"

"Forgive you, Lightfoot?" murmured Cannie, almost inaudibly, "why, what have you done?"

"What was wrong," said the young man, shaking his head, sadly. "I cannot conceal anything—my father always made me act honestly—I have tried to be the son of War Eagle in truth, and this puts the words in my mouth. I have done wrong, because I have spoken with my eyes to the Dove, as a young pale-face may speak—and said, 'I love you.' I am not a pale-face, I am a poor Indian, and inferior to the tribe beyond the Big Water. It is not right that my father's son should do this—that he should come to the little white Dove when she has no friend near her—when she is a captive in the hands of Lightfoot's tribe—and say, 'I love you, and would have you love me as your chosen warrior.' No, no," said the young Indian, his cheeks filling in spite of every effort, and his voice trembling, "that is wrong, and my father's spirit frowns upon me from the sky!"

And turning away his head, the speaker uttered a deep sigh, which, but for his immense self-control, would have turned into a groan.

The girl blushed and avoided his gaze as he spoke; but now recovering her voice, said in low, broken accents:

"You pain me, Lightfoot! You hurt Cannie. Do not talk thus. I am only a child, and you must love me as before—for—for—I love you dearly—dear, dear, Lightfoot!"

She had not intended it. She never would have uttered the words had she reflected for a single instant upon the meaning which he must attach to them. It was an impulse of irresistible pity and kindness which carried her away—of woman's tenderness for one who loved her and suffered—of admiration and old affection, and lonely weakness. She burst into a flood of tears as she spoke, and then suddenly drew her hand away.

The young Indian had seized it with passionate tenderness, and covered it with kisses.

"No—no!" she sobbed; "do not! do not, Lightfoot! I did not mean—how unhappy—how miserable I am!"

And the voice died away in an inarticulate murmur. The Indian drew back, and folded his arms. He saw his terrible error in an instant, and in its whole extent. His heart turned cold, and with close-set teeth he remained as silent and rigid as a statue, his dark eyes burning with a fixed and immovable despair. The girl spoke first: her voice was broken and agitated. Sobs interrupted it, at every instant.

"I was—wrong: it was cruel to—mislead you. I will not affect—any ignorance of your meaning! Will you—pardon me? I am not strong and calm like you, Lightfoot," she continued, wiping her eyes, and continuing more calmly, "I am only a child, and I could not help saying how much I—loved you, as my dear, dear friend and playmate, at our dear little home! I did not think—but I will not speak of that any more! Indeed, you are very dear to me, for you have been kind and good to me always, and to grandpapa, and I admire, and look up to you, Lightfoot. I am only a child yet, and not a woman. You will love me, will you not, as a child—as you always loved me—and I will love you. You'll be my brother and friend, will you not, Lightfoot?"

And Cannie, with all the simplicity and innocence of a child, looked into the young Indian's agitated face, smiling through her tears, and appealing to him, as it were, for care and protection.

A last contraction of the Indian's features betrayed the depth of the despair which he controlled with a will of iron. He had conquered himself. His face grew calm and grave again—he returned the confiding look of the girl with one of brotherly kindness and affection.

"I thank the Great Spirit, who has blessed the poor son of War Eagle with these moments," he said, raising his noble head and eyes toward heaven, "I thank the Master of Life more than all for placing me where I may show the young Dove of the mountain that I am her friend. Let her cease to remember the wild words which Lightfoot has uttered—they came from his lips without asking him to let them. But the blood shall flow out of his heart as readily for the Dove who has spoken to him so kindly. Yes, yes, I will be your friend, Mountain Dove—the hour is near when I will prove it. Forget now the words I have spoken, and sleep. But pray for the poor son of War Eagle first."

"Oh, yes!" said Cannie, wiping away her tears, "let us

pray together as we have often done at home, Lightfoot!"

And taking the Indian's hand, the young girl knelt at his side, and murmured a prayer for him, for her grandfather, and for all whom she loved.

It was a touching spectacle, to see the young man and the girl thus kneeling beside each other in the gloomy cavern, only half revealed by the stray gleams of the dying fire. They were of different and hostile races—they were in deadly peril—the hours that came rapidly would decide life or death for them—but they prayed. They prayed as tranquilly and hopefully, their humble prayer, as though they knelt at home in the little mountain dwelling. And mortals may do as much everywhere.

When Lightfoot slowly retired, his face was quite calm. His great soul was untroubled. He had yielded his heart and future to the "Master of Life," and was tranquil.

Fifteen minutes after he had disappeared down the staircase, the Half-breed, who had been concealed in a dark nook at the entrance, glided out, and entered the cavern from which he had just emerged.

LXIV.

THE SLAVE AND HIS MISTRESS.

EXHAUSTED by the painful conflict of emotion, in the scene with Lightfoot, Cannie had quickly followed his injunctions, and fallen asleep.

When the Half-breed stole, with the stealthy step of a creeping tiger, into the apartment, the girl was lying upon her couch of dry grass, and breathing regularly as she slumbered. The hideous being paused for a moment upon the threshold; and then, with a cowed and humble air, approached the group, his eyes fixed on the form of Miss Argal.

This man, if he may be called such, was one of those strange and anomalous beings who appear from time to time on the earth, to falsify, it would seem, every rule and maxim in relation to human character. Deformed in body and mind—a revolting monster to the eye, and no less a repulsive object to the mind—he yet possessed a strange sensitiveness to beauty and nobility, and cowered before them as a slave before the whip of the master whom he recognizes. We have seen that in the interview with Lightfoot, the Half-breed, in spite of his hatred and jealousy, was unable to meet the eye of the young chief. The presence of the son of War Eagle defeated all his calculations—his influence in the tribe was seriously lessened—the youth had called him a slave, and what was more terrible still, had used the word which made his blood boil within him—the word "*lâche!*" Yet in spite of all this, in spite of his most powerful efforts, he had been compelled, by some irresistible power, to crouch before the youth, and bend his back to the lash, and submit his own will to the nobler nature of his insulter.

This singular submission of the lower nature to the higher, now influenced him in his feelings for Miss Argal. His training and previous life had all tended to degrade the female sex in his mind. Among the Indians they were scarcely more than beasts of burden, and to say that he resembled a woman was the most terrible insult that could be inflicted on a brave. Nevertheless, the young lady ruled him despotically from the first moment of their meeting. Her strange and extraordinary beauty, the brilliant fascination of her eyes, her exquisite grace of attitude, and undulating movements, all impressed him deeply, and made his pulses throb. He had killed her father with his own hand, and quartered the body. It was the Half-breed who stuck the bleeding head upon the stake, and inflicted a last gash, as he danced gaily around it, like a goblin of darkness. It was his iron clutch which had dragged Miss Argal from her chamber, into the light, and his tomahawk had been lifted above her head, to dash her brains out.

The tomahawk had not fallen. The torches had no sooner poured their bloody light upon the beauty of the young lady, than true to his strange instinct, the Half-breed recognized his superior. His arm fell—he recoiled, as it were, before her; and then, thrilling with a vague and secret pleasure at the thought that she was in his power, he had protected her from insult and injury, with the fury of a father who guards the person of his beloved daughter.

At the thought that she was in his power! Such was really the first reflection of the Half-breed—the flattering unction which he laid to his fierce and degraded soul. He soon discovered that their relative positions were reversed. He was the slave of her beauty and exquisite grace, and like a slave he applied himself to the task of waiting on his mistress. The burdens which the tribe had placed upon Miss Argal's pretty round shoulders, and beneath which she had bent down, crying, were indignantly removed. He took them on his own enormous back, to appease the Indians, and walked by her side, grinning hideously, and conversing with the captive.

She had soon discovered the influence which she possessed over her conqueror, and had applied herself to the task, throughout the march, of deriving benefit from it. Fortunately, a falsehood of the Half-breed prevented the poor girl from being bowed down to the ground by the horrible recollection of her father's dissevered body. She had been removed from the building before the Half-breed slew him; and the monster coolly informed her that he had escaped in the darkness, and was unhurt. Thus, Miss Argal, unoppressed by this terrible tragedy, and convinced that her father, whom she loved dearly, was safe, gave her attention to the conquest of her captor, without effort. She had dazzled him with the magnetic lustre of her eyes; sent a shiver through his deformed and rugged frame, by touching his huge, knotty hand with her own little white one, as soft as satin; she had smiled upon the Half-breed, as she alone knew how to smile; and very soon perfected her conquest. Before they reached their place of concealment, she had not only secured for herself every comfort and convenience, she had also induced her slave to treat Cannie and Mrs. Butterton without cruelty, even respectfully. She would pass her arm around Cannie when the child grew faint, and send the Half-breed to the stream to procure water for her. He was her captive, and she used her power to ameliorate the condition of her companions, with whom she shared every comfort.

And on all this, the strange being had looked with approbation and a species of pleasure. It evidently delighted him to humble himself before the beautiful woman. He seemed thus to approach nearer to her. He was less her abhorrence when she smiled on him, than when she trembled before him, and recoiled as his captive. And here we notice another trait in this bloody animal. His physical deformity had been, throughout his life, as sore a point with him as a clubfoot or a cast in the eye is to a beau or a fashionable young lady. He had found himself the terror and horror of the Indian maidens. They retreated hastily when he approached them and avoided any chance of meeting him. One and all of them had striven vainly to conceal the mingled fear and disgust which they felt for his person, with its crooked, gnarled limbs, its gigantic torse, its low, flat forehead, wide mouth, and protruding tusks. He had loved one of these maidens—as he could love—as her slave. Her beauty had attracted him and he had sued for her hand; but the maiden had almost fainted when his sallow face approached her own—when his huge mouth expanded into a hideous grin of servile admiration. When he took her hand in his great rugged paw, on which the black veins stood out like whip-cords, she had shuddered, and drawn it hastily away. When he pressed her to tell him what her feeling toward him was, she had replied, with a trembling voice, that she was afraid of him; but he read in her pale, sick face that she regarded him with irresistible disgust.

Such had been the weakness, such the fortune of the Half-breed throughout his life. He had early left the peaceful home of his tribe, and joined the predatory band of the Catawbas. On the war-path, in the midst of blood and peril, his deformity would not be observed. His great strength and ferocity had soon gained for him a conspicuous position in the tribe. He became a chief, and was what in other walks of life we would call a rapidly rising man. But the recollection of his deformity never left him. He yearned for some object upon which to expend his pent-up feelings. What those feelings were he never stopped to inquire, nor do we feel able to describe them. The Half-breed was a monster of ferocity and blood, but he was still human, and not wholly destitute of human emotion. At times his craving for something—if only an animal—to love him, was enormous, irresistible almost. He would remain for days in his wigwam, scarcely tasting food, brooding over his condition, and struggling in his benighted and sullen mind to understand why he had been created, and what his life would be. When he came forth, and the tribe whispered and nodded at him, and followed him with their eyes as his squat figure went by—muttering fearfully that the Yellow Serpent had been communing with spirits—he would gnash his teeth with scorn, and despise the shallow fools, and feel that he was alone in the world. Then he would return to the war-path with a bloody ardor, which struck terror into all hearts; he would slay women and children without mercy; he would reap undying honor from his associates—to go back and writhe and growl in his den like a wounded wild animal, whose body is festering with poisonous blood and corruption.

This was the thorn in the ferocious soul of the Half-breed —the secret wound which made him mad with pain almost. He knew his own mental and physical deformity, the disgustingly hideous body and mind which he possessed; and he cowered before those who were superior to him. He crouched in the presence of a pure and noble soul like Lightfoot's. He obeyed with the alacrity of a slave the commands of the beautiful woman who was in his power. He waited upon her, and followed her directions like a servant. It is true that at times, as he had attempted in the presence of Lightfoot, he would struggle to assert the supremacy which he really possessed—the power which he could exert over the band—his authority; but the endeavor was vain. True to his instinct, as we have said before, he would yield in the struggle, bow his head before what he recognized as above him, and take the position of the slave again, awaiting the order of his superior.

Thus the Half-Breed was almost delighted when Miss Argal commanded him to do anything. Her subtle instinct soon taught her that this was the best manner of treating him. The penetrating eyes of the young lady discerned the secret of her power, and she was not backward in availing herself of it. His respect and submission seemed to increase with her arbitary demeanor. There was a strange charm, too, in thus humbling the master of her fate. As we have already said, she used her power like a kind, tender woman, to soften the lot of her companions, especially Cannie. She had taken a strong fancy to the child indeed, and supplied her with every comfort she had. She took off her own wrapping and threw it around the little shoulders, and seemed really distressed when Cannie would not receive it. At least the girl should have everything which she could procure for her, however; and the slave-master, the Half-breed, was calmly directed to bring this or that object for Cannie, and attend to all her wants and even wishes. The savage would grin and hasten to obey. His reward was the approving smile of his empress—that smile which said to him, as he basked in it with fierce pleasure, "Others may think you are hideous and repulsive, but I am fond of you, because you comply with my wishes." It was the long sought balm for his degraded soul—the salve which softened his festering wound. He could thus forget for a time his debasement, and submit his fierce head, like a conquered wild animal, with grumbling delight, to the soft white hand which caressed it without fear or disgust.

Once arrived at their place of concealment, the Half-breed had applied himself assiduously to the task of making the young lady's retreat, and that of her companions, as comfortable as possible. He had gone to some distance and procured a large quantity of dry grass for their couches. This he had arranged in the most convenient manner; and then he had brought a quantity of the linsey shawls which had been stolen, to protect them from the cold air of the cavern. A fire had then been kindled, some supper brought, and the savage had retired as a servant retires after fulfilling the commands of his mistress.

Every arrangement connected with the concealment of the tribe had been hurried through by the Half-breed—every trace of their presence obliterated. He had finally gone to make a last survey of the horizon, before returning to the magnet which attracted him in the cavern above. We have seen how he was detained by Lightfoot, how they conversed for a time, and how the young Indian re-entered first. When the Half-breed followed him, he found that he had mounted to the upper cavern where the three females were; and he stealthily glided up the staircase behind him. Concealed in a dark nook of the cave he had heard the entire conversation between Lightfoot and Cannie, had thrilled with a strange awe as they prayed, and remained in his place of concealment until the young Indian had retired, and Cannie, as he knew by her regular breathing, was asleep.

He then entered and approached Miss Argal.

LXV.

CALIBAN AND MIRANDA.

THE young lady stirred in her sleep, and a tremor ran through her frame. The vicinity of the crouching and hideous figure seemed to exert a magnetic influence upon her.

The Half-breed remained for some time silent and motionless at her side, gazing with a species of ferocious and yet servile admiration upon the beautiful countenance, around which fell the profuse ebon curls—afraid apparently to awaken the sleeper. Finally he grew bolder; he crawled like a stealthy panther toward the pillow of the girl, and took in his huge knotty fingers, one of the dark curls and gazed at it with the air of a child who holds a toy which fills it with delight.

The movement awoke the sleeper, and for an instant she gazed with a dreamy air into the revolting mask, rather than human countenance, upon which the red gleam of the firelight fell, lighting up every repulsive detail—the snake-like eyes, the grinning mouth, the hooked nose, and narrow forehead, like a dog's or an ape's. Another tremor ran through Miss Argal's form, and she quickly rose, leaning upon one hand, and looking silently at the Half-breed. In this gaze, however, there was no trace of fear. Despite the wild and frightful scene, the horrible appearance of the intruder, and the half-darkness of the cavern, she did not tremble or exhibit any sign of terror. On the contrary, she recovered almost instantly the air of mistress, which we have referred to, and said in a tone of anger:

"Why did you come and wake me?"

The savage cowered, and retreating two paces, said humbly, but cunningly:

"I came to see if the White Raven," such was the name he had given her, "was well wrapped up and warm. The cave is cold and damp—and she is weary with the journey."

"Well," said Miss Argal calmly, "you see that I am provided for—and now leave me."

The Half-breed made an unconscious motion to obey, following his instinct—but some other impulse counteracted the first.

"Let us talk a little, first," he said, grinning with a polite air. "Let the White Raven talk to the Yellow Serpent."

"I am weary."

"Nevertheless you must talk," returned the Half-Breed obdurately, "you are my captive, and I am not sleepy."

Miss Argal saw from the tone of these words that she had lost a portion of her former power over him, and her marvelous tact made her instantly change her manner and expression.

"Well," she said, "if you treat me as your captive, I must submit, and obey you. Of what shall we talk, Yellow Serpent?"

The old fascinating glance which had charmed Falconbridge came back; and the dangerous smile of the dazzling beauty played upon the ugly dwarf, as it had played upon the young cavalier. The Half-breed thrilled with a vague delight as she looked thus at him, and said:

"We will talk of the future, when you will be the Yellow Serpent's wife."

"Your wife!"

"Yes," was the resolute, almost savage reply, "you shall be my wife! I have sworn it, and it shall be so. I am unmarried, I am a great brave, and you shall be my wife, or I will keep you from being any other warrior's wife—you must die, or be mine!"

The ferocious eyes glared as he spoke, and the lips curled fiercely. Instead of becoming angry, Miss Argal smiled more sweetly than before. The will of the strange animal pleased her, whilst it put her upon her guard and aroused all her *finesse* to meet the occasion. She assumed the pouting air of a child, and with a glance filled with blandishment, said:

"Why do you wish to have me for your wife, Yellow Serpent? You say that you are a great brave, if so, why have you not selected some maiden of your tribe?"

The hideous face was darkened: the eyes scowled bitterly:

"Because the maidens despise me, and get sick when I go near them," he growled; "they are frightened by my ugliness! You only are not frightened, and I have sworn by the Evil Spirit that you shall be mine, White Raven—mine only! You need not try to escape me! I will kill myself rather, but I will kill you first. I will be your slave if necessary—but rather than see you leave me, or spurn me, I will plunge my knife into your heart, and we will die together!"

He was ferocious, imperial, as he thus spoke. There was something almost attractive in the fierce animal's air. He resembled an aroused tiger. It was the beauty of strength and bloody determination.

And instead of frightening Miss Argal, it drew her. Her feminine nature, in spite of the disgusting figure of the speaker, recognized his power and passion. She looked at him almost with pleasure, and said smiling:

"Well, but suppose you were my husband, how could I live away from home, in your land?"

"You need not," returned the savage, returning to his submissive air, "I will follow you back and become a white. Still there is much to make you go with me. I am no common Indian. I am a great chief, and my squaw will be a great woman in the tribe. She shall live daintily, every one shall wait on her. I will be king in the band, but she will be the king's king—his beautiful queen. The tenderest game shall be brought to the table of the White Raven—the finest plunder shall be her own—the maidens shall dance before her, and she shall wear the handsomest clothes to be got in the settlements."

"That is well; I like that, but I cannot go."

"Why? You must!"

"I cannot."

"You shall!"

Miss Argal became submissive and tranquil. She put her hands to her eyes and murmured:

"Why do you speak to me so cruelly?"

Some sobs succeeded, and she looked through her tears at the Half-breed, with such a lovely air of uncomplaining sorrow, that he felt all his anger leave him. He cowered before her, and said:

"The Yellow Serpent did not mean to make the White Raven cry. He is her slave."

The young lady dried her tears, and shaking her head, replied:

"You act like a master, and I no longer have any regard for you. When you were kind to me, I liked you; but now I hate you."

And she turned away her head with an air of offended dignity. The Half-breed was conquered by his captive. As she yielded to his will, so now he submitted like a slave to her displeasure. The resolute expression disappeared—his eyes sank before her, and he said humbly:

"The Yellow Serpent did not mean to speak roughly. He is no savage—he is almost a white, and knows how tender-hearted the white maidens are. Let the White Raven become the wife of the Serpent, and he will be her servant for life. He is a Half-breed, he cares nothing for the Catawbas. He will go and live like an Englishman in a house, and hunt game, and till the ground, and wait on the White Raven. He is her friend."

"You do not prove it," said Miss Argal, coldly.

"How must I?"

"Rescue me and my companions."

"When?"

"To-night."

The savage hesitated and reflected. He evidently doubted.

"If I do so," he said at length, "will you go away with me!"

It was Miss Argal's turn to hesitate—it was only for an instant however. With her former fascinating smile she said:

"I will go away with you."

"And be my wife?"

"Yes,"

The hideous mask flushed with joy, and a broad grin revealed the long hog-like teeth. The young lady almost recoiled before the horrible countenance—she grew faint as she saw the Half-Breed gaze upon her as a hawk does upon a dove which he has nearly caught in his clutches. He seized her hand, and would have pressed it to his ugly mouth, but she suddenly drew it away, and said with a quick return to her air of offended dignity.

"Let my hand go, and now let us talk of the means of escape. How will you devise it?"

The Half-breed drew back humbly, and said:

"I must think of that. But it will be impossible to take the others."

And he pointed to Mrs. Butterton and Cannie. Miss Argal assumed an air of resolute determination, and replied:

"Then I will not go with you."

"Not go!"

"No—unless you rescue them, too!"

"Why, what do you care for them?"

"They are my friends—I love the little one dearly."

And bending over the young girl, she smoothed with a soft hand Cannie's disordered tresses. Her smile, as she thus caressed the little head, was one of exquisite sweetness, and showed how much warmth of heart was concealed beneath the warped and strangely disturbed nature of the poor girl. Her savage companion was not unaffected by the manner of the young lady. He was evidently pleased, and said at length :

"I will try. But you at least shall be rescued. I am tired of my life in the band, and have been thinking that you are right in wanting to return to the white settlements. Yes, I will give up the war-path! I will go back with you—White Raven, you shall make me a pale-face, like my father."

The snake-like eyes grew thoughtful, and even soft, as the man spoke, and he plainly returned in memory to some scene of the past. Miss Argal caught the changed manner, with her quick and acute instinct, and said :

"Was your father a white ?"

"Yes," returned the Half-breed, "he was a hunter who married an Indian girl, of the Catawbas. My mother died when I was a baby, and my father soon afterward. The tribe took me, and one day my old granny, who nursed me, showed me where my father and mother were buried in the woods by Belle Rivière—which the English call the Ohio. I never cried but once—I cried that day. Yes, I did cry afterwards when granny was killed by a white—I split his head with my tomahawk though! I wanted him to come to, afterwards, to stick burning splinters in his body, and roast him till he yelled and died in the flames!"

The scowl had come back,—the bloody instinct was revived:—but it disappeared again, very soon before the smiles of his companion. She had evidently marshalled all of her attractions for the task of subduing to her will, and making a slave of, the singular being in whose power she found herself. No one could have discovered in her air or expression the least indication of disgust, as she looked at and spoke to him. Her smile was as dazzling, her eyes dwelt upon his countenance with as pleased and gratified a look, as if it was the face of a gallant young gentleman, and not a sallow, deformed ape. In half an hour her dominion over him was complete. He was gazing at her with a species of submissive ecstasy: the soft hand, figuratively speaking, had smoothed with its caresses the bristling head of the animal, and with delighted growls, he crouched and cowered at the feet of his mistress and keeper.

The details of the project of escape were quickly arranged. At daylight the Half-breed would return to the cavern where she slept—and pass through the fissure in the roof of the highest cave to the area above, with the three women— he would leave Mrs. Butterton and Cannie at a place of safety, near a neighboring fort,—and then he and Miss Argal would proceed to a spot in the Alleghanies, where a New Light missionary lived, and be married. Afterwards they would seek the northern settlements.

This was the Half-breed's plan. It is unnecessary to say that it was not Miss Argal's. Her design was to escape without the assistance of the Half-breed;—her colloquy on the subject had a very simple object. That object was the discovery of the means which her captor would make use of to effect the escape. She had attained a knowledge of all now:—the fissure in the upper cave would permit them to pass:—and long before daybreak, they would all be far away.

As this thought passed through her mind, Miss Argal bestowed upon the Half-breed, her most winning and confiding smile. She graciously gave him her hand to kiss—submitted to the ceremony without moving a muscle—and then, declaring that she needed rest, smiled him out of the cavern.

The animal went away, shuddering with ill-concealed delight, and gazing on the young woman until an abutment of the rock hid her from his view.

With a sneering smile, Miss Argal then turned, and hastily, but with a wary hand, awoke her companions.

LXVI.

LIGHT SHINING IN DARKNESS.

THE three women consulted for some time in animated whispers, and their plan was rapidly formed.

They would remain quiet until the Indians went to sleep; and then, when the cavern was all silent, and occupied only by slumbering forms, would steal up the staircase into the cave above, ascend to the next, then to the next—and finally make their exit through the fissure in the roof of the last. Thereafter, escape would not be difficult. As soon as day-light came they would be able to make their way back by the path which they had followed in coming —the broken twigs would direct them.

"And then, Cannie," said Miss Argal, placing her arm around the girl, drawing the little head down to her bosom, and kissing the white brow; "then, Cannie, dear, you will get back to your grandfather, and we will all be happy again."

"Oh, yes! I long to see grandpapa!" returned the girl, clasping her hands; "he is miserable about me, I know, and would be following me, if he had not been wounded—Oh! so cruelly wounded!"

A sob accompanied the words.

"There, don't cry," said the young lady, smoothing the girl's curls, "hope for the best—and one thing which I rely upon more than all, is just what you have spoken of—a party must be coming to rescue us. I know they are coming."

"Yes," said Mrs. Butterton, "Captain Wagner will not stay long—but oh! my poor, poor father!'

And a sob, deeper than Cannie's, came from the warm-hearted woman's lips.

"Captain Wagner will surely come," said Miss Argal, a shadow of anguish passing over her countenance, "and—Mr. Falconbridge!"

She paused a moment, overcome apparently by some cruel memory: then controlling her emotion, added :

"We must go, however, and meet them. That is part of my plan. The Indians will follow us, unless they are afraid, but the pursuers will not suffer them to re-capture us."

"We will trust in God, at least," said Cannie, with touching simplicity; "you know if we trust in Him He will not desert us; and all He does is for the best."

Miss Argal did not reply. She seemed suddenly absorbed in painful reflection, continuing to caress the girl's hair. Then she turned her dark eyes upon the little face, and gazed at Cannie with an expression of such hopeless anguish that it made the girl's countenance flush with pity and sympathy. No one could have recognized in the changed features of Miss Argal, the proud and imperial woman of the past. The penetrating eyes no longer glittered with their dazzling and seductive magnetism; the lips no longer curled with disdain or provoking coquetry. The eyes were bathed in moisture—the lips quivered. The drooping lashes nearly rested upon the pale cheek; and as Cannie gazed, tear after tear flowed silently down, and fell upon her upturned face.

"You are crying!" said the girl. "Oh! what are you crying for?"

The arm of the young lady tightened its fold around the slender form, and bending down her head, she pressed a kiss upon the girl's lips, and burst into tears.

"I am crying because I am so bad, and you make me so ashamed," she said in a broken voice; "I am so untruthful and bad, and miserable! Oh! Cannie! what you have said breaks my heart!—for I do not trust in God! I have tried but I cannot! I cannot! I am evil and miserable! and He hates me!"

"Oh, no!" returned the girl, mingling her tears with those of her companion, "He does not hate you! He cannot, if you feel that you have done wrong and ask His forgiveness!"

"I cannot ask it! I am unfit to pray! Once I prayed at mamma's knees—but I have not prayed for years—I have done so much evil! But—but—Cannie—do you know!"—

And the poor girl sobbed convulsively.

"Do you know—I am—my mind is not sound—I am out of my head—sometimes!—always, I think:—and I have thought that He will pardon a poor—miserable—insane girl —for her wickedness! Oh! teach me to pray, Cannie—you pity me and do not turn away—I almost think God will forgive me if you kneel and ask Him to. May I kneel down with you?"

Cannie scarcely knew how, but in a moment she was kneeling upon the floor of the cavern—between the two women in the same posture—and praying in a low, broken, but earnest voice. She could not tell how the words came—she did not hesitate an instant, nevertheless; her prayer was tearful, impulsive, and filled with deep feeling.

When she rose, Miss Argal leaned her head upon the tender bosom, encircled Cannie's neck with her arm, and sobbing, exhausted, trembling with emotion, whispered faintly in her ear:

"I think God has heard me, and forgiven me."

The dying firelight no longer fell upon a countenance full of anguish and shame:—a sad smile played over the lips and half-closed eyes:—the heart pressed to the heart of the child, beat tranquilly.

At the same moment Lightfoot entered the cavern.

LXVII.

THE RIVAL OF THE HALF-BREED.

THE young Indian approached the group with the silent tread of his race, and pausing before them, folded his arms and said :

"I have come to show the Mountain Dove and her companions that they have a friend."

Cannie raised her head eagerly, and fixing an earnest, blushing look upon the Indian, murmured :

"Will you go away with us, Lightfoot?"

The Indian inclined his head.

"The tribe are going to sleep. Soon they will be slumbering. Then I will carry you off, and place you on the homeward path."

Cannie clasped her hands and gazed so gratefully into Lightfoot's face, that the blood rushed to his cheeks, and it required all his self-control to suppress the tremor which ran through his frame. He did suppress it, however : in a moment he had recovered his presence of mind: and obeying a gesture from the girl, he came silently, and sat down near the group.

Their plans were quickly communicated to him, and the expression of eye which greeted the announcement, was one of unmistakable satisfaction. His reply was, that their plan was his own. He had thought at once of the fissure in the upper cave, and he came to prepare them for the moment, when he would silently conduct them to the place.

They conversed thus for a quarter of an hour in whispers, and arranged all the details of the scheme. As soon as the savages, in the lower cave were sunk in deep sleep, they would be able to put their project in execution: and as there were many indications of the fact that the braves were, one by one, yielding to their long day's journey, the realization of the hopes of the party did not seem very far distant.

Lightfoot remained then, silent and motionless in his place, listening with the keen ear of the Indian, to all noises which ascended in muffled murmurs from below. One by one these noises died away :—the muttered "Oughs" of the warriors, as they wrapped their blankets around them, and addressed themselves to sleep, became less and less frequent :—finally all sounds lapsed into silence, with the exception of the heavy breathing which indicated the slumber of the tribe.

It was no part of the young Indian's plan, however, to carry out his enterprise at once. He was well acquainted with the echoing peculiarities of the cavern—and his design was to wait patiently until the troubled sleep of the warriors became a very heavy, log-like insensibility : and this would not take place for an hour or two. By that time, the sentinel also would be nodding over the fire, and they might proceed without difficulty to their undertaking.

This had been communicated to the three women, and by the advice of Lightfoot, they had lain down to snatch the hasty slumber requisite to support them in their flight. All obeyed, and worn out with excitement, were soon asleep.

Lightfoot remained thus silent and motionless for two or three hours, wearily listening, when, all at once, a cautious step descended the winding staircase from the upper cavern. He rose, for this could scarcely be one of the Indians. With his hand on his knife he waited. Then at sight of the figure which appeared at the mouth of the cavern, he uttered a low exclamation of astonishment.

It was the figure of Falconbridge.

LXVIII.

THE MARCH OF THE HUNTERS.

THE appearance of Falconbridge is easily explained.

Captain Wagner and his companions had no sooner crept to their hidden position on the brow of the opposite precipice, and concealed themselves beneath the heavy foliage of the dense pines, than a council of war was called.

The question to be determined was a simple one. Should they make an attack before nightfall upon the occupants of the cavern, trusting to their superior arms, or wait until midnight, when the band was asleep, and then surprise them, and put them to the knife? Some members of the party advocated the former plan, and urged the fact that the Indians were, no doubt now, according to their invariable habit, overcome with liquor. They had certainly carried off from the Ordinary as much rum as sufficed, by the account of the servant who had escaped—and nothing would be easier than to pile up brush at the mouth of cavern, set fire to it, and force the Indians to an open combat, as the alternative of being suffocated by the dense smoke.

This proposition found favor with numerous members of the party, but they waited to hear the opinion of Captain Wagner. The Borderer, who had listened attentively, and when the speaker ceased, closed his eyes, and with knit brows reflected rapidly, now shook his head, and growled:

"It won't do! Friend Huger, your scheme is a good one, I don't deny, and shows that you have been after this sort of game before—but there's a flaw in it, that kills. I don't object to smoking the copper-faced devils, and suffocating 'em; if I could do it, I would put every Injun in America in the big cave I've heard of, in the Blue Ridge up the valley yonder, heap up whole pine trees at the mouth, set 'em afire, and smoke my pipe with pleasure as I heard 'em yelling and howling in the death agony. That would be good sport, or the devil take me! But it won't do here! These varmints are not the only people in the cave.

"To our certain knowledge there are three ladies in the hands of these miscreants. Mrs. Butterton, Miss Argal, and little Miss Caunio from the mountain yonder, George says. Now the smoke would suffocate the women, too, and that's not a part of our plan. I accordingly reject it, as commandant of the troop, and will give my own views, which I shall carry out, unless they are met by others better. I know the 'Devil's Garden' by heart. There is a path from this ridge along the precipice, which will take us from one side of the gulf to the other. I propose that we wait until past midnight, when the scoundrels will be dead asleep—and then we can make the attack. We can approach in either of two ways. The cave can be entered from the opening yonder where the two savages were talking, or through a cleft in the rock above, near the strange rock like a man. We may then rescue the women, and make an end of the whole party."

This proposition was unanimously approved of, and the hunters concealed themselves more carefully, awaiting the hour when they were to commence their march along the winding path toward their enemies.

The moon had risen some time before, slowly ascending like a shield of fire above the wild eastern ranges, and now poured a flood of splendor upon the gigantic pinnacle which towered above; on the yawning chasms and glimmering masses of piled up rock: on the gorges bristling with drooping evergreens; and on the river which glittered in its rays like a writhing serpent. The great orb shone tranquilly, and the yellow light slept on the weird scene as peacefully as though it were untenanted by mortal—not the lurking-place of deadly foes who would soon grapple in a mortal struggle.

At ten paces from the rest of the hidden party, George and Falconbridge conversed in low tones of their fears and hopes, and all the emotions of their hearts. Long before, indeed from the first moment of their meeting almost, they had become bosom friends: heart spoke to heart: each recognized a brother: and now, on the perilous border, in the wild night, with those whom they loved more than life in mortal danger, the bond of brotherood was drawn closer still, until the two natures almost were combined into one. Each trembled with vague dread of the result of the intended attack. Would they arrive in time? Had not the Indians, even now, put their captives to death? Were Bertha Argal and Cannie Powell still breathing, or had they fallen victims, hours before, to the savage cruelty which had slain young children at the Ordinary, and dismembered the dead body of the unhappy Mr. Argal?

So the two young men passed the long hours in shuddering dread—impatient, longing, panting for the contest—eager for the signal which would solve their doubts and end their fears.

At last it came. Captain Wagner passed the word cautiously along the line, and taking the head of the party, set forward on the precipitous and almost imperceptible path which wound down the steep declivity. It was only to be followed by careful observation, leading, as it did, beneath the dense foliage of the evergreens, along the edge of the precipice, where the moon's rays scarcely penetrated—and more than one of the party, winding, single file, down into the gorge, had to grasp the drooping boughs to prevent themselves from being hurled into the chasm beneath.

At last the bed of the small stream was reached, and the body of hunters commenced the ascent of the towering pinnacle. This would have been entirely out of the question near the outer edge, which was, as we have said, a sheer precipice of five hundred feet, but at the point which they had reached, about a quarter of a mile from the precipice, it was possible to ascend, though this even was an undertaking of great difficulty. The masses of rock in the path of the party were huge and almost impassable—the tangled underwood very nearly a complete barrier—but the trianed and active hunters overcame all obstacles, and slowly made their way, preceded by Captain Wagner, toward the summit.

It was nearly daybreak. Already faint streaks began to appear in the eastern sky, the harbingers of dawn; and all was more profoundly quiet in the wild scene than even upon the night before.

At last the party reached the top, and a hurried consultation was held. The result was that an examination of the fissure, and the entrance to the cavern beneath the man's bust, should be made, and to the latter Captain Wagner addressed himself. Falconbridge, his second in command, repaired with a portion of the hunters to the fissure.

He soon reached it, and bidding the men await his return, let his body down through the yawning aperture, into which the moon's rays plunged, and felt his feet base themselves upon a jutting crag near the entrance. From this abutment, he found no difficulty in picking his way, though it required great caution, into the cavern nearest the summit.

From this he descended, directed by chance gleams of fire-light, playing upon the roof, to the next, then to the next, and so to the cave in which Lightfoot was watching over the slumbers of Mrs. Butterton, Cannie, and Miss Argal.

LXIX.

THE SON OF WAR EAGLE.

AT sight of the young man, as we have said, Lightfoot, who had risen to his feet, with his hand on his knife, uttered a low guttural exclamation of astonishment.

The two persons, who represented so nobly the great races from which they drew their blood, remained for some moments motionless, surveying each other without speaking. They were strongly contrasted, and yet singularly alike in those subtler and less perceptible traits which underlie the mere outward appearance. There was the same frank gaze, clear, penetrating, unshrinking—the look of the eagle upon the sun : the same proud simplicity of attitude ; the same erect carriage of person. They stood thus, no inapt representatives and types of the Caucasian and the Indian—the civilized European and the untutored North American—the court and the trackless wilderness.

Their glance was not one of hostility or suspicion. Each had recognized in the other a pure and noble soul—but still the inevitable circumstances of their position made them use due caution. It was not two boys filled with chimerical ideas of human goodness and unwavering confidence, who stood thus, confronting each other. They were strong men—with their feelings deeply aroused—opposed at a critical moment, on a critical occasion.

Lightfoot, without removing his hand from his knife, said in a low tone ;

"Why is the young pale-face in the heart of his enemies?"

Falconbridge pointed to Miss Argal, and replied:
"I came to seek her."
"She is your friend?"
"More than my friend."

"The young man uttered the words with such dangerous animation and distinctness, that Lightfoot raised his hand quickly, and said in a whisper:

"Hist! Beware how you speak so loudly. The members of the tribe will wake at the noise, and your blood will flow."

"I care not," returned Falconbridge, who gazed with flushed cheeks at Miss Argal as she slumbered serenely, a happy smile playing fitfully upon her lips; "so she is saved from the diabolical cruelty of these savage beasts, I count my own life as nothing."

The words affected Lightfoot like a blow. His head rose haughtily, and he fixed upon Falconbridge one of those burning glances which seem to measure the foe—as a tiger measures the enemy upon whom he is about to spring. But the emotion of rage was plainly instinctive. It did not last. The expression of menace disappeared almost as quickly as it came, and a deep sadness fell like the shadow of a cloud on the flashing eyes and proud lip. With drooping head, the Indian murmured:

"Be silent! I am the son of War Eagle, and in other days the blood of him who uttered such words would have run out of his heart! But my heart is changed. Lightfoot no longer strikes in this quarrel. His heart says, 'Yes, my tribe is cruel, is bloody'—but he is still a Catawba, a chief. Let the young pale-face respect the feelings of a chief."

The noble voice went to the heart of Falconbridge. His cheeks reddened with impulsive shame, at thus wounding, unnecessarily, the feelings of his companion. He stretched out his hand, and said, frankly:

"I would beg forgiveness—I meant not to hurt you, son of War Eagle. Let us speak not as foes, but as brothers, for I know, I feel, that you are here as the protector of women and children. I would know that even if one of those children were not this one before me."

And he pointed to Cannie.

The Indian gravely took the proffered hand, and then said :

"Does the young pale-face come to rescue the young woman ?"

"Yes."

"Does he come alone ?"

And the penetrating eyes of the Indian chief looked full into the eyes of his companion. Falconbridge replied, with ready presence of mind, that he alone had made his way to the cavern. He felt instinctively that in this critical moment, when the aid of Lightfoot was of inestimable value, it would be wholly unnecessary and equally cruel to present to him the tragic alternative of acting with his own tribe against the whites, or with his adopted people against the Indians. He evaded thus the question, and added quickly :

"What plan of escape have you devised?"

Lightfoot, in low, rapid tones, explained everything, and added :

"The hour has nearly arrived. The band are sleeping— I will go and reconnoitre. But before the son of War Eagle goes, let him say to the young pale-face that his tribe are not wholly fierce and cruel—they are very noble often, though their eyes are different from the eyes of the whites. The Good Spirit made the world of land and water, and valley and mountain—he traced out the rivers, and rolled round the seasons, through the hours of unremembered years, for all the tribes of all the mighty nations. He gave to one of these great tribes, the whites, another land—to us he gave the prairies blooming with a hundred flowers—the great wide forests—the pathless lakes—and lofty mountains. We lived in the prairies, and upon the mountains—we paddled on the lakes. The Evil Spirit often made us fight with each other; but not always. Then came the pale-faces, and they dyed the soil with the blood of braves. Wherever an Indian met a white, he met an enemy—it was life or death. This has made all the tribes so bloody—this makes the Evil Spirit laugh, and triumph. The son of War Eagle felt his heart turn cold within him—he wandered from his tribe—one day a prophet of the whites spoke to him of the Son of the Great Spirit, and he listened. Then he left his people, and became a believer. To-day he would not bear his knife against either—he would turn away, and bury his sufferings in silence. If the knife strikes him, let it strike—he will die a Christian chief of the Catawbas!"

With these words, the young Indian left the cavern, and noiselessly descending the winding stair to the cave beneath, disappeared from the eyes of his companion. Falconbridge looked after him for a moment, then hastily going to Miss Argal's side, laid his hand upon her arm.

The young lady opened her eyes, and gave a quick start, as she saw Falconbridge. Then covering her face with her hands, she murmured with burning blushes:

"Do not speak to me—I am not worthy!"

CHAPTER LXX.

THE CONFESSION.

FALCONBRIDGE displayed an emotion even greater than that of his companion. His face flushed with passionate emotion, and his breast heaved, as he gazed upon the woman whom he loved, even more than ever it seemed to him, now that she was helpless and surrounded by bloody enemies.

The nature of this man was one of those which remembers the good and forgets the bad. He no longer recalled the terrible wrong which the young lady had inflicted upon him—he no longer thought of her as the woman who had trifled with him, broken his heart, and laughed in his face when he suffered. She was only the poor stricken girl whose will and heart were diseased by an awful visitation of the Supreme Ruler of the universe—he thought of her, as she struggled in her father's arms that day, and cried, "I loved him only"—as she looked when she came with streaming eyes, and broken accents, and prayers for pardon, to return his mother's ring. As he looked at her now, and heard her murmur, "Do not speak to me—I am not worthy," his heart was filled with an inexpressible love and pity."

Of the feelings of the young lady herself, it is scarcely necessary to speak. The change which had taken place in her whole being has been described—we have rapidly touched upon, with a sort of fear, at undertaking such a picture, the scene when another light than that of earth illuminated the gloomy depths of her soul:—and we know thus what she felt in looking upon the victim of her untruth and cruelty.

She scarcely dared to meet his eyes, and turned away,

covering her blushes of shame, as we have said, with her hands. For more than a minute Falconbridge did not speak —emotion had overcome him. Then he regained his self-possession, and said:

"Do you think that I remember the past, with bitterness? No, I do not. Look up, it is a faithful, devoted friend who speaks to you."

"How can I?" murmured the young lady, removing her hands from her face, but averting her head; "I am filled with such shame, sir, that it almost kills me!"

"Do not speak thus! Do not even refer to the past!"

"I must," she said in a low tone, glancing with unutterable sadness at him, and then looking away again, "I must, Mr. Falconbridge, for I have acted toward you in so base a manner, that it almost breaks my heart to think of it. But do not think too cruelly of me! One of my bitterest pangs, even here in this gloomy place, where I have so much else to make me miserable, is the recollection of my dishonorable conduct toward yourself. Do not interrupt sir," she said, as he was about to speak, and gazing now with sorrowful and shrinking modesty into his face; "do not stop me, Mr. Falconbridge. You know I am a poor insane creature, and I know not whether I shall have the mind or memory to speak as I wish to speak to you, if I do not go on now. I say, that I have been guilty of dishonor to you, and I *must* confess it all, before I can feel that you have forgiven it—I do not know if you can. You came to the Valley, and from our first meeting I determined to engage your affection, that I and my father might be compelled to live no longer in this solitude. I practiced upon you those wiles which it is the sad misfortune of woman to possess—I succeeded in my aim—and then I deceived you, basely, dishonorably, shamefully!"

Her face was crimson as she spoke. The effort which she made in thus speaking, was plainly immense, passionate, cruel.

"I met Lord Fairfax," she went on, "and I broke my faith with you—I treated you as no lady can treat a gentleman without degrading herself; I sneered at you when you complained; turned my back when you remonstrated; when you begged me with that deep love which should have been my pride, and honor, to be true to my plighted word, I laughed in your face. Mr. Falconbridge!" said the young lady with quivering lips and hands which trembled so much that they were almost unable to put back the mass of raven curls which fell over her face, "Mr. Falconbridge, it almost kills me to utter these words!—it makes me sick at heart!—I am so humiliated and degraded in my own eyes, that I could sink through the earth for shame! But I must speak! Yes, sir, I behaved toward the most honorable and noble gentleman I've ever known in a manner which I can scarcely believe as I think of it—I repeat it, with base, base dishonor!—and on my knees I beg, I pray your forgiveness! Stop, Mr. Falconbridge!—do not speak—let me add what I know you are thinking at this moment—let me tell you my only excuse for this terrible conduct. But I need not—I see in your eyes that you have recalled it. Oh, yes, sir! that is my sole excuse—it is something, is it not, sir? I was only a poor miserable creature—with my head whirling, my mind unsound—my heart depraved and awfully wicked! I was not always so, sir! Once I was true and pure—mamma taught me to be good and tender—but I could not remain so! Against my better nature I acted with awful deception—I wounded you, and made you suffer without pity! —but—but, through it all—I can scarcely find strength to confess it, for you may misunderstand me—it escaped me, papa says, in that mad attack which you witnessed—I—loved you,—Edmund!—as you loved me—with my whole, entire heart!—you only! Do not think me unmaidenly!" she sobbed, turning away, and blushing to the roots of her hair; "do not think that I wish you to return to me! That can never be, if you even desired it! We must part forever, after this terrible night! We can never meet more, but I am changed, and I can pray for you—I can pray to God to forgive me my great sin—as I pray you humbly to do so—you, whom I have wronged so terribly and basely!"

She stopped, sobbing convulsively,—overcome by the woful confession, so repugnant to a woman: shaken by a depth and poignancy of shame and anguish which no words can describe.

And Falconbridge was as passionately moved as herself. Her words had struck him like sharp arrows, recalling as they did all his suffering, his long agony, his despair. This was not the dominant feeling in the breast of the young man, however. An unutterable compassion and tenderness made his heart throb. His frame trembled, and he vainly essayed to speak. In a few moments, however, he had mastered his agitation, and had opened his lips, when suddenly Lightfoot stood beside them.

"Come!—there is no moment to lose!" said the Indian in a low, quick voice, "the sentinel is asleep, and the day is breaking!"

The Indian cautiously awoke Mrs. Butterton and Cannie as he spoke—and they silently rose from their couches. Falconbridge had only time to bend over Miss Argal, to press her hand to his lips and say in a deep broken voice:

"I forgive you from my heart! May God forgive all my sins as completely!"

LXXI.

THE FLIGHT.

THE three women quickly made their preparations, and signified their readiness to follow their guides.

Lightfoot went in front, cautioning the members of the party, in a low tone, to make no noise; and thus gliding like shadows, they ascended the first flight of steps, leading to the next cavern above.

There, Lightfoot paused a moment to listen. His quick ear seemed to have caught some slight sound of hostile import. Bending his head, like a crouching wild animal, his keen eyes plunged into the half-darkness, his acute ears strove to discern the repetition of the noise. It seemed to have existed only in his imagination; and with a silent movement of the hand, he motioned to the party to follow.

The ascent became steeper and more difficult. In more than one place the steps of the huge staircase were wanting, and the women had to be lifted in the arms of their companions. Falconbridge and Lightfoot, it may easily be believed, experienced singular emotion as the forms of those whom they loved were thus clasped in their arms, resting upon their hearts. The young Indian was still agitated by the cruel scene of his disappointment in the cavern: his face glowed as he lifted the girl, and with all the respect and tenderness of a brother, placed her safely upon the ledge above. And if such an emotion invaded the breast of Lightfoot, what a rush of painful delight must Falconbridge have felt, as Miss Argal's cheek nearly touched his own, as her dark curls brushed against his bosom!

But it was no time for reflection—no time to indulge these inevitable emotions of the youthful heart. The moments rushed onward, winged with terrible peril—all was at stake; the issues of life and death must soon be decided.

The party hurried onward as rapidly as the broken and jagged pathway would permit. They had ascended thus very nearly to the entrance, and were mounting the last precipitous staircase leading to the fissure in the pavement above, beyond which lay hope, freedom, life. Lightfoot again raised Cannie, and then assisted Mrs. Butterton to ascend. Falconbridge held out his arms for Miss Argal, and she obeyed his gesture.

The young man and the girl were thus clasped, as it were in each other's embrace, when a roar like that of a furious wild beast was heard, and followed by twenty Indians, the Half-breed rushed up the staircase. He had gone to seek Miss Argal, had discovered the escape of the three women, and hastily calling to his companions, followed them.

He had arrived just in time to see Miss Argal clasped to the bosom of Falconbridge, and the sight aroused in him the furious devil of blood and death. By a superhuman bound he reached the plateau beneath the fissure, just as the three women were thrust upward by their companions—but in spite of his reckless daring he recoiled.

Falconbridge had seized a huge mass of rock, and lifting it above his head, hurled it downward. The Half-breed avoided it by a movement to one side as rapid as lightning, and it rebounded from the jagged floor, burst into fragments, and sent throughout the gloomy caverns a sombre roar, echoing and rebellowing from side to side.

Lightfoot and Falconbridge took instant advantage of the diversion, and passing through the opening, found themselves in the air above, in the midst of the party of hunters who were rushing to their assistance.

The Indians appeared at the fissure, their red faces distorted with rage and ferocity—above all, the hideous countenance of the Half-Breed, which resembled that of some horrible demon, wild with rage and disappointment. But at sight of the hunters armed to the teeth, with levelled rifles, the heads disappeared, amid cries of fury and fear. A volley from the whites followed, and a howl from the cavern replied to it. More than one of the savages had been killed by the unerring balls.

Then a new phenomenon appeared. At the moment when the hunters were hastily reloading their pieces, a dense cloud of lurid smoke rose slowly through the fissure, and ascended in the first rays of morning. Captain Wagner's quick eye had discerned, from his position at the mouth of the cavern, the escape of the captives—he had quickly heaped together vast quantities of dry boughs—these had been set on fire, and in the midst of the thick smoke his men advanced to the attack.

The smoke swept upward toward the more elevated cavern in which the entire tribe, by this time, were assembled. Thus the captives huddled together upon the lower floor were unharmed. Their bonds were quickly cut, and the women escaped—the men seized arms from the floor and joined the whites.

At the head of his party, thus swollen in numbers, Captain Longknife rushed up the staircase of the cavern, firing his pistols. Volleys from the hunters behind him were added—and very soon they had arrived within sight of the fissure.

The huge borderer presented an appearance almost frightful. His shaggy black hair and beard were singed by the flames—his bulky form looked gigantic amid the clouds of smoke—with his immense sabre whirled above his head, he struck right and left with a fury which made him resemble some mad giant of the old mythology.

More than once the cry of "Longknife! Longknife!" issued from the terrified savages, who seemed to regard him with superstitious awe and horror. They recoiled before him, and crowded tumultuously toward the fissure. At every moment the advancing hunters stumbled over dead bodies —they breathed heavily in the lurid smoke: but with wild shouts and discharges of fire-arms rushed upward.

The black fissure then disgorged before the eyes of the party above, a furious crowd of savages. Their enemies followed, and in an instant the final struggle commenced upon the plateau of the gigantic pinnacle, which now shone brightly in the light of day.

LXXII.

THE BORDERER AND THE HALF-BREED.

THE struggle was furious, horrible, mortal. All the most intense and acrid passions, which agitate the human soul, were spurred to wild and incredible activity, and the combatants seemed to have made up their minds to conquer or die, without thought of retreat or flight.

The enemies were nearly a perfect match. It is true, that the Indians exceeded the hunters in numerical strength, but the superiority of the arms used by the latter gave them a decided advantage, and more than made up for the inequality of numbers. The area upon which they contended —the summit of the dizzy precipice—was limited, and thus the whites fought under favorable circumstances, for they could not easily be surrounded.

Captain Wagner led the party of hunters: and beside him Falconbridge advanced into the press, dealing such blows with his sword that every opponent went down before him. The two men seemed possessed with the battle ardor in its fullest extent—that fury of the soul which animates the blood of men, as animal ferocity does the blood of beasts, turning the mildest human beings into wolves and tigers. Captain Wagner did not lose his presence of mind, however. He led his men with the reckless courage of one who commands a forlorn hope; but with the cool generalship, also, of a veteran campaigner. He advanced, step by step, beating down every opponent—delivering his orders in a loud, strident tone, which rose above the uproar—and embracing, even at the instant when he gave his blows, the entire field of action at a glance.

Falconbridge was beside him—and beside Falconbridge was George. The youth was thoroughly aroused. His habitual calmness and amiability had completely disappeared. His head was tossed back with fearless pride, and in his heaving bosom, his burning eyes, his lips set close together, might have been seen the evidences of a nature of immense depth and strength—of dauntless will—of inflexible hardihood and determination. There was no longer anything of the boy about him—he was the full-armed warrior, rejoicing in the deadly contest. His sword descended with unerring precision upon the writhing phalanx of Indian warriors, and he was beside Falconbridge wherever he advanced.

It was in the midst of this mad struggle, that all at once, George heard a woman scream—and this scream he recognized as issuing from the lips of Cannie. It was so wild and piercing, so filled with distress and anguish, that the young man's heart turned cold with apprehension. With a hurried assurance to Falconbridge that he would return in an instant, George threw himself backward, and clearing at a single bound, two or three dead bodies, rushed in the direction of the spot from which he had heard the cry of distress.

A few words will explain it.

Cannie, Mrs. Butterton, and Miss Argal, had been hastily conducted to the rear of a large mass of rock, on the eastern edge of the plateau, not far from the curious granite bust, in order to screen them from the balls of the savages, a large portion of whom carried rifles and pistols, procured from the dwellings which they had plundered on their march. A cleft in the rock afforded a favorable hiding-place, and in this cleft, accordingly, the three women crouched, listening with terror, to the noises of the desperate conflict. Beside them Lightfoot leaned, with folded arms, depressed head, and heaving bosom, against the rock. A terrible struggle was going on in his breast. All the old instincts of the savage chieftain were aroused within him, by the din of the combat—by the clashing weapons, the discharge of fire-arms, the yells and shouts, as the enemies closed in the mortal contest. His limbs trembled—a shudder passed through his frame—and his glowing eyes resembled balls of fire. But those eyes were not directed toward the place of combat—his nervous fingers did not clutch the weapon at his girdle. He could take no part against either of the bands, for neither was his foe. He was a Catawba, it is true, but he was also a friend of the whites —a Christian; and to terminate any indecision which he felt, came the thought that his presence was necessary to the safety of Cannie.

Thus he curbed the wild battle instinct raging in his breast—suppressed the tremor which agitated his frame ; his feet rooted themselves in their place, and with folded arms he awaited the end of the contest.

The three women were less capable of controlling their feelings. They listened with terror to the shouts and discharges. Every rifle shot, to their excited imaginations, rung the death-knell of the person for whom they felt the deepest solicitude. Above all, Cannie thought of George, and the peril in which he must be, with blanched cheeks, and eyes full of wild anguish. She saw him pale and bleeding, beneath the trampling feet—her imagination conjured up, for itself, a horrible spectacle—and unable longer to bear the terrible suspense, she rose to her feet, passed hastily by Lightfoot, and going to the edge of the rock, looked toward the combatants.

As she reached the point, she suddenly recoiled with that cry of terror which George had heard and obeyed.

An Indian, with a hideous scowl upon his features, met her face to face, and raised above her head a long, glittering knife, which descended like a flash of lightning toward her bosom.

But the weapon did not bury itself in her heart. It found another sheath. Lightfoot had seen her peril—his face flushed crimson—and arriving at the spot, with a single bound, he had thrown himself between the girl and the descending knife.

It entered his bosom, and buried itself to the very hilt.

The savage recognized his brother warrior, and chief, too late, and uttering a howl of terror at his action, disappeared in the direction of the main contest, at the moment when George reached the side of the girl.

Cannie had thrown her arms wildly around the young Indian, vainly endeavoring to sustain him from falling. Her strength was unequal to the task, however; Lightfoot tottered faintly, raised his eyes to heaven, and extending his arms, fell backward, dragging the girl with him, to the earth.

George hastened to their assistance, but he had come too late. The weapon had evidently inflicted a mortal wound. Almost fainting at the awful sight, at the pale, calm face, and half-closed eyes of the dying man, Cannie supported his form in her arms, and looked up at George with an expression in her eyes which haunted him to the day of his death. There was in it such a depth of anguish, a tenderness so profound and passionate, that the young man felt his cheeks flush in unison with the girl's emotion, and his pulses throb.

Cannie spoke to the dying man in quick, hurried tones, which were scarcely recognizable. She bedewed his forehead with her tears—besought him to speak to her—and used every means to arouse him, and recall him to consciousness. Miss Argal and Mrs. Butterton hastened to her assistance—and all three of them chafed his brow and hands. It was of no avail—the young Indian exhibited no signs of life beyond a faint movement of the chest—and George saw, with inexpressible anguish, that his friend was dying. As he gazed at the serene face, drooping languidly

toward the bare shoulder, at the eyes veiled by their long
black lashes, at the slowly heaving bosom, which, at every
pulsation, forced a few drops of the Indian's life-blood
through the wound, the young man's throat seemed to
choke with tears, and a groan issued from his lips.

But it was no time to indulge in regrets. The combat in
which his friends were engaged, began to roar more furiously than before. The cries of his companions recalled
him to the contest; and at the moment when he roused
himself to a consciousness of his duty, these shouts were
redoubled, and replied to from the slope, by which the peak
was reached.

. A quick glance in the direction of these latter cries, revealed their origin. At the distance of a quarter of a mile
Lord Fairfax, who had found the trail of the hunters, was
seen sweeping onward toward the pinnacle, followed by
twenty mounted men, who plunged their spurs into their
foaming animals, and rushed upward, to the relief of their
friends. The sight banished completely the softer emotion
which George had experienced. His face flushed again with
the animal instinct of war—and hastily stooping, he raised
the languid body of Lightfoot in his arms, and bore it to
the cleft in the rock, where the women could minister to
him, if he revived, without danger from the bullets of the
enemy.

He then bade them, in hurried accents, keep close within
their place of concealment; and in the midst of a hundred
frantic shouts, hastened back to the scene of contest.

The Indians, in his absence, had been slowly driven back,
step by step, and were beginning to revolve the propriety
of flight, when they heard the cries of the party coming up
the mountain. At the same moment another incident took
place, which completed their despair, depriving them of all
"heart of hope."

Captain Wagner, as we have said, plunged, at the head of
his men into the very centre of the savages, and with his

sabre, of immense weight and length of blade, hewed down every opponent who stood in his path. Breathing hoarsely, dealing gigantic blows with a ferocity now thoroughly aroused, and shaking from him, so to speak, as a bear shakes off the dogs, the most powerful warriors who assailed him, he had left behind him a long train of dead or dying, who had bit the dust beneath his arm. He was destined, however, to find a foeman worthy of his steel. This was the powerful Half-breed, who had hitherto fought in another part of the press, but who now advanced toward the soldier, uplifting, with both hands, a huge axe, which he had seized from a pile of stolen utensils in the cavern.

The countenance of the Half-breed resembled, at this moment, the mask of a fiend, or rather the veritable physiognomy of a demon incarnate, let loose upon the material earth. His eyes were blood-shot, and burned with a lurid lustre, suggestive of blood and death. His hideous mouth was distorted into a sneer, which rendered it a thousand times more repulsive; on his broad chest, and enormous arms, the muscles stood out like knots, or excrescences.

He advanced straight upon Captain Wagner, and aimed a terrible blow at his head—a blow which would have felled the most powerful ox. The soldier parried it with his sword, but the result was unhappy for him. The sabre yielded to the immense stroke, and snapped within six inches of the hilt.

The Half-breed uttered a howl of triumph, and throwing his chest backward, whirled the axe with both hands, and all his strength, above his head, delivering the blow with the full swing of the deadly weapon.

But he had met an enemy as wary and self-possessed as himself. The axe did not descend. With a bound of astonishing rapidity, Wagner leaped upon the Half-breed, and seized him by the wrist and throat. The axe was no longer of any use to him—the grasp upon his throat required the use of his hands—with another howl, more furious than the former, the savage dropped the weapon and clutched his enemy in a terrible and deadly embrace.

Then commenced a struggle awful for its ferocity and the mortal determination of the combatants. It was a contest for life or death, and each felt that the result must be doubtful. Both were men of immense physical strength—both aroused to the last fury of passionate hatred; neither gained, at first, any advantage. The superior stature of Captain Wagner counted in his favor; but the deformed Half-breed had trained his huge muscles, by constant exercise, until they were as hard and elastic as steel; and this more than balanced his want of height. He wrapped himself around the frame of the Borderer like a deadly boa-constrictor, tightening the grasp of his crooked arms and legs, and striving, it seemed, to crush the breastbone of his adversary.

Thus locked in a deadly embrace, the enemies made gigantic efforts to terminate the struggle. The Half-breed had no arms—having discharged his pistols, and dropped his knife and tomahawk in the melee. The Borderer had a knife, but it was tangled in his belt, and he could not draw it, until his foe was prostrate beneath him, and his own arms free from the paralyzing pressure. They staggered from side to side, stumbling and nearly falling over the dead bodies; writhing like wild animals, and uttering hoarse growls; exerting their great strength to an extent almost supernatural in the breast to breast contest for life.

Then a new and more terrible feature was added to the struggle. Step by step they had detached themselves from the rest of the combatants, and now they found themselves rapidly approaching the ledge of rock which ran around the brink of the precipice. The Borderer's back was turned to it, and he was not aware of his peril until it was almost too late to guard against it. He heard, at the instant, a sort of hissing growl, and a sudden and diabolical grin distorted the face of the Half-breed. Breathing heavily, and gnashing his boar-like tusks, he forced his enemy toward the dizzy precipice, and suddenly, as they reached the very verge, buried his sharp teeth in the Borderer's throat.

Wagner uttered a hoarse cry, and staggered back. The dog-like bite, deep into his throat, had taken him unawares, and nearly paralyzed him. His head grew dizzy, his right hand released its hold upon the Half-breed: clinging like a tiger, to the Borderer's throat, the malignant savage pushed him, inch by inch, to the verge.

A glance behind him showed the soldier his awful peril. He saw the sheer descent of five hundred feet beneath him, the plateau at its foot, a bed of shattered rocks: and upon that plateau, his mangled corpse would be lying in three seconds, unless he could disengage the hideous monster's teeth from his throat.

His brain reeled. A shudder passed through his frame— and a sort of chill invaded his breast. The heart of this man, who had braved a thousand perils, who had led his men into the bloodiest gulfs of battle, who had set his life, a hundred times, upon the hazard of the die, without giving so much as a thought to the event—the heart of this stalwart soldier, who had never felt fear in the midst of any danger, now recoiled and died within him at this horrible thought—at the idea of death in a shape so hideous and revolting.

He summoned all his remaining strength, and made a final effort to hurl from him the monster, whose fangs were buried in his bleeding throat. The effort was vain. The jagged teeth clung closer still—their grip was firmer, and they gnawed at the quivering flesh with hound-like ferocity. The Borderer uttered a stifled cry, and let fall his other arm, with which he had endeavored to repel his enemy. The act preserved him. The Half-breed had forced his opponent to the very brink, and was about to hurl him over, when he felt a blade, keen and mortal in its stroke, enter his breast. The Borderer's hand had fallen upon the knife in his belt—he had drawn it and struck. The monster's hold relaxed, the teeth clutched at his enemy's throat with a last despairing effort—and uttering a hoarse growl, he endeavored to drag the Borderer with him in his fall.

Captain Wagner had just strength enough to recover himself. His body oscillated, as it were, upon the brink; and he staggered back, as the hideous form of the Half-breed disappeared like a mass hurled from some war-like engine in the yawning chasm, where it was dashed to pieces upon the rocks.

As the Borderer turned from the terrible contest, wiping his streaming brows, and breathing heavily, he saw the Indians give way. Then, all at once, with loud shouts and the discharge of pistols and carbines, the party, headed by Lord Fairfax, bore down upon them, and completed the rout:—the remnant of the band disappeared in the forest, with howls of hatred and despair.

At the same moment the sun rose above the eastern mountain, and poured his tranquil light upon the spectacle of blood and death.

LXXIII.

THE YOUNG INDIAN.

AT the mouth of the cleft in the rock, where the women had concealed themselves, Cannie holds upon her breast the head of Lightfoot, who is dying.

The young chief exhibits no evidences of suffering—no fear of his impending fate. His countenance is calm and untroubled; his eyes are filled with a serene, happy light; the courage of his race and his new-found faith, have come to nerve him for the journey through the vale of shadows.

As he looks up into the face of the young girl, who gazes at him with inexpressible anguish and compassion, a faint smile wanders over his countenance, and a sigh escaping from the parted lips, seems to indicate deep happiness.

"The Dove of the Mountain is unhurt," he murmurs; "the head of the son of War Eagle rests upon her heart! Has the day dawned, Mountain Dove, and is the combat over? Have the children of the Catawbas gone away?"

"Yes," murmured Cannie with a sob.

The Indian caught the almost imperceptible sound, and said:

"Why do you cry? Is your heart sad for me? Do not cry for me—I am not unhappy—oh, no, not unhappy!"

"You are dying, Lightfoot," returned the girl, suppressing, by a violent effort, a rush of tears.

"Dying? Yes, that is true, little Dove," he said; "but is that anything to grieve at? The world is very dark and sad, and I go from it to another land where there is never any darkness. *You* gave me this hope and happiness, for you taught me what to believe, and what my duty was. Without you, I should never have been anything but an Indian warrior—I am dying, but I am happy."

17

"And for me! oh, you are dying for me!" exclaimed the girl, nearly beside herself with anguish; "you gave your life to protect me from that blow. Would I had died before you—in your place, Lightfoot—dear, dear Lightfoot; my heart is breaking as I think"——

She stopped, nearly suffocated by emotion, and crying bitterly.

"Do not weep!" said the Indian, earnestly, with glowing cheeks; "you wound me! I thank the Master that he permitted the poor Indian to save the little friend who gave him the great hope of another land! See the sun! there he rises! Before he rests in the mountains the son of War Eagle will be smiling as he stands in the presence of the Master of Life!"

As he spoke, a slight convulsion passed over his frame, and his eyes began to grow dreamy and absent. The girl saw, through her tears, with a sudden chill at the heart, that his mind had commenced to wander, as the spirit does when it approaches death.

"Oh, yes!" she exclaimed, "you will stand in the presence of God, and he will smile upon you, for you are pure and good—oh, so good and kind, dear, dear Lightfoot! You are dying because you protected a poor child, and the Saviour will receive and bless you!"

"Ah!" murmured the Indian, his head slightly drooping, "was that my father's whisper? Does War Eagle talk from the happy hunting-grounds to his child? I will go to meet him!"

And the young chief attempted to rise, but fell back faintly.

"No, no!" cried the girl in a low, frightened tone, and trembling, "do not try to rise—lean on me—you are dying, Lightfoot!"

The words arrested his failing attention, and he looked up into her eyes with a sad smile.

"Dying?" he said faintly; "do you say that the son of

War Eagle is dying? Yes—now I see, I remember! The knife! You are the Mountain Dove, are you not, little one? I loved you—did I not try to save you? I thought—but that shadow! Why does it creep so slowly, slowly? And the wind! Is it the wind or the voices of other years in the forest where I roamed as a chief of the Catawbas? It is a brave, great tribe—the son of War Eagle is a chief! There, the wind again—and it blows from the mountain where the old man lives with the maiden. Is that a rose in your hair, little Dove, and who is wandering with you? A youth of the palefaces! He is a noble-looking boy, but he can never love you as the poor Indian loved you. You are more to him than the skies and rivers, than the prairie and the forest—you are his life; without you he would die!"

A glow came to the face, upon which the pallor of death was slowly settling. By a last effort, he raised his drooping head, with a parting gleam in the joyful eyes, and it fell back upon her shoulders with the face turned upward to the sky.

"It was not the wind!" he murmured, close to her ear; "it is my father, who is whispering to his child, and blesses me as I go. Do you hear—'My son dies well!' Yes, the son of War Eagle, the child of the Catawbas dies well, since he dies for the little Dove. Farewell, I am going to the Master!—the sun, how it shines!—how the Master smiles!"

And the voice died away. With a bright light on his face, the young chief fell back into the arms of Cannie, and expired upon her bosom.

At the distance of ten paces, and not far from the strange granite bust, Lord Fairfax held, in the same manner, upon his breast, the head of Falconbridge, who was dying in his arms.

Within five yards of the young man lay the body of Bertha Argal—beautiful in death as in life.

LXXIV.

THE YOUNG CAVALIER.

THE young girl who has played so woeful a part in our drama—who, under the influence of some Fatality, it would seem, had wrecked in their freshest bloom the hopes and happiness of a noble heart—this child of error and unhappy weakness, had blotted out the record of her fault, by one supreme and all-embracing act of courage and devotion.

She had sacrificed her life in the vain attempt to preserve that of her lover.

It was at the moment when Lord Fairfax was ascending the slope, when Captain Wagner was struggling with the Half-breed, that Falconbridge, finding himself nearly surrounded by a number of the savages, retreated, fighting desperately, toward a rock, against which he designed to place his back.

The tide of conflict had rolled in another direction, and borne George and his companions from his side; he was thus left alone to oppose his enemies.

Thus contending with all the desperation of a knight of the Middle Ages surrounded by a cloud of Saracens, Falconbridge retreated, step by step, toward the rock which we have mentioned—on the opposite side of which was the cleft in which Miss Argal and the two others were concealed.

Cannie and Mrs. Butterton were bending over Lightfoot, and did not hear the clash of Falconbridge's weapon, as he parried the blows aimed at him. But Miss Argal heard it

—and something in her heart told her that the man whom she loved was in danger.

With the impulsive and daring girl, to determine was to act. She hastily left the hiding-place, and passing round the rock, found herself in the midst of the Indians.

She did not look at them. Her burning eyes were fixed upon the youth, who contended single-handed against his adversaries. At the same instant she saw the Indians draw back, as by a concerted movement—one of them, who was behind, levelled his rifle at the breast of Falconbridge—and fire leaped from the muzzle.

The ball which was intended for the young man, entered the bosom of Miss Argal. With the activity of a tigress whose young is threatened, the girl had bounded forward, and thrown one arm round his neck, protecting his body with her own.

He heard the discharge—the young girl's wild cry of anguish; he felt her form weigh heavily upon his breast. An awful horror for a moment made his heart ice—but then the blood rushed back like a torrent of raging fire. With the hoarse cry of a lion lashed to fury, he deposited the form of the girl upon the ground, and throwing himself with insane rage upon the crowd of savages, plunged his sword right and left into every breast which opposed him. His mad passion was so frightful and deadly, his face so terrible in its menace, that the bravest of the savages recoiled before him with superstitious dread.

But the unseen Ruler of the world had decreed that all the courage, all the strength, all the immense passion of Falconbridge should avail him nothing; his last hour approached. In his headlong advance, his foot slipped in blood; he fell upon one knee, and his sword striking against the rocks, was broken close to the hilt. As he essayed to rise, one of the savages levelled his pistol, and the ball entered his breast.

With a last look toward the sky, Falconbridge, like

Lightfoot, fell backward, the blood welling from the wound, and staining his white ruffles with crimson.

The Indians had begun to waver already, as they saw the advance of Lord Fairfax; the form of the Half-breed had disappeared in the gulf beneath; as Falconbridge fell, they hastily retreated, and finally disappeared down the slope beneath the boughs of the evergreens.

When Lord Fairfax leaped from his horse, the first object which greeted his gaze, was the body of Falconbridge. He seized it in his arms with a hoarse cry, and at the pressure of the father's heart to the son's, the young man opened his eyes and gazed about him faintly.

"My son! my child!" cried the Earl, with inexpressible anguish; "my boy, speak to me! Where are you wounded? Oh! in the bosom here!"

And with trembling, but rapid hands, the Earl tore open the young man's waistcoat and shirt. Pushing hastily aside a small gold locket which hung from Falconbridge's neck by a fine steel chain, he searched for the wound. He did not search long; turning suddenly pale, the Earl seemed about to faint.

Immediately over the heart, a circular spot of blood indicated the place where the ball had entered.

He saw that all was over. His knowledge of gunshot wounds told him this one was mortal—and turning away his head, the stern old nobleman uttered a sob which tore its way from his inmost heart, like a cry of agony and despair.

"Yes, yes!" said a panting and broken voice at his elbow, "yes, friend, you are right; you are not deceived; he's as good as gone from this earth! Falconbridge! Falconbridge! look at me once more, comrade! It is Wagner that speaks to you!"

And the rude Borderer, who had hastened with giant strides to the spot, threw himself upon his knees at the side of the young man, and inclosed his pale hand in a grasp of iron.

"Look at me, comrade!" growled the Captain, in hoarse and tragic accents, "you see me, don't you? Come, open your eyes! I'm Wagner, the old bear that loved you, and here's George, who's got hold of your other hand. Don't be talking, for your wound is sure to bleed, only look up, companion! Black day! miserable hour!" groaned the speaker despairingly; "a bullet has done for him—all's over with the boy!"

As he spoke, the young man slowly opened his eyes, and looked round with a dreamy glance, at the faces beside him.

"Companion!" he muttered, as his glance fell on Wagner, "is she saved?"

"There, stop talking!" cried the soldier, with a glow in his cheeks, "stop that talking, I say."

"Ah! comrade, you are there," he murmured, "and she —she is—gone! I remember!"

As he uttered these words, which were almost inaudible, the cheeks of Falconbridge flushed, and then turned white again: a convulsion passed over his frame, and made the hot blood gush from his bosom. With a faint attempt to rise, he fell back with a low cry into the arms of Lord Fairfax, whose strength seemed about to desert him.

"Rouse! rouse! my child!" he exclaimed in an agony of despair; "do not die without looking at your father—it will kill me!"

And the grim Earl strained the fainting and languid form to his breast so wildly, that it seemed to infuse a portion of his own life into Falconbridge.

He slowly opened his eyes. His glance fell upon the face of George, which was bathed in tears. The boy held his white cold hand, and kneeling, pressed it to his throbbing heart. The wandering eye of Falconbridge arrested itself as it fell upon the agitated countenance—his lips moved, and he endeavored, vainly, to speak.

"Bend your ear to his lips, George," groaned Wagner, "he's going, and has got something to say."

George quickly obeyed, and placed his ear to the mouth of Falconbridge.

"I am dying," was the low murmur; "I am going—to leave you, George! I always loved you—dear companion—as I know that you loved me! You will do me a last favor," he said, raising his hand feebly to the locket on his breast; "see that I am buried on the mountain yonder—by the pine which—we looked at on that autumn day—and bury *her* beside me!—this locket—it contains a woman's hair—her hair—don't let them remove it from my bosom, George!"

"Oh, no! I swear it! I will protect it with my life!" exclaimed the weeping youth.

"And now, farewell!" murmured Falconbridge, a sorrowful smile passing over his pale face; "I am dying—am I not?"

"It won't be long!" muttered Captain Wagner, his fiery eyes moistened with tears; "five minutes I give him!—miserable day! Oh, why did he ever come on the trail! Falconbridge! Falconbridge! look here, comrade! Look at Wagner, who's crying like a baby at your knees!"

The young man heard the appeal of the Borderer, and turned his eyes upon his face.

"Friend!—true and tried!" he murmured, faintly, "we must part! Remember me—when I am gone!"

"Remember you! Until my grave is dug, I'll love and think of you, my boy, and cherish you! My heart is bleeding, look you!—my poor old heart!"

He stopped, overcome by emotion.

The face of Falconbridge grew soft and serene: then a slight color came to the pale cheeks; and by a great effort he turned his eyes in the direction of Miss Argal's body, and faintly stretched out his hands.

"He wants to have her by him when he goes!" groaned the Borderer; "he's faithful to the death!"

And the soldier rose quickly, and going to the spot where the pale, cold form of the young lady lay, took it in his arms, and brought it to the side of Falconbridge. The face of the Borderer was white, and his frame shuddered, as he thus held close to his breast the body of the woman whom he had seen so often, smiling and beautiful in life. But he did not falter—he deposited the inanimate figure at the side of the youth.

As the eyes of the dying man fell upon the pale features, the exquisite face, as of one who was sleeping tranquilly and happily, his lip quivered, and a tremor agitated him, making the blood well, in a crimson stream, from the wound in his bosom.

"She is gone before me!" he murmured in a whisper; "is the day about to wane, companion?—this darkness! 'Tis a grand, beautiful world—with its flowers and sunshine!— but—another land!—see how it shines above me as I go!"

These words were his last. With a final movement, which exhausted all his strength, he bent toward the dead body of the young lady, and encircling it with his arms, died with his head upon her bosom.

CHAPTER LXXV.

THE DAUGHTER OF THE STARS.

WITH the death of him who has illustrated our poor pages more than all his co-mates, the chronicle might fitly terminate.

Falconbridge once dead, his figure removed, his eyes no longer dwelling upon the prairie, the mountain, and the river,—both the scene and the actors appear dreary and sad: the life of the drama has departed.

But we linger for a brief space before bidding the reader farewell. The vortex which drew into its bloody depths so many forms, did not spare, in its final effect, another being.

The bodies of the whites and savages, who had been slain, were buried; and the hunters, at the head of whom rode the Earl and Captain Wagner, returned toward Greenway Court.

Scarcely a word was uttered by the two leaders upon the march. They scarcely turned their heads, for, in a litter of boughs behind them, were borne the dead bodies of Bertha Argal, and Falconbridge.

Then a procession of hunters, bearing a litter upon their shoulders, ascended the mountain, and the young man and the girl were laid at the foot of the great pine which he had looked at that day,—beneath whose shadow he had wished to be buried. The cavalcade returned to the lowland again —silent and sorrowful; all were thinking of the youth and maiden who were sleeping their last sleep.

One murmur, alone, was mingled with the hoof-strokes of the horses. The leader of the troop, with white, cold lips, whispered strangely:

"It is well!"

Then, many days afterward, the silence of the mountain fastness was broken by the noise of a horseman ascending the winding road to the dwelling, which we have visited more than once.

This horseman is George. He is going to see Cannie, and his face is very pale:—for the child is lying dangerously ill.

The exposure upon the march with the Indians had aggravated, terribly, her tendency to disease of the lungs; and soon after her return, she had been seized with an acute attack. A physician had been hastily sent for from the settlement east of the Blue Ridge; but after an examination of the condition of the sufferer, he had shaken his head, and turned away hopelessly.

The disease had invaded the vital organs, and the death of the child was only a question of time.

She lingered until the cold, sad winter had passed away, till the violets of spring were blooming in the grass, till the birds were carolling in the mild blue sky, which drooped like a canopy above the headlands and rivers, and the prairie glittering with a million flowers.

Then the life of the little sufferer waned rapidly.

George was ever beside her—controlling the sobs which tried to force their way from his lips—and smiling upon her hopefully and sweetly.

She knew how much he had loved her now—she knew that this love had increased until it came to be a portion of his life. She would often take his hand, and with smiles of deep tenderness, and swimming eyes, thank the boy for his kindness and goodness, through all the days since he had met her, and saved her life.

And George would laugh and chide her for her sorrowful air—for her talk about dying, and seeing her "last violets" —then his feelings would overcome him, and throwing himself down on his knees at her bedside, he would bury his face in the counterpane and sob: or press his quivering lip to the little white hand, and cry like a child, until he was exhausted.

Beside her, day and night, the old gray-haired man watched her every movement—the color in her cheeks—the quick, short breaths—the brows knit at times with sudden and acute pain. His life seemed absorbed in his child; and as her strength became weaker and weaker, his very heart's blood seemed to ebb away with her own.

Thus the winter waned away, and the spring came gladly —but it brought no life to Cannie.

She had clearly drawn near to that mysterious world which lies beyond the stars, and yet only a step from every human being. Lying serenely on the little white couch beside the window, she resembled rather a pure white flower than a mortal maiden—a snow drop, delicate and fragile, and transient—which the first breath of wind would blow away.

She would lie thus for hours with the old man's hand in her own, gazing out on the wild landscape of mountain and gorge, with a dreamy smile—very happy it seemed, in some thought, which came to her; wholly willing to submit to the fate which now awaited her at any instant.

At last the invisible hand was stretched out. It was a beautiful evening of May. The sinking sun threw a flush of crimson light on the opposite mountain—on the lofty pines —and far down on the gliding waters of the Shenandoah, the "Daughter of the Stars," which murmured and died away, as the soft breeze of evening came and went, bearing up from the prairie the delicate odor of flowers.

"The time has come, dear, for me to leave you," she said faintly; "don't grieve for me, grandpapa—I shall be happy, and I will meet you in heaven."

He pressed his lips with sudden agony to her thin white hand—but the low soft voice again begged him not to grieve for her.

As she spoke, she saw George come at a swift gallop up the mountain, and her cheek flushed gladly. He was soon beside her.

"I thought I never should see you any more," she murmured, smiling; "I am going away from you, George."

The young man sobbed and fell almost powerless upon his knees at the bedside.

"Oh do not! do not speak thus!" he said; "you will live! you will live to be my own! oh, you *must* not die!"

"God has called me," she answered; "I cannot stay. Remember me, grandpapa, and George, when I am gone—remember little Cannie, who loved you so!—who—will meet you where—suffering never comes!"

She never spoke again. Bending over her couch, they caught her last sigh.

The old man clasped his hands, and slowly raising his eyes to heaven, murmured with a low, terrible groan:

"God take the spirit of my child, and may I follow her!"

George buried his face in the counterpane, and pressing his lips wildly to the pale cold hand, only moaned.

When he rose and looked at her with streaming eyes, she was smiling upon him, even in death.

Thus she passed away, like a flower, a leaf, a dream of the spring,—and they laid her as she had desired them—by the side of Falconbridge. The story of her life became known to the inhabitants of the region, and it was said that a young gentleman from the low country had nearly died of grief. Then a song began to float about, set to plaintive music—the production it may be of some native bard. of some youth, who was touched by the pathetic story, and who, personating George, sang his grief and despair. He sang it in these simple and unpolished lines, which, handed down traditionally, tell of the sweetness and tenderness of the maiden—the sorrow of her lover:

"Down on the Shenandoah roving,
   Long time I lingered by the shore,

Cannie by my side, dear and loving—
Now she is laughing there no more!

"Bright as a sunbeam on the mountain;
　Fair as the lily by her side,
Fresh as the water in the fountain,
　Was Cannie, my young Virginia bride

"Oh! all the world is sad and dreary
　Nothing brings me solace all the day—
Daytime and night-time I am weary—
　Cannie's forever gone away!

"Long time I loved her; now a-roaming
　Wide o'er the world cold and poor,
Ofttimes I think I see her coming,
　Ofttimes I hear her by the shore!"

Such were the homely lines, to which were attached this chorus, full of pathos;

"Oh she was an angel,
　Last year she died,
Toll the bell, a funeral knell
For my young Virginia bride!"

The melody was sad and plaintive—like the whisper of the wind in the mountain pines—the sigh of the autumn breeze in the broomstraw at twilight;—like the gentle and murmurous lapse of the waves, as they glide away beneath drooping boughs, or under the bending flowers of the meadows.

By the side of her cousin, whom she had loved so dearly, near the grave of Falconbridge, the pure and noble, the child thus serenely slumbered. In the vast wild solitude, on the brow of the great precipice, beneath the outstretched arms of the mighty pine, which bent in the wind, or swayed under the feet of the eagle, these children of nature slept in peace.

A few words will terminate our chronicle.

LXXVI.

THE HEART OF LORD FAIRFAX.

SINCE the events which we have related, more than thirty years have passed.

The month of October, 1781, is drawing to its close.

In a house in Winchester, a man of about eighty, with long gray hair, thickly powdered; a thin, worn countenance, bearing the marks of illness; and an attenuated figure clad in a richly embroidered dressing-gown, sits in a large arm-chair, supported by pillows, extending his hands from time to time toward a cheerful blaze in the wide fireplace.

At three paces from him, erect, silent, and watchful, stands an old servant, with hair as gray as his master's, but a face still hale and ruddy in spite of his great age.

"John," says the invalid, in a thin, weak voice.

"My lord."

And the old servant approaches his master.

"What noise was that, which I heard? They were shouting in the street, I thought. Has any intelligence arrived from the army? You came in a moment ago, and must be informed. What intelligence?"

Old John hesitates. Upon his countenance it is easy to read an expression of acute pain.

"Speak!" Lord Fairfax says, in his weak and faltering voice. "Lord Cornwallis has not evacuated Yorktown? It is not possible!"

"No my lord," is the low reply.

"What then?"

John hesitates again. His master turns toward him with querulous energy.

"Am I to have a reply, or are you dumb?" he says.

Old John sighs, and looks at Lord Fairfax with deep affection and sympathy.

"The news is bad, my lord," he says, "and I would rather not tell it."

"Bad? speak! I am not a baby! Cornwallis has not evacutated Yorktown, you say—what then?"

"Worse than that, my lord."

Lord Fairfax rose suddenly erect in his chair.

"Worse? what do you mean?"

Old John groans this time.

"I thought to keep the news from you, my lord. But you order me to speak, and I obey your order. My lord, Cornwallis has surrendered his army."

"Surrendered!"

"Yes, my lord!" groans old John.

"To —— George Washington?"

"Yes, my lord."

Lord Fairfax sinks back, and a groan of inexpressible anguish tears its way from the trembling breast.

"That boy! that boy!" he murmurs, "the child whom I brought up! The English dominion in North America overturned by that curly pate!"

A spasm passes over the features of the old earl, as he utters these words. He totters in his chair. Suddenly he extends his arms toward the old servant, closes his eyes, and murmurs.

"Take me to bed, John, it is time for me to die!" *

Six months afterwards he was dead.

---

* His words.

LXXVII.

THE HEART OF GEORGE.

 A MONTH after this scene—that is to say, in November, 1781—a cavalier coming from the east by way of Ashby's gap, forded the Shenandoah, and entered the Valley.

He was a man of about fifty, tall, powerful, as straight as an arrow, and with something proud and imposing in his appearance and carriage. His eyes were clear and penetrating, his lips firm, the poise of the head indicative of command. He wore the full dress uniform of a general of the American army, and rode an excellent horse, which went along gaily beneath his powerful rider, through the November sunshine.

Passing to the left of the little village of Millwood, the stranger threw a glance toward "Saratoga," the residence of General Morgan, which was seen on a hill across the woods, on his right; then he continued his way, reached the town of White Post, turned to the left at the post, which still stood in the main street, and pushing on, reached Greenway Court, in its great lawn, backed by woods.

Dismounting in front of the deserted mansion, the stranger tethered his horse to a bough, pushed open the decayed door, and entered the house.

All was silent and dreary. The rooms were bare and desolate. The panes of the windows were broken; the spiders had woven their webs everywhere; and the dust lay half an inch deep on the discolored floor.

The stranger gazed around him for a moment. Threw a

glance toward the staircase, as if he thought of ascending it; but apparently gave up the design, and a moment afterwards left the house, going back to his horse.

He had not uttered a word. With a parting glance at the mansion, he mounted, and rode in the direction of the Massinutton.

He crossed the river, and entered the gorge, along the bank of Passage Creek, as the sun was declining.

Pushing on, as though he were afraid of being benighted, he followed the narrow and winding road up the slope of the mountain, and in half an hour came in front of a small house, with a great rock at its back.

A moment afterward, he had dismounted, approached the house, and forced an entrance through the creaking door.

The house was deserted. Some broken furniture alone indicated that it had once been occupied. The stranger looked around him with painful earnestness, and then went toward a small apartment, upon one side of the main room, his heavy heels armed with huge spurs clashing upon the decayed floor, and arousing a hundred echoes.

The smaller apartment was bare like the larger, but the stranger suddenly stooped and picked up an object from the floor. It was a small portion of a woman's or a child's ruffle, apparently—such as at that period decorated the upper edge of the bodice. An imperceptible tremor passed over the stalwart frame of the personage as he gazed at the object in his hand; then having satisfied his curiosity apparently, he placed it in his bosom.

Returning to the front door of the mansion, he cast a final look around him, taking in at a glance every feature, every detail. All was ruinous, deserted; the spot had a melancholy air about it—and the stranger slowly remounted his horse, and left it, muttering:

"I can scarcely realize that it is the same!"

Instead of returning by the same road, he directed his way along a devious bridle-path toward a mighty pine which raised its trunk against the sky, on the very summit of the mountain, at the point where it sank suddenly into the valley. After great exertion, his horse stumbling frequently, he reached a spot beyond which it seemed impossible to proceed. He solved the difficulty by dismounting and advancing on foot. Even then the ascent was arduous. The huge masses of granite were piled up like a Titanic pyramid, but he finally surmounted all obstacles and reached the foot of the great pine.

It grew in a narrow patch of soil, encircled by rocks; at its foot were three graves, marked by moss-covered slabs of marble.

The stranger stopped to breathe for an instant, and his glance swept the immense horizon of mountain, valley and river. From his great elevation he looked down upon a vast extent of country stretched beneath him like a map, and the view was sublime in its wild magnificence.

But the wanderer had evidently come with no intention to gaze at the landscape. He dwelt upon it for a moment only—then his glance was directed toward the grave-stones.

He stooped down, and pushing aside the moss, read the inscription upon the largest of the three.

The inscription was as follows:

" Beneath this ſtone lies.
EDMUND VISCOUNT FAIRFAX, only ſon of THOMAS
LORD FAIRFAX, of Denton, England.
God rest him."

The stranger gazed long and sorrowfully upon the words, recalling plainly some scenes of the past which the name on the stone suggested. His head drooped, and a deep sigh issued from his lips as he murmured:

"There lies the noblest heart I have ever known—a great, true soul, full of kindness and honor—a gentleman of the antique days of knighthood. Yes, yes, God rest him! The Supreme, the All-seeing, the Rewarder of charity and love, and faith—has He not received to his eternal rest this noble suffering soul? Who was ever like him? I have met with no other human being so great! Falconbridge! Falconbridge! your death was a glorious one! You died as you had lived—a true gentleman!"

The head drooped lower as these almost inaudible words escaped from the lips of the stranger. He remained for some time, gazing at the stone, his shoulders drooping, his breast heaving—then drawing a long breath, he fixed his eyes upon the one beside it, which bore this inscription only

"To the memory of

BERTHA ARGAL,

Beautiful and unhappy."

"Yes, yes," the stranger murmured, "very beautiful—very unhappy—poor child of misfortune!"

And his sad glance wandered toward the third tombstone. He seemed almost to dread deciphering it—but setting his lips close, knelt down and read what was cut upon the marble.

These were the words:

"Here lies the body of CANNIE,
the daughter of an Englifh
gentleman :
Born in England, May the 10th, 1733,
Died in Virginia, May the 9th, 1749.
'*And he took them up in his arms, put his hands upon them, and blessed them.*'"

The stranger riveted his eyes upon this inscription with an expression of such anguish that it was plain the stone covered a great sorrow. His broad breast was shaken, his clear, penetrating eyes slowly filled with tears, and his cheeks flushed with passionate emotion.

Mastered by a sudden impulse, he took from his pocket a pencil, and after the words:

"Here lies the body of CANNIE...."

wrote, in addition:

... "And the heart of GEORGE,
Born in Weftmoreland, Virginia,
February 22d, 1732:
Died the fame day and hour,
May 9th, 1749.

As the stranger finished the addition to the inscription, two tears rolled down his cheeks, and fell upon the stone. Burying his face in the long grass growing upon the grave, he sobbed, rather than said, in a hoarse and broken voice:

"Farewell youth! farewell happiness! farewell dream of my boyhood! The earth is dreary since you went away. Farewell until we meet again!"

THE END.

NEW BOOKS
And New Editions Recently Published by
G. W. CARLETON & CO.,
NEW YORK.

GEORGE W. CARLETON.   HENRY S. ALLEN.

N.B.—THE PUBLISHERS, upon receipt of the price in advance, will send any of the following Books by mail, POSTAGE FREE, to any part of the United States. This convenient and very safe mode may be adopted when the neighboring Booksellers are not supplied with the desired work. State name and address in full.

Victor Hugo.

LES MISÉRABLES.—The celebrated novel. One large 8vo volume, paper covers, $2.00 ; . . . cloth bound, $2.50
LES MISÉRABLES.—In the Spanish language. Fine 8vo. edition, two vols., paper covers, $4.00 ; . . cloth bound, $5.00
JARGAL.—A new novel. Illustrated. . 12mo. cloth, $1.75
THE LIFE OF VICTOR HUGO.—By himself. . 8vo. cloth, $1.75

Miss Muloch.

JOHN HALIFAX.—A novel. With illustration. 12mo. cloth, $1.75
A LIFE FOR A LIFE.— . do. do. $1.75

Charlotte Bronte (Currer Bell).

JANE EYRE.—A novel. With illustration. 12mo. cloth, $1.75
THE PROFESSOR.— do. . do. . do. $1.75
SHIRLEY.— . do. . do. . do. $1.75
VILLETTE.— . do. . do. . do. $1.75

Hand-Books of Society.

THE HABITS OF GOOD SOCIETY; with thoughts, hints, and anecdotes, concerning nice points of taste, good manners, and the art of making oneself agreeable. The most entertaining work of the kind. . . . 12mo. cloth, $1.75
THE ART OF CONVERSATION.—With directions for self-culture. A sensible and instructive work, that ought to be in the hands of every one who wishes to be either an agreeable talker or listener. . . . . 12mo. cloth, $1.50
THE ART OF AMUSING.—Graceful arts, games, tricks, and charades, intended to amuse everybody. With suggestions for private theatricals, tableaux, parlor and family amusements. Nearly 150 illustrative pictures. . 12mo. cloth, $2.00

Robinson Crusoe.

A handsome illustrated edition, complete. 12mo. cloth, $1.50

LIST OF BOOKS PUBLISHED

Mrs. Mary J. Holmes' Works.

'LENA RIVERS.—	A novel.	12mo. cloth,	$1.50
DARKNESS AND DAYLIGHT.—	do.	do.	$1.50
TEMPEST AND SUNSHINE.—	do.	do.	$1.50
MARIAN GREY.—	do.	do.	$1.50
MEADOW BROOK.—	do.	do.	$1.50
ENGLISH ORPHANS.—	do.	do.	$1.50
DORA DEANE.—	do.	do.	$1.50
COUSIN MAUDE.—	do.	do.	$1.50
HOMESTEAD ON THE HILLSIDE.—	do.	do.	$1.50
HUGH WORTHINGTON.—	do.	do.	$1.50
THE CAMERON PRIDE.—*Just Published.*		do.	$1.50

Artemus Ward.

HIS BOOK.—The first collection of humorous writings by A. Ward. Full of comic illustrations. 12mo. cloth, $1.50
HIS TRAVELS.—A comic volume of Indian and Mormon adventures. With laughable illustrations. 12mo. cloth, $1.50
IN LONDON.—A new book containing Ward's comic *Punch* letters, and other papers. Illustrated. 12mo. cloth, $1.50

Miss Augusta J. Evans.

BEULAH.—A novel of great power.		12mo. cloth,	$1.75
MACARIA.— do. do.		do.	$1.75
ST. ELMO.— do. do. *Just published.*		do.	$2.00

By the Author of "Rutledge."

RUTLEDGE.—A deeply interesting novel.		12mo. cloth,	$1.75
THE SUTHERLANDS.—	do.	do.	$1.75
FRANK WARRINGTON.—	do.	do.	$1.75
ST. PHILIP'S.—	do.	do.	$1.75
LOUIE'S LAST TERM AT ST. MARY'S.—		do.	$1.75
ROUNDHEARTS AND OTHER STORIES.—For children.		do.	$1.75
A ROSARY FOR LENT.—Devotional readings.		do.	$1.75

J. Cordy Jeaffreson.

A BOOK ABOUT LAWYERS.—Reprinted from the late English Edition. Intensely interesting. 12mo. cloth, $2.00

Allan Grant.

LOVE IN LETTERS.—A fascinating book of love-letters from celebrated and notorious persons. 12mo. cloth, $2.00

Algernon Charles Swinburne.

LAUS VENERIS—and other Poems and Ballads. 12mo. cloth, $1.75

Geo. W. Carleton.

OUR ARTIST IN CUBA.—A humorous volume of travel; with fifty comic illustrations by the author. 12mo. cloth, $1.50
OUR ARTIST IN PERU.— do. do. $1.50

www.ingramcontent.com/pod-product-compliance
Lightning Source LLC
Chambersburg PA
CBHW022114290426

44112CB00008B/666